English Pronunciation Secrets:

The Game-Changing Guide to Mastering the General American Accent

By Rebecca Bower

PROactivePronunciation.com

About the Author

Rebecca Bower, MHSc. is the owner and founder of PROactive Pronunciation, a consultancy specializing in empowering her clients to speak English with clarity and confidence. Rebecca is a Speech-Language Pathologist with more than 12 years of experience and a global educator working in the field of articulation. Rebecca is a COMPTON P-ESL Certified Accent Modification Consultant and Instructor and author of the book *English Pronunciation Secrets: The Game-Changing Guide to Mastering the General American Accent.* Find out more about Rebecca at www.proactivepronunciation.com

Disclaimer

English Pronunciation Secrets: The Secrets You've Been Searching For!

A complete English pronunciation program

Have you ever tried to correct a word you've mispronounced, only to be told by a friend, "Nope, that's not quite it." Have you ever been frustrated because you can't actually tell the difference between some English sounds, and your native-English-speaking friends can't explain what they are doing to make the sound because they have no clue either? Can you hear and pronounce the differences in the words "pill, peel, Paul, pal, pail, pile, pool, pull, poll, with confidence? The problem is that just repeating native speakers does not always help. Repetition is not the answer when you can't hear the difference to begin with!

Accent reduction coach, international dialect instructor, and Speech-Language Pathologist, Rebecca Bower has unveiled the hidden mysteries of English pronunciation in *English Pronunciation Secrets*. She has created a comprehensive simple-to-follow guide to achieve clear, more accurate North American English pronunciation. If your goal is to learn the secrets of how native North American English speakers actually pronounce the English language and to master those skills for yourself, then this is the book for you! This guide is designed to help you speak with more precise and clear General North American English pronunciation. Unlock the secrets in this book so you can finally speak English with clarity, confidence, and accuracy.

This is the guide for you, if:

- You struggle with being understood when speaking English
- Your English pronunciation skills are affecting your confidence, social life, working relationships, or career
- Your knowledge and skills are being undermined by your communication skills, specifically your English pronunciation
- Your English pronunciation is affecting your ability to freely and confidently speak to new people
- You avoid speaking and interacting at work and in social situations because you do not feel confident in your speaking skills

4

This guide is not your ordinary English pronunciation/accent reduction book. In *English Pronunciation Secrets,* all of the mysteries of English are finally revealed! The topics that you didn't know you didn't know are all here. A typical pronunciation book touches on basic topics, but this guide dives deep into the comprehensive subject, including in-depth examples and extensive practice activities to hone your skills. You will learn the unique method for how to physically "feel" for your correct pronunciation. You will be given the keys to mastering English pronunciation, not just to learn words and sentences but to master *conversation*. Because isn't effective conversation the point of it all?

In *English Pronunciation Secrets*, you will learn how to:

- Speak more clearly. Easily pronounce all of the most challenging sounds that non-native English speakers encounter, with stress and intonation exercises, and so much more.

- "Feel" the correct pronunciation with incredible detail. The goal is not to repeat words because how has repetition worked for you so far? The goal is to be able to correct yourself and KNOW that you are pronouncing the sounds in the goal accent. You can finally feel confident when speaking!

- Complete comprehensive practice exercises that move you from the simplest level (sound level) and progress you slowly up the ladder to syllables, words, phrases, sentences, reading, and finally, conversation practice, so you don't get stuck.

- Perfect your stress patterns, intonation, and linking to speak English clearly and fluently so you can actually enjoy your conversations with others.

- Speak using common English reductions, silent letters, different spellings, and use all those crazy exceptions in English.

This comprehensive guide includes simple and clear activities, so you can feel confident that you're doing it right. No more guessing!

Imagine actually looking forward to a conversation with a co-worker or new acquaintance instead of shying away.

Imagine being able to order your morning coffee without a thought as to whether you'll be understood or not.

Imagine feeling confident that your skills, knowledge, and personality will shine through, not just your pronunciation.

Now, grab a coffee (or beverage of choice) and get cozy. This is going to be a fun journey!

Acknowledgments

This world is a better place when we share our knowledge, skills, and experience with each other. We help each other grow and reach our goals by doing so. Thank you to all of my clients who have demonstrated real motivation and hard work. You have shown me time and time again what it means to go after what you want with needle-like precision and to grab hold of the knowledge you need to help you get there. My desire to share what I know gets stronger with each new amazing individual with whom I work. Thank you.

Without the incredible patience and unending positive support of my husband, Trevor Bower, even the idea of writing this book would not have happened. He has this knack for broadening my perceptions to consider a bigger picture, look outside the box, and strive for more. His encouragement and sacrifice to support me in writing this book is a testament that he is a true gem of a man! He's my greatest example of taking action. I am so lucky to have such an amazing partner to sail through life with.

Introduction

Jay was a wreck!

He was nervous. It wasn't because he wasn't ready for his presentation. He was very familiar with presenting to high-stakes CEOs on alternative energy technology. Jay knew his stuff! He was nervous because he knew in the pit of his stomach that he would have to face the inevitable confused looks and requests to repeat himself during his presentation. Jay knew that the audience would likely get lost and that he would have to do his best to be clear and precise as he spoke. He also knew that no matter how much he tried to do that very thing, it didn't help, and he ended up with the same result, repeating himself constantly. So here he was, ready to demonstrate his skills and expertise, only to be undermined by his English pronunciation once again. The feelings of anxiety, dread, and hopelessness filled him.

Jay had been speaking English for nearly 20 years. He had the vocabulary and grammatical proficiency in English to which many people only hope to aspire. What Jay did not have, however, was a clear foundation of English pronunciation which created misunderstandings regularly. He had tried to speak slowly and "enunciate," but the problem was that he didn't know what sounds he needed to change or how to even do that! He was mispronouncing the words, stress patterns, and intonation of English, and it was negatively impacting his career.

Jay worried that he would continue to be passed by for leadership positions if he continued on this path. Jay knew he had the skills and expertise for these positions, yet he did not have the communication skills to relay that to decision-makers. Jay worried that if he continued to let his communication skills undermine his expertise and confidence, his clients would not see the tremendous knowledge he brought to the table. Jay would lose clients and potentially big contracts, and this was not a situation he was willing to live with any longer.

You are likely reading this right now because you find yourself in a similar situation. You feel anxiety when you speak English. You feel frustrated and even stuck, and you don't know where to start to improve your English pronunciation. I meet with intelligent, successful, talented individuals every day, just like you, that dread speaking because they struggle with English pronunciation.

Most people who learn English as their second language eventually master the grammar and vocabulary of the language. Unfortunately, English pronunciation is rarely ever taught. Worse yet, the pronunciation of your non-native English

Instructors has an impact on your pronunciation as well. Truthfully, most native English speakers do not even understand the details of their own pronunciation like a Speech-Language Pathologist does. That's where this guide comes in. You are finally going to learn the techniques, the missing links of English pronunciation. How much you can improve depends on how open and willing you are to sound different than you have sounded your entire life.

Unclear English pronunciation has cost talented people advancement in their careers, connection, and even income due to lost potential. Excellent communication skills are a necessity in a competitive job market. It's as simple as that. Without learning the secrets of English pronunciation, you have to guess what to change. The unfortunate truth is that most people find themselves sounding exactly the same as they did after speaking English for 20+ years!

And what became of Jay, you might ask? Well, Jay learned the tools, tips, and secrets laid out for you in this guide. He applied what he learned. His performance appraisals improved. His confidence when speaking is at an all-time high. His clarity of speech is like it has never been before! Jay benefited because he learned the little-known secrets in this guide and applied them to his life. His career outlook is bright, and he is no longer held back by the barrier of his communication skills.

This guide will show you the exact steps to follow to experience the freedom of speaking English with clarity.

This guide will show you how to:

1. Identify your problem sounds, stress patterns, and intonation so you can finally fix your main issues

2. Practice with no-brainer exercises that start from the simplest level to get you to your goals

3. Adjust your tongue, lips, jaw, and voice to improve your pronunciation through simple-to-understand directions

4. Speak English clearly and confidently in conversation

How do you know this works? I have compiled all of the information that I have obtained through my training and clinical practice. I have gathered all of the practice materials that have helped my accent reduction clients achieve their goals through over 12 years working as a Speech-Language Pathologist and during my time as an

Accent Modification Instructor. I have compiled this information just for you in one simple-to-use guide.

I have worked with countless clients worldwide, from India, China, Thailand, Bangladesh, Brazil, Spain, Germany, Russia, the Czech Republic, Poland, Ukraine, Romania, Serbia, Croatia, Nigeria, Sudan, and so many more! I have created this guide to share the secrets of speaking English clearly and confidently, the secrets that even native English speakers don't know that they use every day!

I wrote this guide because I looked at what was out there and knew there was so much more to share. I saw lots of boring super-dry guides that share only a limited amount of information with no real progression to work through simple sounds to conversation. I didn't see any guides that gave readers an understanding of what to "feel" when learning new sounds (because sometimes you just can't hear or differentiate the difference quite yet!). This realization led me to write a book with a fresh take on the subject with a more exciting and effective way to practice English pronunciation. I wanted to provide you with more in-depth information and practice to help you get the results you want.

It is a passion of mine to help people with their communication skills. The quality of your communication skills affects how you express your needs, desires and how you connect with others. Your communication skills can even contribute to your source of income! When people come to me for help with accent reduction (also referred to as accent modification), these are the reasons that drive me to share my knowledge.

So what's in this guide anyways?

Well, in part one, we discuss all the basics.

You will understand how speech works. You will learn everything you need to know about accents and basic anatomy without having to take a Master's degree course.

In part two, the guide covers all consonants that cause non-native English speakers to struggle with their pronunciation. You will not only learn the secrets of the General North American English accent, but you will learn how to compare it with your own pronunciation. You will learn to train your ears to hear the difference and learn all the little tips and tricks to "feel" when you are producing the new sound correctly. You will learn how to practice your skills from sounds to syllables, words, phrases, sentences, reading, and finally to conversation.

Part three explains the tricky vowels. Now, unlike many guides, this book goes into great detail to help you "feel" when your tongue is in the correct position. This guide will reveal all the vowel secrets to get you from the simple sound level to the conversation level, where you can finally use your skills when speaking to others.

Part four explains all of those exceptions in English. The secrets of silent letters, when you can pronounce sounds in multiple ways, and words that have numerous accepted pronunciations are all revealed. Part Four also covers topics such as why English speakers seem to drop the /t/ in the word "button" and why certain words sound as if the vowels disappear altogether. This part of the guide also deals with certain English words that don't sound like they are spelled.

In part five, the guide shows you the secrets of the "music" of English. It covers stress patterns, intonation, and all the little secret linking rules and retractions to make English flow fluently and easily.

This guide reveals to you in great detail exactly why we stress the words **OB**ject and ob**JECT** differently. Stress rules are essential in English, but most of the time, it's just never discussed. This guide is jam-packed with examples and easy-to-understand directions to help you speak English with confidence and clarity.

After working through this guide, you will achieve a clear understanding of your issues. You will gain confidence in knowing exactly what to do. You will have practice materials provided to hone your new skills. You will finally be able to overcome the obstacle of clear English pronunciation that has been standing in your way.

Do you want to chat with your friends and colleagues without worrying about how you pronounce your words?

Do you want to present your knowledge in work meetings, presentations, or video conferences without being filled with anxiety and losing sleep the night before over how you will sound?

Do you want to be acknowledged for the skills and knowledge you have at work because you can precisely articulate that expertise?

Do you want to speak with ease, confidence, and clarity? Wouldn't it be amazing to no longer see puzzled faces from your listeners who are trying to understand your meaning?

This guide covers all the necessary topics, including incredibly detailed information in the most straightforward, easy-to-follow language. This book is a simple guide that includes all of the materials and **SIMPLE** practice activities you need to achieve your goals in one place. The very fact that you're looking at this book right now is a sign that you are ready to take your communication skills into your own hands. You are ready to make a significant change, one that could bring you incredible outcomes in your career, working relationships, social relationships, and even impact your income.

Be like Aphrodite, a finance manager from China who, through learning these secrets, now holds power and confidence with her English pronunciation. She has been asked twice in one month by her Uber drivers if she was born in North America!

Be like Jian. With the knowledge and skills learned from the secrets in this guide, he finally understands his English pronunciation issues. He can now speak English with confidence.

Now, you might be saying to yourself;

Do I have time for this?

Do you have 15 minutes to set aside each day? Do you talk to anyone in your day-to-day interactions? If you can answer yes (and unless you are completely isolated, yes should be your answer), you absolutely do have time to impact your English pronunciation significantly. Improved speech does not take multiple hours out of your day, but rather it requires understanding, tiny adjustments, and intention to achieve your goals. With just 15 minutes a day and the motivation to implement what you learn into your daily conversations with others, you can make significant changes to your pronunciation and clarity.

What if I get stuck or give up?

This guide explains everything you need to know in the simplest easy-to-understand steps. It helps you move from YOUR level at YOUR pace, so you'll never get stuck. It's a guided-hand-holding type of experience. This guide is jam-packed with examples and precise explanations to make learning so much easier! The list of common pronunciation differences in this guide is exhaustive and gives you examples of what you are already doing and what to do about it, so there's no guesswork. There are endless practice examples to walk you through the simplest steps, from isolation (saying a sound on its own repetitively), syllables, words, phrases, sentences, reading, and finally, conversation.

The secrets are all laid out here for you. All you have to do is follow the simple steps. If you apply the secrets outlined in English *Pronunciation Secrets: The Game-Changing Guide to Mastering the General American Accent*, you can achieve clear, fluent speech and finally experience the confidence and freedom of speaking English clearly!

English Pronunciation Secrets is not your typical boring English pronunciation workbook. This guide includes the information that I, as a Speech-Language Pathologist, have gathered throughout my education, clinical practice, instruction from over 12 years of experience working in the area of articulation. This guide is for those who are motivated and willing to expand their pronunciation skills.

If you have been working hard to improve your English pronunciation but need one incredible source that provides simple-to-understand secrets about the General North American English accent, this is it! So congratulations, you have found that book and are that much closer to achieving your goals.

I wish you well on your journey to clear and confident English pronunciation. My goal is to transform your understanding of the secrets of English that even native English speakers are not aware of.

So, let's do this together. Imagine we're meeting and grabbing a coffee together now to chat about what you can do to achieve your English pronunciation goals. Let's finally learn the secrets of English pronunciation that have been holding you back. Are you ready? Let's do this!

Table of Contents

PART ONE: Starting: Let's do this!

Chapter 1: Speech 101

What Is An Accent?

An accent is any distinctive pronunciation of a language. Generally, an accent is associated with a particular nation or location. We all have an accent. Everyone! An accent is a relative term. It is a localized speech pattern, meaning it is a pattern that is different only to another person that does not use that pattern. No matter where you are from, if you go to another location with a foreign language pattern than yours, you will have an "accent."

Those who master the English language often speak English using the sounds of their native language, resulting in an accent.

Dialects And Regional Accents

An accent occurs when a speaker learns another language but uses the sounds and patterns from their first language while speaking the second language. Often, speakers use the closest sound options from their first language to substitute as they speak. These substitutions can be quite similar for some sounds and not so similar for other sounds. In some cases, these pronunciation differences are only a mild variance and are so slight that they do not result in others not understanding the meaning. In other cases, the sheer number of differences in pronunciation and the relative difference of sounds themselves can significantly impact one's ability to be understood.

Every speaker is different. One thing to consider here is that not all speakers of a particular language will have the exact same accent. Many factors can impact your level of "accentedness." One element to consider is how long you have spoken your first language and at what age you learned your second (or third) language. Another aspect to consider is if you are fluent in various other languages in addition to your first language. Each language to which you are exposed regularly through speaking and listening will impact your overall speech pattern. If, for example, you had a nanny growing up, who spoke with a different accent, even this could affect your pronunciation!

Pronunciation is incredibly complex, and many elements impact the changes that occur. For this reason, considering ONLY your first language when learning how to adjust your pronunciation is often not adequate enough information from which to work. It is recommended that you receive an intensive speech assessment before working on your English pronunciation. You will want to know precisely what your speech differences are, compared to your goal language, in this case, General North American English pronunciation. It is not always enough to make assumptions about your typical language differences based on your first language since you are an individual. You may end up wasting time learning sounds you didn't need to work on or miss important speech distinctions specific to you as a speaker. If you would like to book a thorough speech assessment, you can book a consultation at my website to discuss this option: https://www.PROactivePronunciation.com.

While for some, their accent poses no real issues and adds a desired exotic characteristic to their speech. For many, unfortunately, what often occurs is that their pronunciation gets in the way of being understood. Over the time I have worked in this field, my clients have repeatedly explained how frustrating and emotionally difficult it is for them when they are not understood. They know all too well the looks of confusion on others' faces when they speak. They cringe at the questions for clarification, "can you repeat that?" and "can you say that again? I didn't understand." Like so many of my clients, their anxiety when speaking to others in English is real. It affects their work life, social life, and even their professional goals and aspirations. Research indicates that speaking confidence affects the types of roles and jobs people apply to. My clients often explain their experiences of frustration and desperation when communicating with colleagues, clients, and supervisors, in their attempts to be understood, to speak clearly, and to feel confident when speaking English. Yes, for most, an accent is an attractive characteristic of one's origin. Still, for some, an accent can be a barrier that impacts their ability to be understood, express their knowledge and skills, and affect their career and income. I will never fully know or understand the feelings and emotions that my clients experience when their professional skills and knowledge are undermined by their difficulty communicating. I will, however, continue to help my clients overcome this obstacle.

I am honored to share my skills and knowledge to empower my clients to achieve their pronunciation goals. It is the best job ever, and I feel renewed excitement with each new client I work with. To watch a client finally understand what was standing in their way of pronouncing English clearly and help them learn and use the skills to improve their pronunciation is incredible. There is nothing better than hearing a client say, "I get it now!", "I wish I learned this information 20 years ago!" and "I finally know what to do!" So, I wanted to share my knowledge with you here so that you, too, might get closer to overcoming your issues with speaking English clearly and confidently.

So that brings me to a common question.

Is Learning A New Accent Even Possible?

Yes. Absolutely, yes. There are some considerations to this answer, though. A few factors can impact how difficult this process might be for you. First, we must realize that age can be a factor in the speed and ease of pronunciation change. The older we are, the longer our motor muscle memory has been ingrained as a habit. These speech "habits" can be challenging to retrain. It absolutely is possible, no matter your age. Still, you must consider that someone who has practiced speaking patterns for two years while speaking English versus someone who has done so for 40 years will have different experiences adjusting their speech. Again, this does not mean it is impossible, but we should expect that some sound habits will be trickier to change as a result.

Another thing we should consider is motivation. Motivation is a fundamental element of change in all things, but this goes for pronunciation as well. Having the motivation to change your accent can go a long way in helping you achieve your goals. Suppose your employer urges you to brush up on your communication skills for work presentations, but you genuinely do not feel your pronunciation inhibits your meaning. In that case, it is unlikely that you will be motivated to put in the time and effort required to make a meaningful change in your pronunciation.

Consider your expectations. The goal of accent reduction or modification is to reduce the barriers experienced by pronunciation issues and improve your overall clarity and confidence when speaking English. Very rarely I do come across prospective clients that want to "eradicate" their native accent. Eliminating all traces of your accent is not the goal of accent modification instruction. First, this goal not only would likely take years of intensive work, but it would also take a characteristic of a person's heritage away. I always like to ask my clients what their goals are and get a grasp of how realistic their ideas are about accent modification instruction. You, too, must ask yourself what your personal goals are regarding accent reduction or accent modification.

As with all things, the results you see are related to the work you put in. Practice is essential for any significant change. How much? Well, I often like to explain to my clients that there is drill work to complete daily. Repetitive practice is necessary to ensure you are getting the fundamental movements down in a quick natural way. The primary way to practice, however, is to use what you learn in everyday conversations. The more you use these changes in your speech, the more you can get out of your comfort zone and begin to try out your new pronunciation with other people. It is a slow process, and at first, it can feel very much like you are mimicking someone else. This brings me to some good advice...

Embrace The Strangeness!

Nearly every client, at some point, expresses to me that it was like they were "acting" at first. This "imposter feeling" is a common reaction since you will be using entirely different speech patterns than what you have been used to your entire life. The feelings of weirdness will pass. I also encourage my clients to record themselves. Either use your phone, audio, or video or just sit at your computer and record yourself there. Recording yourself is really helpful in seeing and hearing your progress. Another useful recommendation is reading aloud and highlighting your target sounds on a document as you record yourself. You can then review the video or audio while reading along and hear your pronunciation differences. What is essential, though, is that you take the time to be intentional about your pronunciation when you speak. A big mistake is to believe that your speech will just improve or change by knowing what to do. No, you must be intentional about your pronunciation until the pattern becomes habitual. Habituation will only occur with repetition and practice. So throw your inhibitions to the wind, my friends! This is going to be an exhilarating and "out of your comfort zone" experience.

When people ask me how they can truly improve their pronunciation, I talk about the quality of their practice. You can practice the wrong information in the wrong way for years and see little to no change, or you can get the information YOU need and see significant differences in your pronunciation. If you identify your pronunciation differences and receive accurate instruction about how to hear the speech sounds (differentiation) and how to produce sounds (elicitation), then absolutely yes. Unfortunately, many people believe that it must be impossible since they have been practicing by repeating the English they hear around them for years, and it has not yielded any results. Receiving accurate feedback and identifying for yourself when you are producing sounds accurately are essential elements to any accent modification program.

This book hopes to shed some light on the details of General North American English pronunciation. I hope this book will help you understand the nuances of English articulation and the often-unknown rules of English stress, intonation, and pronunciation. So let's dig right in, shall we?

Let's Talk About The Elephant In The Room

Again, it is important to remember that we ALL have an accent. We all have a distinct pronunciation pattern derived from our environment. If we move to another country, we would expect that our non-native speech will be the accented speech, and of course, this applies all around the world. An accent is a relative term; it implies a difference in pronunciation from another goal language pronunciation. Some linguists and professionals in the field of Speech and Language have in some ways deemed the word "accent" as a dirty word. Many feel that it implies that one language's pronunciation is superior or somehow more legitimate than another. Others, however, see the term as globally relative and therefore has no inherent positive or negative connotation. However you view the term, here it is used in a relative manner, and English is discussed as the "goal" language, only because this particular guide is for people who want to learn English pronunciation. However, keep in mind that accent modification instruction can occur for any speaker who wishes to learn another language's pronunciation, no matter the goal language.

Why Is Pronunciation So Difficult To Change On My Own?

A quick explanation:

I want to touch on the research that explains a little more about why an accent exists and lingers and in what situations an accent changes. Many people ask me why they have such a strong accent after speaking English for over 30 years, when their Brother, for example, has been speaking English for the same amount of time has no accent at all? I often answer with a question. How old were you and your Brother when you first were regularly exposed to the North American English Accent? When the answer reveals, "I was 18, and my Brother was 9", it becomes much more apparent.

There is a phenomenon called the "critical language acquisition period." It's just a fancy way of saying that there is an age at which your pronunciation will be effectively solidified if you receive no specific instruction. Learning a new language at different ages will impact your pronunciation in different ways. The age at which you learned your second language is the strongest predictor of whether or not you will speak with a strong accent or if you will speak with no accent of your first language at all. Most people believe that the level of exposure to English would likely have the most significant impact on their accent. Many people think their English pronunciation is bound to improve if they only had MORE exposure to English and MORE practice, read MORE English books, or listen to MORE English podcasts and movies. Unfortunately, a person's level of exposure to a language is not a very good predictor of accent acquisition. It is the AGE that you learn and use your second language regularly that makes most of the difference.

So, why is an accent more likely to "stick" if you learn your second language after the age of 10? The overarching understanding is that our brains develop the ability to distinguish and "attend to" our native language from birth. As we are exposed more and more to our first language's pronunciation, stress, and intonation patterns, our brains' neural connections become stronger and stronger. These strong connections help us to attend to and eventually replicate those patterns in our speech. As we age, these connections become stronger and stronger. If we are not regularly exposed to other languages' pronunciations and accents, our brains eventually stop "listening" to new sounds and patterns. The critical period exists up to the age of around 10. After age 10, speaking your second language without a foreign accent becomes less and less likely.

Train Your Hearing: Differentiation

If the lack of exposure to another language extends beyond puberty, people experience difficulty even "hearing" differences in subtle variations of other languages. People who experience this truly cannot "hear" or distinguish the difference in pronunciation between many sounds of other languages. The ability to hear and distinguish the difference between sounds is called "differentiation." Issues with differentiation often occur with subtle variations of vowels in English, for example. Many non-native English speakers have difficulty distinguishing between words like "heat, hit, hot, hat, hut, height, and hate" or "Pete, pit, pet, pat, pot, put, pout," for example. If you have ever repeated a native speaker and were SURE that you have perfectly copied their pronunciation, only to be told you were not pronouncing it the same, then you have experienced this phenomenon! It can be a genuinely baffling experience for second language learners.

So all of this sounds like terrible news, doesn't it? Our brains seem to be fixed at a certain point in our lives to solidify our pronunciation and determine our accent. The result is a reduced ability to differentiate between unfamiliar sounds that do not exist in our first language sound repertoire. So, is there any point in even trying to change your pronunciation?

Yes. There is hope! Not just hope, but REALLY strong evidence to show that these seemingly fixed characteristics of speech are, in fact, quite flexible if you consider a particular set of factors. The good news here is that this learned pronunciation pattern does not have to be permanent at all. In fact, the research clearly shows that you can achieve native-like pronunciation AFTER this critical period if you have adequate intelligence and receive intensive and specific learning experiences with native speakers of your goal language. So many people who have received the explicit knowledgeable instruction they need go on to speak with clear English pronunciation. It is possible. With motivation, focus, and the right instruction, it is very likely that you will achieve this goal for yourself.

Accent Reduction vs. Accent Modification vs. Accent Neutralization...What's The Difference?

Okay, so here's the deal. Because of all the discussion around the term "accent" and various views on what it means to change one's pronunciation, there have been plenty of varied opinions on which term to use. The term accent reduction implies that you can reduce your previous accent. This term is not quite accurate in that your old pronunciation is never actually reduced. What really happens is that a person learns new speech patterns to sound more native to their goal language; they are ADDING an accent. The old accent is never reduced. It is just replaced as desired. Accent modification, on the other hand, comes a little closer to accurately describing what occurs. When you learn new pronunciation skills, you are modifying your way of speaking. Accent neutralization means that pronunciation is neutralized to limit the apparent pronunciation differences of your goal language. This term is not widely used, and in my opinion, still does not really capture the goal of many of my clients. For the most part, the term accent modification is most accurate, but as professionals in the field, the term accent reduction is widely used by our clients when searching for help and instruction. For these reasons, you will see the terms accent reduction and accent modification used interchangeably.

When you learn to change your pronunciation to match your goal language patterns more closely, you are not getting rid of your native accent. What actually occurs is you learn new skills to use a new "accent" in addition to your native pronunciation. You do not lose your native accent unless you truly never use it again.

Code-Switching

You will be able to use your old pronunciation patterns and your newly learned pronunciations at will whenever you so choose. Just as when you might switch your language for different situations, you can do the same by switching your pronunciation style. Changing your tone to adapt is called "code-switching." Code-switching is a term used to describe switching a language, dialect, or language style according to one's speaking situation. People code-switch for many reasons. For example, people code-switch to change from formal to informal speech, when discussing specific topics, quoting someone, fostering rapport, for group identity, softening or strengthening a command, or fitting in. The point here is that, when working on accent reduction or modification, you are learning a new skill, a new "tool" to use in your communication toolbox. You are not losing one.

IPA: The International Phonetic Alphabet

When you look in the dictionary, beside each word, you will see those strange and unworldly symbols; THAT is IPA! IPA is an alphabetic system devised in the late 19th century to standardize all speech sounds in written form. IPA shows a written symbol for all the sounds that humans create, and therefore can represent the "pronunciation" of speech sounds through symbols. IPA is uniform across all languages.

Most people have seen those crazy symbols in the dictionary next to words but do not truly understand what they are. It is a select few phoneticians and speech-language pathologists who are proficient in IPA transcription.

It is important to understand a little about IPA because it helps students who wish to improve their pronunciation by having an unmistakable "symbol" to represent the sound they say. It is not based on English spelling rules, does not change, and there is no variation. Each symbol represents a sound. It's as simple as that! It makes understanding the process of changing pronunciation so much simpler and is an invaluable visual element to learners. You do not need to know IPA by any means, but you will learn many symbols associated with the sound differences you produce. It will help you to identify and compare the goal sounds. Overall, you will likely learn only a handful of symbols that apply to your particular needs, but these symbols will be a huge help when improving your pronunciation. IPA symbols take away the confusion that comes with using English spelling as a description; because English spelling does NOT equal pronunciation; IPA DOES!

To start, let's take a look at some important IPA (International Phonetic Alphabet) symbols in English:

IPA Symbol: Consonants

/p/ pot, lap	/L/ like, bowl	/ʃ/ shoe, flash
/b/ bad, lab	/n/ no, noon	/tʃ/ chew, match
/t/ top, mat	/m/ more, home	/dʒ/ Just, badge
/d/ dot, toad	/ŋ/ going, singing	/ʒ/ vision, beige
/f/ food, if	/w/ we, window	/θ/ think, with
/k/ cat, black	/v/ very, give	/ð/ the, this
/g/ go, frog	/r/ road, car	
/j/ yes, yellow	/s/ so, moose	

IPA Symbol: Vowels

/ʌ/	"uh"	up, gum
/a/	"ah"	on, top
/æ/	"aa"	at, cat
/ə/	"uh"	(the same as /ʌ/) today, animal
/i/	"ee"	eat, very
/I/	"ih"	it, in
/ʊ/	"ouh"	look, good
/u/	"oo"	who, do
/ɛ/	"eh"	bet, said
/aI/	"ah ee"	my, lie
/eI/	"eh ee"	day, say

/oʊ/	"oh oo"	s<u>o</u>, <u>low</u>
/aʊ/	"aa oo"	h<u>ow</u>, c<u>ow</u>
/oI/	"ow ee"	t<u>oy</u>, b<u>oy</u>

I highly recommend going online and searching for "interactive IPA English charts." These charts allow you to hear the pronunciation for each symbol. There are endless examples online to listen to. At the time of this writing one good example would be https://www.ipachart.com/.

I want you to take some time to look through each symbol and the word examples with each. Most are pretty self-explanatory, thank goodness! Others look super weird, and you will need to pay a bit more attention to those as you practice through this book. Don't worry. You don't need to know these by heart. The symbols you do need to learn are the ones that apply to you. You will see so much throughout this book that it will be difficult NOT to memorize by accident! Just know that this is here as a little reference for you, should you need it.

Don't Let English Spelling Steer You Off Course!

Put plainly, spelling in English does not equal pronunciation. Without a doubt, you have already noticed there are peculiar irregularities in English pronunciation as compared to how words are spelled.

First, English has words with silent letters. "thumb" silent "b," "knife," silent K, "talk" silent /L/

English has words with silent letters in some, but not in others, with no seemingly apparent rules to help explain why: "calf, half, talk" have a silent /L/. BUT "self, shelf" have an audible /L/.

English has homographs: words that have the exact spelling as other words but have a completely different pronunciation and meaning:

- Lead "leed" /Lid/ (to direct in front of), lead "lehd" /Lɛd/ (a metal)

- Wind "waiynd" /waind/(a course that is not straight), wind "wihnd" /wind/ (a gust of air)
- Bass "base"/beis/ (low, deep sound), bass "baas" /bæs/ (a type of fish)

English has homophones: words that have the same pronunciation but are spelled differently and have different meanings:

- to/two/too
- there/their/they're
- pray/prey

English has homonyms: Words that we pronounce the same, we spell the same, but have different meanings:

- Pen: This can mean both "a holding area for animals" and "a writing instrument."
- Book: This can mean "something to read" or "the act of making a reservation."

English has spelling that we pronounce in different ways in different words

- Chess: pronounced /tʃ/ as in "chicken"
- Chef: pronounced /ʃ/ as in "shoe"

- Is: the "s" we pronounce as a /z/
- Of: the "f" we pronounce as a /v/

- Think: pronounced with /θ/ as in "three"
- This: pronounced with /ð/ as in "the"

What this means is that you cannot rely on the spelling of English to speak English clearly. What a bummer, eh?

In this guide, there will be a lot of talk about "sounds" in speech. The sounds of speech are entirely different than the letters representing those sounds in English.

So, I want you to pay keen attention to how a word is actually said rather than how it is spelled. There are only 26 letters in the alphabet, but there are 44 sounds that those letters represent in spoken English. Trying to override your current knowledge of letters and sounds is important to grasp the General American English Accent.

Types of English Sounds

Okay, so here I'm going to go into a bit of linguistic jargon, so stay with me here. I promise it's not a waste of time! These are terms that you will find helpful when working to improve your English pronunciation, and they will help explain some of the differences and nuances of English pronunciation.

Below are terms used to describe which parts of the mouth we use to make a particular sound.

Bilabial is a Latin term that means "two lips." The term bilabial refers to the making of a sound by making our top and bottom lips touch. Feel how your lips touch for /m/, /b/ and /p/. These are bilabial sounds.

Labio-dental means "lip-tooth." These types of sounds are made when your bottom lip makes contact with your upper teeth. E.g., /f/ and /v/ are labio-dental sounds. Sounds fancy, doesn't it?

Interdental means "between teeth." The "th" sound is interdental. We use this term to describe when we place the tip of our tongue between our front teeth. E.g., "Think."

Alveolar refers to the alveolar ridge. The alveolar ridge is that bump you feel on the roof of your mouth, right behind your front teeth. We often place our tongue tip there to make sounds, E.g., /d/.

Palatal refers to the roof of the mouth or the hard palate. The entire front part of the roof of your mouth is the hard palate, and it becomes soft as you move farther back. Palatal sounds include the "sh," "ch," and "j" sounds.

Velar refers to the back of the roof of your mouth. We produce velar sounds using the back of your tongue when it contacts the far back soft part of the roof of the mouth. E.g., /k/ and /g/ are velar sounds.

Glottal refers to the glottis. The glottis is the area between the vocal cords in your larynx or throat. When you constrict or close the glottis and release the airstream, there is an audible sound produced. E.g., when you cough, you're constricting your glottis.

Manner of articulation describes HOW we make sounds.

Stops: Stops are produced when you completely block the air from coming out. E.g., when you make the /p/ sound, the air stops completely until you release that air (aspiration).

Fricatives: A fricative is a type of sound that is produced by friction, creating turbulent airflow. The friction is caused by narrowing and blocking the airflow partially in the mouth to make a sound. These sounds can be prolonged, unlike a stop, which is quick. Example of fricatives include /s/, /z/, /f/ and /v/. See how you can make these sounds long if you want, but not so with stops like /d/?

Affricates: An affricate consonant starts with a stop and ends with a fricative. The two sounds are produced quickly after each other. The "ch" is a fricative because if you dissect it into its parts, we pronounce "ch" with a /t/ sound followed by a "sh" sound: t+sh=ch. Cool eh?

Nasals: We produce nasal sounds by letting the air come out of our noses. If you place your hand in front of your nostril, you can slightly feel the air out the nose. You can see the airflow if you place a mirror under your nostrils while saying the /n/ sound. If you were to hold your nose and try to make the /n/ sound, the sound would stop altogether. Sounds like /n/, /ŋ/ as in "ing," and /m/ are nasals.

Liquids: Liquids involve sounds that have qualities of both vowels and consonants. Often these sounds vary slightly depending on what other sounds are produced before or after them. They're like shape shifters. We make liquid sounds when the tongue is "approximating" or close in contact with the palate. /L/ and /r/ are examples of liquid sounds.

Blends: Blends include two or three consonants together. Put plainly, we smoosh two or three consonants together, usually with /r, L, or s/. E.g., **pl**ay, **pr**ess, **spr**ing are all consonant blends.

Glides: These sounds become like the vowel that follows them. /w/ and "y" as in "yes" are examples of glides.

Vowels: If we change the positions and shape of our tongue in our mouth, the oral cavity space changes. The tongue position changes how we release the air from our mouth. That is how we create vowels. Different languages have different vowels. Some languages have more vowel sounds than others.

Diphthongs: This term is a fancy way of saying we pronounce two vowels side by side, sliding quickly from one to another. We have four main diphthongs, /aʊ/ as in "how,"/eI/ as in "day,"/aI/ as in "my," and /oI/ as in "toy."
If you say these words in slow motion, you should feel how there are two vowels produced.

Phew! You got through the driest part of this guide. Congratulate yourself. Let's learn about how the voice works now.

Let's Talk About VOICE!

It is extremely important to understand the distinction between voiced and unvoiced sounds in English. The reason is, if you don't have a good grasp of this concept and you don't fully gain the skill to turn your voice on when you need to, the entire meaning of English words can be lost! Many non-native speakers of English omit the voice in voiced consonants, and the result is confusion because the meaning has been lost. An example of this is seen in the word "crab" (a crustacean in the ocean). The /b/ at the end of the word is voiced. If you were not to turn your voice on, the word would sound like "crap," another word for feces. These voicing issues have the potential to cause embarrassment, as you can imagine.

We create our voices when our vocal cords or vocal folds make contact and vibrate. You can feel if your voice is on by placing your hand on your neck and feeling a buzz of vibration. Voiceless sounds have no vibration, like a /h/, and therefore you should feel no buzz at all on your throat. However, if you were to make the /z/ sound, you should feel the buzz vibration on your throat.

In English, we have many consonant sound pairs: meaning two sounds are produced in EXACTLY the same way, except one is voiced and the other is not. I like to call them "sister pairs"; there is only one difference, one has the voice on!

These are the voiced consonants in English: B, D, G, J, L, M, N, Ng, R, Th (as in the word "then"), V, W, Y, "ZH," and Z.

These are the voiceless consonants in English: Ch, F, K, P, S, Sh, T, and Th (as in "thing").

All of the vowels in English are voiced sounds.

<u>"Sister pairs"</u> E.g.

Try the sounds below and feel how one sound has no vibration on the throat, and the other does.

- the /z/ is voiced, and the /s/ is voiceless
- the /g/ is voiced, and the /k/ is voiceless
- the /b/ is voiced, and the /p/ is voiceless
- the /v/ is voiced, and the /f/ is voiceless
- the /d/ is voiced, and the /t/ is voiceless
- the "j" is voiced, and the "sh" is voiceless

Blowing Wind: Airflow, And Why It Matters In English

Now, I'm guessing that you have never really put much thought into how much blowing of air you do when you speak. Really, only phoneticians and speech therapists spend very much time thinking about these things! However, for those who are learning English as their second language, this is something you must begin to pay attention to if you hope to grasp the various nuances of English pronunciation.

Let's go over the basics here, and we'll get into the specifics later when we discuss different sounds in English.

Airflow refers to the air that you expel when you create a sound. As we had talked about before, we have different types of sounds. Stops will create a quick puff of air because the airflow has been obstructed, then released like a "pop". /p/ /k/ and /t/ are examples of this. It is impossible to make these sounds long. Fricatives will have a longer continuous airflow. Let's say, for instance, that you make the /f/ sound. You should feel and hear the air releasing past your teeth and onto your bottom lip. You can make this sound short, or you could elongate it if you want to. Affricates, if you remember, have a stop followed by a fricative, so you should note the airflow releases from the stop and transitions to the fricative sound. Airflow from liquids, glides, vowels, and diphthongs are not as turbulent, so you likely won't feel any airflow at all.

Location of airflow:
Just for clarification, the airflow you feel should be "central," meaning you should notice the air is coming out on the center of your mouth and lips. For instance, if you produce a /s/, you should feel the air on the center of your lips. The only sound where airflow should be lateral or out the sides of your mouth is with /L/, but again, you would not feel this airflow, so you don't need to worry about that. If you notice the air is coming out the sides of your mouth in /s/, for example, or you notice that your /s/ sounds "sloshy" or unclear, it is best to seek the advice of a speech-language pathologist for a phonetic assessment. There may be a speech disorder present.

Aspiration:
There are sounds in English that are "aspirated." Aspirated sounds are produced with a small puff of air directly after the sound. Essentially, it sounds like a tiny "h." Aspiration occurs in /p/ /t/ and /k/ sounds at the beginning of stressed syllables, e.g., "pole, tie, and kite." Keep in mind; this is not always the beginning of words. It has to do with stressed SYLLABLES. So, the words "appear" and "attack" would have an aspirated "puff of air" at the P and T as well because the aspirated sounds are at the beginning of the stressed syllable. The exception is if it occurs after an /s/ like "spy." The reason the aspiration is dropped is complex and has to do with how long it takes to produce the voiceless stop consonant and the time when your voicing vowel is starting, or "voice onset time." Now, that sounds like a lot of crazy jargon, but all you really need to know is that you can feel the air puff when you say /p/ /t/ and /k/.

Oral (mouth) vs. Nasal (nose) airflow:
Another thing to consider is whether air is coming out of your mouth (oral airflow) or out of your nose (nasal airflow). All consonants and vowels require airflow out of the mouth. The only exceptions are /n/, /m/ and /ŋ/. For these nasal sounds, you

should be able to feel the vibration on your nose when you produce them. If you put a mirror under your nostrils, you could see the glass fog up from the airflow. Similarly, if you were to plug your nose while producing these sounds, they would stop when the air is blocked from your nose.

Syllables

There will be some discussion on syllables in this book, so I want to describe for you exactly what a syllable is. A syllable is a single unbroken string of sounds within a word. You can think of a syllable as a "beat" in a word. You can clap to each beat to find the syllables. Syllables have nothing to do with how many sounds it contains. It has to do with how many vowels a word contains. Clapping to each part of a word with a vowel can help you identify a syllable. Syllables usually contain a single vowel and include consonants.

For example:

<u>Hat</u>: you can clap once for the single beat

<u>Pa</u> <u>per</u>: you can clap twice for two beats

<u>Oc</u> <u>to</u> <u>pus</u>: you can clap three times for three different beats

<u>He</u> <u>li</u> <u>cop</u> <u>ter</u>: you can clap four times for four different beats

<u>Un</u> <u>in</u> <u>ter</u> <u>rup</u> <u>ted</u>: You can clap five times for five different beats

Try to find the syllables in words you regularly use to get the hang of identifying syllables in speech.

An Important Question: Who Was Your English Teacher?

No, it's not that I have any particular interest in who your English teacher was EXACTLY, but I ask because it's important to know whether or not your English teacher was a native English speaker. I ask this because this one factor can have a significant effect on your learning. Pronunciation is one area of teaching which is often neglected in most second language instruction. The lack of information about pronunciation is evident in how pronunciation is discussed in most English learning course books. Pronunciation becomes an afterthought. At most, only a small handful of "common differences" might be addressed during instruction. In my research, countless articles demonstrate that few teachers say they try and do some pronunciation in most lessons. Still, the majority either does very little or no pronunciation work at all. In my experience working with clients over the years, there is a resounding commonality; clients are often taught nothing specific to pronunciation or were taught rules that were just plain incorrect. I cannot tell you the number of clients that have said to me, "What? You're kidding! My teacher told me to do this…[insert an incorrect made-up rule]". Of course, non-native teachers do not neglect pronunciation out of malice but possibly out of a lack of knowledge or confidence in the area of pronunciation. It is challenging to teach others a skill that you have yet to understand or develop yourself.

If there is a lack of understanding of the speech mechanism and how sounds are produced, instructors are left with a "repeat after me" teaching method. Repetition-type instruction leaves the learner to rely on the teacher for accuracy cues, which often are difficult for non-native speakers to provide with any amount of confidence. Without any development of "differentiation" skills to be able to distinguish and hear differences between new sound systems of the goal language, and without any specific explanations of how to produce particular sound systems, learners are left with next to no tools to be able to self-correct and improve their pronunciation. If students are provided with incorrect instruction on top of this, it is no wonder that pronunciation is a skill that lingers far beyond language proficiency.

A Note About Practicing

You will find extensive and exhaustive practice materials in this guide. Practice will start with identifying your ability to hear the goal sound (differentiation) and then practice producing the sound (production).

Practice examples are presented to you in order of complexity. We will start in isolation, practicing just the sound on its own. We will then work up the ladder to syllables, words, phrases, sentences, reading, and conversation. The phrases and sentences presented will often be silly tongue-twister drill practice. The goal here is to maximize your motor movements to get used to the new pronunciations and increase your speed. Although some of the sentences will be crazy, they present a distinct opportunity to super-charge your pronunciation practice. There will also be a few funny little vocabulary items to be aware of. Please do not be offended if there are some "off-colored" words in the vocabulary. Although crass, I feel leaving these words in practice is necessary to increase your awareness of potential embarrassment. I do this, so you do not find yourself in an even more embarrassing situation in real life. So I apologize in advance. You will come across a few swear words!

I hope this book will help you, someone who has gone through the painstaking work of learning English as a second language. I want to help bridge the gap between what you have already learned and your English pronunciation goals.

I want to give you a clear warning. I will say this now and likely many times more throughout this book. Self-directed learning is a valuable activity, and with it, new understanding and skills will undoubtedly occur. However, there is no substitute for learning from a certified Speech-Language Pathologist (SLP) who is also certified in accent modification Instruction. If you hope to see significant improvements in your English pronunciation, the greatest results are to be expected when working with a knowledgeable and experienced professional. A knowledgeable instructor can work through differentiation, clear instruction on eliciting accurate productions, providing feedback, and teaching you the skills you need to turn that knowledge into a functional skill. You can make improvements on your own, but as with any DIY projects you take on, you risk wasting time, resources and potentially not achieving the outcomes you desire. Visit my website for information on the PROactive Pronunciation Program and individualized assessments at www.PROactivePronunciation.com.

Chapter 2: Speech
How It All Works

Talking seems so natural. But, do you know the parts that we use to create speech and how it all works? Why even bother to learn this? Well, by understanding the basics, you can better adjust the elements of your speech. We all understand that our lips and tongue move in specific ways to create sounds. You may be surprised, however, to learn just how much more complicated speech is. Speech is a truly fascinating ability!

Let's take a crash course in the anatomy and physiology of how we produce speech to better understand what is happening when we speak.

Airflow And Voice

We produce all speech sounds with air from our lungs. The /h/ sound is literally just air flowing from our lungs, past our mouths, with no constriction.

Air flows from our lungs up through the trachea to the glottis. The larynx is the area where our vocal folds sit. If you feel where your "Adam's apple" area is, this is the larynx.

Our vocal folds are two flaps of tissue that vibrate together to produce a sound. Voice can only occur if the airflow passes by these flaps of tissue. If you place your finger against this area and say "ah," you will feel a slight vibration. The vibration occurs when the two flaps, the vocal folds or "cords," make contact with each other. Our voices will go up and down in pitch depending on how tightly the vocal folds are pulled or how lax they are loosened. We can change the loudness by adjusting how much air pressure from the lungs goes through the vocal folds. If the airflow were to run out, we would slowly press the muscles surrounding our larynx and lungs to "push" out whatever air remains to allow the voice to continue. For many non-native English speakers, their first language does not have some voiced consonants as does English. Remember, voicing consonants can change the meaning of a word.

In English, we have these "sister pairs," meaning one version of the sound is voiced and another is not, and that difference creates a difference in meaning. The pronunciation and the mouth's position are the same, with one difference; the voice is either turned on or off. Here is an example: "Pick" to pick up something from the ground (the "CK" is not voiced) vs. "Pig," a farm animal (the g is voiced).

Again, both sounds /k/ and /g/ are made in exactly the same way. Only voicing is different. Voicing is an area we will discuss in greater detail later in this book. Still, it is crucial to understand the basics of voicing. It is especially important to be able to identify when your voice is on vs. off. Your vocal cords vibrate to make all vowels. Voiced sounds like "B," "D," "G," "Z," etc., are vibrated with voice, and the vocal folds don't vibrate for voiceless sounds like "P," "T," "K," "S," etc.

When you add your voice to voiced consonants, you increase the overall power of your speech. Increased voicing raises your overall volume, making you sound louder, clearer, more confident, improves your resonance, and can even help you speak with a deeper voice. Improving your voicing of voiced consonants even helps to eliminate word confusion and enhances the rhythm and timing of your speech. It's worth working on!

Nasal vs. Oral Sounds

Another often unknown part of how we produce sounds is the velum. If you have ever wondered what that "hangy ball" at the back of your throat is, well, it is called the "uvula." The uvula is the farthest protrusion of the velum. The velum is part of the soft palate that hangs near the back of your throat. This soft flesh is anchored by muscles that allow it to tense and rise to block air from going through the nasal passage or the nose. So, when the velum is up, all the air from breathing and speaking will come in and out of our mouths. If the velum is down, the opening to the nose is unobstructed so that air can pass through the nose. When we make nasal sounds, this velum hangs down. Most people cannot physically feel that they are controlling this movement. You can feel, however, the air that is released.

If you make a /n/ sound, the velum is down, and the tip of your tongue is on the roof of your mouth. The whole oral cavity (mouth) is blocked off, leaving the airflow no choice but to travel out your nose. Sounds like /n/, /m/, and /ŋ/ are produced nasally.

The Palate

If you run your tongue along the roof of your mouth, you will feel a hard top. This hard top is called your palate. The palate is divided into a few parts. If we press our tongue along different parts of the palate, we will create different speech sounds.

The Alveolar Ridge:

The alveolar ridge is the area just behind your top front teeth. If you run your tongue along it, you will feel a bumpy area that's lower and close to your teeth. The alveolar ridge is where we produce sounds like /t/, /d/, /s/, and /L/. If you run your tongue too far back, you will hit the hard palate.

The Hard Palate:

The hard palate is the smooth roof of your mouth, just behind the alveolar ridge. This area should feel hard if you press your tongue on it. If you notice, the top of your mouth is not flat but quite vaulted upwards, like a cave. The sides of your palate are lower as they reach your teeth. The hard palate is where we produce sounds like "sh," and "ch," and "J" with the sides of our tongue up.

The Soft Palate:

If you run your tongue even farther back, you will feel that the hard bony palate turns soft. Many people have difficulty feeling this area as it is pretty far back! The soft palate is where the back of the tongue will contact to make sounds like /k/ and /g/. Try and feel for yourself.

The Tongue

So let's get to the main Character: The tongue!

We can divide the tongue into parts: the tip, centre, back, and sides.
Each part of the tongue moves in a particular position to help create different speech sounds as the air flows past it.

The tip of the tongue:

The tip is the very end or point of your tongue. The tip of the tongue is responsible for many of the sounds we produce in English. For example, when placed between the teeth, the tip creates the "th" sound, as in "think." The tip of the tongue also touches the alveolar ridge to create the /t/ and /d/ sounds. Try for yourself, and see if you can feel where your tongue tip touches. The tip of the tongue also produces sounds like /s/ and /z/, only it nearly touches the alveolar ridge and area just behind the top front teeth.

The middle of the tongue:

The middle of the tongue is the area behind the tip. This part of the tongue adjusts to produce differences in vowels. For example, when the middle of the tongue is high and forward, you create the sound /i/ or "eeeeee" as in "seed." When the middle of the tongue is down, you make the /a/ sound as in "pot" or "mop." If you compare /i/ and /a/, you should feel the middle of the tongue going up and down, up and down. Notice, the tip of the tongue is not involved in these sounds. The tip of the tongue is resting neutrally in the mouth, touching nothing at all.

The back of the tongue:

The back of the tongue is far more difficult for most people to sense in speech. It is the part of the tongue that feels as though it is beginning to go to your throat. The back of the tongue is responsible for sounds such as /k/ as in "can" and /g/ as in "go." If you repeat /k/ and /g/ over and over, you should be able to feel a slight contact of the back of your tongue to the roof of the mouth. For many, this will require a little more investigation to feel what is truly happening. If you grab a mirror or your phone, record your tongue when you say /g/. You will have to do this with your mouth slightly open, of course. You will notice that the back of your tongue goes up to the palate. Notice, too, that the tip of your tongue is staying down and neutral. The tip is not involved in these sounds at all.

The sides of the tongue:

We often ignore the sides of the tongue when talking about pronunciation, but this is a mistake. The sides of the tongue can be looked at as "anchors" of the tongue. The sides rise, contacting the top teeth for many sounds helping to anchor the tongue into position. Certain sounds require the sides of the tongue to rise to the roof, like /ʃ/, or "sh" as in "shoe" and /tʃ/ or "ch" sound as in "cheese." We also raise the sides of the tongue for the infamous /r/ sound. It is important to feel how the sides of your tongue raise upwards for these sounds when learning correct pronunciation. Becoming aware of these parts of the tongue and increasing your understanding of the movements within your mouth will go a long way towards fully "feeling" your pronunciations. Increased awareness of the feeling of your tongue positions is essential since it is the basis for being able to self-monitor your pronunciation and be able to self-correct. Feeling the pronunciation is especially important if differentiating between sounds that are difficult for you.

The Teeth

There's not much to say here, as your teeth are not exactly mobile. There's really nothing to be aware of except that we use our teeth in pronunciation in English. The "th" /θ/ sounds as in "think" and the voiced version /ð/ as in "this" are both pronounced using the front teeth. The tongue tip is placed between the teeth as we blow air above the tongue to produce the sound. Many languages do not have this particular sound in their phonemic repertoire. Hence, it is an important sound to master when speaking with a General North American English accent.

The Lips

Most people know how the tongue plays a major role in speech, but the runner-up, the lips, are not often noticed. The details of lip movements in speech are essential to master, as their position highly impacts English pronunciation. Positions include:

- spread in a wide smile for sounds like "eeeee" and /s/ and /z/
- neutral as in the vowel /ʌ/ or "uh"
- slightly rounded as in /ʊ/ as in "look" or "put"
- fully rounded, as in /u/ and /o/ like in words "you" and "no"

Understanding the intricacies of lip position is important to speak clearly and be truly understood using the General North American English accent.

The Jaw

Jaw positioning is our final consideration when we look at the anatomy involved in speech. The jaw is another essential element that we must be aware of when we discuss pronunciation. The jaw plays such an important role because it affects the position of the tongue in many ways. Since the jaw is where most tongue muscles are attached, its position will dictate the height of the tongue. If your jaw is closed and your teeth are together, the tongue has a free-range within the oral cavity to move. If the jaw is opened slightly, the tongue goes downwards with the jaw and is lower. When the jaw is open and lower, the tongue will have a greater area to move or range of motion. If the jaw is open completely, the tongue goes down farther still, along with the jaw.

For this reason, vowels with low tongue positions include the jaw being opened completely, and vowels with high tongue positions require the jaw to be closed. We can adjust many vowels with slight changes to the jaw position. It's important to understand what position your jaw should be in when working on pronunciation goals to ensure accurate and precise articulation.

Now, I know this might have been a bit more information than you thought you needed to know. The truth is that without understanding these basics, we can miss the intricacies of pronunciation, and along with that comes reduced clarity and accuracy in speech.

Become familiar with these elements of your speech. Begin to think about what your lips, tongue, and jaw are doing to create your speech sounds. The more awareness you have, the easier it will be to begin adjusting your speech patterns. It is often by "feeling" the differences rather than listening for them that my clients can self-adjust their speaking.

Start paying attention to this and give it a try for yourself!

PART TWO: All Those Tricky Consonants!

Chapter 3: "TH": Yes, We Do Speak With Our Tongues Out

So here we are! We can finally begin to implement our understanding of how speech works and how our lips, tongue, and jaw move to create sounds.

A quick reminder about that fun word "Differentiation":

Remember, to differentiate means we can "hear" the difference between the sounds we produce versus the sounds we hope to achieve, also called our "goal" sounds. It is essential to hear the difference between the old and new productions to compare and contrast your speech and make the appropriate adjustments. Another critical element is to "feel" what you are doing differently with your tongue, lips, jaw, airflow, or voice to change how you produce a particular sound. Feeling the difference is important because sometimes our ears can play tricks on us, especially if differentiation is a problem for you. Sounds start to meld together and begin to sound the same, as our brains have not yet become attuned and trained to hear sounds that you have not paid attention to in the past. At the beginning of your practice, you will notice that "differentiating" the nuances between certain sounds is more difficult. As you practice, your brain begins to improve and picks up the differences between different sounds. As you go through the process of change, you will also need to feel how your speech pattern is different and focus on that difference because feeling it will be your way of identifying whether or not you are producing the goal sound correctly. So the mantra here is "hear it," "feel it," "do it." Repeat.

Order Of Complexity

So here, we're going to talk about the process. When changing a speech pattern or replacing a sound with an entirely new pronunciation, you cannot expect just to use it in rapid conversational speech. Change in pronunciation is a process. It takes practice, repetition, familiarity, and habituation. To achieve this, you must work through an order of complexity. First, we practice in isolation, the sound on its own. We then move to syllables, words, phrases, sentences, reading, cued conversation, and finally, natural, spontaneous conversation. To expect yourself to use your new sound or sounds in a quick discussion with work colleagues who constantly interrupt and change topics rapidly would be setting yourself up for failure. Work through the process, and move on to the next phase when you feel ready. Remember, it is quality we are aiming for, so focus on accuracy rather than speed. Speed will increase with practice, but if you do not focus on ensuring your articulation is accurate, then you essentially miss the boat, as they say.

Improving Your Listening Skills

Improving your pronunciation can significantly impact your ability to hear sounds in others' speech as well. Nearly every client I have worked with at some point mentions to me that they can "now hear the sounds when native English speakers talk." They never noticed the sounds before, or they could never identify what the difference was. Generally, this results in a greater ability to understand others. If understanding the rapid speech of a native English speaker is something you struggle with, I am happy to give you fantastic news! Your work towards more precise General American English pronunciation will also be work towards greater understanding and comprehension of other native English speakers. How cool is that?

So, here we go!

Let's now talk about some of the most common difficult sounds produced in English. I will explain each sound in detail, how to create it, compare it to typical errors and substitutions of its pronunciation, and give you practice materials to master using the sound. Let's do this!

TH

Description:

Some people refer to this as the "rude" sound because it is often considered impolite in other cultures and even in English to stick out your tongue at someone. In this case, however, it is necessary. If you do not put your tongue out, your pronunciation will be noticeably different from General North American Pronunciation. This sound is produced by placing the very tip of your tongue and placing it between your front teeth. We produce the "th" sound with only a TINY bit of the tongue tip, so be sure to check the mirror to ensure you are not placing too much tongue out of your mouth. The next element of this sound is breath. The "th" sound requires that you "BLOW" air. You should feel the air flowing above your tongue as it passes past your upper top front teeth and your tongue tip. I often tell my clients to feel the air on their tongue tip to ensure proper airflow.

There are two forms of "th" in English: Voiced "th" and Voiceless "th," and each have a different symbol in IPA.

Voiced "th": /ð/
Voiceless "th": /θ/

The voiceless version just requires that you pull your tongue tip between your teeth and blow. The voiced version of "th" requires one additional step! Add your voice! To do this, you make the sound loud. Often, this is difficult for people to do, so think of it like you will hum while blowing and saying "th." A great way to "feel" if your voice is on is to place your hand on your throat. This is where your vocal folds are, and this is where you can feel your voice vibration. If you do a voiceless "th," you should not feel any "buzz" or vibration on your throat. When you create the voiced "th," you should feel the "buzz" on your throat or a definite vibration sensation when you feel your neck.

Spelling:

Unfortunately, the spelling in English will not give you any hints about whether you must use the voiced or voiceless version of "th." Sorry! English just won't help you out here! I explain to my clients that they must memorize a list of the voiced "th" words. Luckily, there are only a few voiced "th" words. The rest can be assumed to be voiceless.

<u>Common Differences: Hear it!</u>

Voiceless "Th"

For the voiceless "th," people often substitute the /t/ sound: Here is a list of comparison words of the /t/ sound versus the voiceless "th" or /θ/. Go through the list yourself and feel how they are pronounced differently. Be sure to keep your tongue tip out and blow for the "th"!

Listen to the difference as you say each word and compare the sounds to improve your "differentiation" skills! A good tip is to record yourself so you can listen afterward as well.

/t/	"th" voiceless				
boat	both	tank	thank	torn	thorn
fate	faith	taught	thought	trash	thrash
fort	fourth	term	therm	tread	thread
got	goth	team	theme	trill	thrill
mat	math	tent	tenth	true	through
oat	oath	tie	thigh	tug	thug
root	Ruth	tick	thick		
		tong	thong		

Voiced "Th"

"th" is often substituted with other sounds. The voiced "th" is generally replaced with /d/

See the list below. The term "minimal pair" refers to one change in sound that changes the entire meaning of a word. Take a look at these words and see if you make these substitutions in your regular speech as well. As you say the second "th" version, put your tongue tip between your teeth, blow, and add your voice vibration.

<u>D vs. "th" voiced Minimal Pairs:</u>

/d/	"th" voiced				
Dan	than	dine	thine	breed	breathe
day	they	doe	though	load	loathe
den	then	had	hath	sued	soothe
D	thee	laid	lathe	udder	other
D's	these	tide	tithe	bladder	blather
dare	there	read	wreathe	header	Heather
dough	though	bade	bathe	wordy	worthy
die	thy	ride	writhe		
		she'd	sheathe		

Another sound difference people often make with "th" is substituting it with a /s/ or a /z/.

Listen to the difference as you say each word and compare the sounds to improve your "differentiation" skills!

Substitutions for voiced "th" as /s/ and /z/:
"The" would be pronounced as "zuh" or "suh"
"That" would be pronounced as "zat" or "sat"
"This" would be pronounced as "zis" or "sis"
"Those" would be pronounced as "zoze" or "soze"
"Them" would be pronounced as "zem" or "sem"

The "th" is a continuant, meaning that the sound can be sustained or held. It is not a pop of sound that is quick and stops. The "th" sound must be slightly sustained or held to avoid sounding like a /d/ with your tongue out. Practice elongating the "th" sound and holding it slightly longer to ensure you release good airflow.

<u>Feel it!</u>
To feel the differences between these words, you must pay attention to a few things.
1: feel that your tongue tip is slightly between your front teeth. Don't bite too hard! The teeth should only barely graze your tongue to allow air to pass between the teeth and tongue.

2: Feel the airflow as you blow. You can often feel a cold sensation at the tip of your tongue. Some people feel the air on their lips just past their tongue tip.

3: For the voiced "th," feel that your voice is on by placing your hand on your throat. You can feel the vibration there or focus your attention on the slight vibration at the tip of your tongue when you make this sound. Either way, be sure to be aware of the difference in feeling the voiced versus the voiceless "th."

Do it!

Alright, now let's practice! First, we will start by focusing on isolation, the sound on its own. Compare voiced and voiceless versions of each of these:

Isolation:

thhhhh, thhhhh, thhhhh, thhhhh, thhhhh

Syllables:

Hint: Many people get stuck at the syllable level with voiced "th" especially. What often happens is that they produce a nice clear "th" but then add the /d/ right after, as their tongue quickly slips in and touches the alveolar ridge. What you end up with is a "thd." So, the word "this" ends up sounding like "thdis." To avoid adding the old /d/, focus on opening the mouth after the "th," pulling the tongue down immediately. Try it for yourself.

thhhhha, thhhhhe, thhhhhi, thhhhho, thhhhhu
athhhhh, ethhhhh, ithhhhhh, othhhhh, uthhhhh
athhhha, ethhhhe, ithhhhhi, othhhho, uthhhhu

Voiced "Th" Practice

Voiced "th" Words:

Below is a list of all of the voiced "th" words. Memorize this list because all other "th" words will be voiceless.

Beginning of Words:

than	thee	then
that	them	there/their
the	themselves	therefore

therein	they'll	those
these	they're	thou
they	they've	though
they'd	this	thy

Middle of Words:

another	gather	soothing
bathing	leather	tether
brother	mother	tetherball
clothing	other	together
either	rather	weather
father	smoothest	weatherman
feather	smoothie	worthy

Ends of Words:

breathe	teethe	scathe
smooth	lathe	tithe
bathe	seethe	loathe

Voiced "th" Phrases:
Beginning Phrases:

By themselves	Their house	They did
Then you	Them again	This is it
That was	Then again	Those things
The beginning	Therefore I will	Though I agree
The end	These things	

Middle Phrases:

Another building	Light feather	Soothing bath
Bathing suit	Mother dearest	Tether ball
Big brother	My father	Together we stand
Either way	New clothing	Weather station
Fruit smoothie	Other than that	Weatherman said
Gather here	Rather old	Worthy opponent
Leather belt	Smoothest shave	

Final Phrases:

Bathe today	Loathe that idea	Smooth shave
Breathe easy	New lathe	Large tithe

Beginning Sentences:

That tree is so beautiful

The paper is on the desk

This is the book I needed

Their offices are over there

These are my favorite jeans

Those dogs love running in the park

They have been in the sun all day long

Then they went with their friends to the party

These cups are bigger than the ones over there

The children have their homework in their backpacks

They went by themselves

Therefore, we will challenge this bill

Therein lies the question

They'd be crazy to go into that place without a defense

They'll want to find a ride there

They're likely to survive the whole ordeal

They've got a lot of confidence

I believe so, though I could be wrong

Middle Sentences:

My mother called today

That bird lost its feather

I'd love another piece of cake

That was a fantastic smoothie

The weather is wonderful today

Your father is visiting next week

I have never played tetherball before

Tell your brother to come in for dinner

We worked on the project together for six months

They were bathing in the creek

My brother is my best friend

We went shopping for clothing

Either way you look at it, there is a decision to make

Why don't you gather some sticks for the fire?

My belt is made of leather

Where is the other glove?

I'd rather be at home than at this work conference

That is the smoothest shave I've ever had

What an amazing strawberry smoothie

That sauna was really soothing

You'll need to tether that rope to a tree

The weatherman was right again

Are you worthy of this honor?

Ending Sentences:

Don't forget to breathe

He sanded it down really smooth

I bathed the dog in the bath today

I bought this soother so the baby could use it to teethe

Have you ever used a lathe before?

He will seethe when he's seen what you've done

I loathe being bit by mosquitos

"Th" + /d/

This combination of consonants is often tricky, so it's a good idea to practice. To pronounce these sounds together, we will avoid putting a pause or a break between the sounds. We will slide from the "th" position with your tongue between your teeth, then move to the /d/ position with your tongue on the alveolar ridge. There is no vowel or "eh" sound between these two consonants.

Words:

bathed	seethed	tithed
betrothed	sheathed	unbathed
breathed	sleuthed	unscathed
clothed	smoothed	wreathed
loathed	soothed	writhed
mouthed	sunbathed	
scathed	teethed	

Sentences:

Even after the fight, I left unscathed

I breathed in the wonderful fresh spring air

I mouthed out the words to my friend in the library

She smoothed out the tablecloth to prepare for dinner

The calm music easily soothed the baby

I sunbathed all day and got the worst sunburn of my life

He tithed to the church to help the poor

The worm wriggled and writhed in the mud

I have always loathed watching horror movies

Voiceless "Th" Practice

Words:

Beginning:

thank	thing	thrift
Thanksgiving	think	thrifty
thaw	thinly	thrill
theatre	thinned	thrive
theft	third	throat
theme	thirst	throb
theory	thirsty	throne
therapy	thirty	throng
thermal	thistle	through
thermometer	thong	throw
thermos	thorax	thrush
thesis	thorn	thud
thick	thought	thug
thicken	thrall	thumb
thicker	thrash	thump
thicket	thread	thunder
thief	threat	Thursday
thigh	threw	thwart
thin	three	thyroid

Middle:

anthem	atheist	bathtub
anthrax	athlete	Bertha
apathy	author	birthday
atheism	bathroom	breathy

deathly
earthly
earthquake
earthy
empathy
ethane
ethanol
ethical
ethnic
ethos
filthy
frothy

healthy
lengthy
lethal
lithium
menthol
methane
method
methyl
monthly
mouthwash
nothing
panther

pathway
python
rethink
Timothy
toothbrush
toothpaste
toothy
urethra
wealthy
within
without

End:

absinth
bath
beneath
Beth
birth
booth
both
breadth
breath
broth
cloth
dearth
death
depth
earth
eighth
faith
fifth
filth
forth
fourth
froth
girth

Goliath
goth
growth
health
hearth
length
mammoth
math
meth
month
moth
mouth
myth
ninth
north
oath
path
plinth
rebirth
seventh
sheath
sixth
sleuth

sloth
smith
south
stealth
tablecloth
teeth
tenth
tooth
truth
twelfth
uncouth
unearth
warmth
wealth
width
with
worth
wrath
wreath
youth
zenith

Beginning Phrases:

a thing or two
drive-thru
finished my thesis
floral theme
he's a thief
he's a thug
heard a thud
in the thick of it
in the thicket
in the throngs of
lingual thrush
movie theatre
needle and thread
on the throne
report the theft
sore throat
speech therapy
thank you
Thanksgiving Day

thaw the meat
theory of evolution
thermal sources
thermometer reading
these are the things
thick and thin
thicken the gravy
thicker than thieves
thigh-high
a thin piece of wood
think of it
thinly veiled
thinned out the herd
third in line
thirsty for water
thirty-three
thistles and thorns
thong sandals
thorn in my side

thought about it
threat of snow
three or four
threw it to her
thrift store
thrifty shopper
the thrill of the kill
thrive in nature
throbbing thumb
through the path
throw it out
thumbs up
thump on the ground
thunder storm
Thursday is the day
thwart your enemies
thyroid disease
warm thermos

Middle Phrases:

a long python
atheist or religious
author of this book
always apathetic
Bertha is here
birthday party
breathy voice
clean your toothbrush
deathly ill
earthly desires
earthy smell
empathy and
compassion
ethane gas
ethical dilemma

ethnic food
filthy rich
frothy smoothie
healthy people
in the bathroom
it was an earthquake
lengthy poem
lethal weapon
lithium-ion battery
menthol gum
methane gas
method of
achievement
methyl alcohol
minty mouthwash

monthly agenda
national anthem
nothing to do
Olympic athlete
on the pathway
out of toothpaste
overflowed bathtub
rethink your view
Timothy was here
toothy smile
watch for anthrax
watch the panther
wealthy family
within a minute
without a thought

End Phrases:

absinth drink

afraid of death

bad breath

53

beneath the cover

Beth will come

birth control

both of us

breadth of the article

bubble bath

building wealth

clean the cloth

David and Goliath

depth of the argument

eighth time around

faith in God

fifth piece of pie

filth and dirt

fourth time trying

froth on my mug

go forth

goth look

growth of the plant

he was uncouth

he's a sleuth

health and wealth

it's a myth

large mammoth

length of the road

loud mouth

math equation

meth and other drugs

month of the year

moth to the flame

Mr. Smith

ninth time

north to south

on the hearth

path to wisdom

phone booth

planet earth

pledged an oath

round tablecloth

seventh-day

sixth minute

slow sloth

soup broth

south to east

tenth attempt

tooth in the mouth

truth will be told

twelfth time

unearth the truth

warmth of the sun

white teeth

width and girth

width and height

with my friend

worth a penny

wrath of the enemy

wreath on the door

youth versus age

Beginning Sentences:

Thank you for the therapy session

She threw a party at the theatre on Thursday

I thought that Thanksgiving was three days ago

I don't love what has happened to my thighs at thirty

Thank you for thinking of me on my thirtieth Birthday

There was a tight feeling in my throat when I threw that picture away

He taught me a thing or two when I finished my thesis on the topic

The thief and the thug went through the drive-thru

I heard a thud in the movie theatre

He would never report the theft because they were thicker than thieves

The gravy was too thin, so I added starch to thicken it to a thicker paste

I found a thin piece of wood in the thicket

I was thigh-deep in the thick thistles and thorns

I have thirty-three pairs of thong sandals

These are the things that I think of when I'm in the throngs of emotion

I thought about how thirsty for water I was

The thrifty shopper only shops in thrift stores

The <u>thr</u>eat of snow is a <u>th</u>orn in my side
I held my <u>thr</u>obbing <u>th</u>umb as I wandered <u>thr</u>ough the path
I got a sore <u>thr</u>oat on <u>Th</u>anksgiving Day
I <u>thr</u>ew <u>thr</u>ee or four spools of <u>thr</u>ead to her
She <u>thr</u>ew it out on <u>Th</u>ursday
The <u>th</u>ermometer shows the meat has not fully <u>th</u>awed

Middle Sentences:
I got a too<u>th</u>brush for my Bir<u>th</u>day
I spit the mou<u>th</u>wash out of my mouth
One-<u>th</u>ird of weal<u>th</u>y people are heal<u>th</u>y
I felt an ear<u>th</u>quake while I was making a smoothie
The too<u>th</u>paste fell in the ba<u>th</u>tub when I was in the ba<u>th</u>room
I am dea<u>th</u>ly scared of py<u>th</u>ons
An a<u>th</u>eist believes in a<u>th</u>eism
The au<u>th</u>or of the book spoke with a brea<u>th</u>y voice
Ber<u>th</u>a was apa<u>th</u>etic to the fil<u>th</u>y rich
He went wi<u>th</u>out a Bir<u>th</u>day party for all of his life
Clean your too<u>th</u>brush regularly and use minty mou<u>th</u>wash and men<u>th</u>ol gum
Heal<u>th</u>y people avoid sugary foods
I hid in the ba<u>th</u>room for a leng<u>th</u>y period of time as the ear<u>th</u>quake rumbled
Empa<u>th</u>y and compassion are important wi<u>th</u>in a civil society
There's no<u>th</u>ing on my mon<u>th</u>ly agenda
Wi<u>th</u>in a minute, that ear<u>th</u>y smell of e<u>th</u>ane gas filled the room
You must only use e<u>th</u>ical me<u>th</u>ods of research
The weal<u>th</u>y family financially supported the Olympic a<u>th</u>lete
I had to re<u>th</u>ink which pa<u>th</u>way I came from
She dropped the too<u>th</u>paste in the ba<u>th</u>tub
Timo<u>th</u>y sang the national an<u>th</u>em with a too<u>th</u>y grin

End Sentences:
Kei<u>th</u> wanted a boo<u>th</u> wi<u>th</u> a tablecloth
Be<u>th</u> threw a mo<u>th</u> in the ba<u>th</u> as a joke
That was the best Four<u>th</u> of July on ear<u>th</u>
Kei<u>th</u> lost his brea<u>th</u> as he walked down the Nor<u>th</u> pa<u>th</u>
My son put his too<u>th</u> benea<u>th</u> his pillow at night for the too<u>th</u> fairy
She put the wrea<u>th</u> out in the mon<u>th</u> of December to decorate for the holidays
Clean the clo<u>th</u> after your bubble ba<u>th</u>

Both of us are focused on building wealth

Beth will increase the breadth of the article

It's a myth, despite the depth of your argument

He's a sleuth, uncouth, and a loud mouth

Go forth on your path to find faith in God

Even the filthy rich are afraid of death

That was the fourth time this month we assessed the growth, health, and wealth of this business

Mr. Smith found a moth on the North side of the hearth

He pledged an oath on the seventh day to abstain from drinking absinth

We use math to measure width and girth

The youth of this day are worth our attention

He lost the fourth, fifth, sixth, seventh, eighth, ninth, tenth, eleventh, and twelfth race

The mammoth had bad breath

The hot broth hurt every tooth in my mouth

I hid with my friend beneath the tablecloth

/d/ + "Th"

The /d/ sound involves placing the tongue tip on the roof of the mouth just behind the front teeth on the alveolar ridge, which is that bump behind your top teeth. The tongue then must slide out and between the teeth to create the "th." Below are some examples to practice. Feel how you will need to slide the tongue from the alveolar ridge over to between the teeth without releasing or letting go.

Give it a try!

Words:

sad thing	had them here	made this book
mad thug	Did they win?	bold throw
mud throwing	old thug	wild theme park
dad things	kid threw the ball	load the truck
read the book	bald thin man	bird themed
add these numbers	lied then stole	hid them
end that game	lend the tools	

That was a wild theme park

Don't forget to load the truck with apples

She wanted a bird-themed party

The neighbor said he would lend the tools to us for the shed

I need help to add these numbers together

I forgot I had these boxes here

My daughter made this book for you

There will be no mud throwing during recess

I read that book last year, it was great

My dad thinks his jokes are hilarious

He lied then he stole from us

That's one very mad thug

The sad thing is that I can't even remember it

If you end that game of monopoly, we can go out for ice cream

Did they win the baseball championship?

Exceptions:

A few English words are spelled with a "th" but pronounced as a /t/ sound. Here is the list to be aware of:

Thomas	"tah mus"
Theresa	"tuh ree suh"
Esther	"es ter"
Thai	"tie"
Thyme	"time"

Asthma (The "th" here is pronounced as a /z/ "az muh"

Reading:

Choose a favorite book, newspaper, blog, or even your work emails to practice your new pronunciation of "th" while reading. If the reading is digital, you can even highlight all of the "th" sounds to help you as you read along. Press Ctrl + F (or use the 'Find' function), then enter "th" to highlight each one. Another great tip is to record yourself while reading, either on your computer, laptop, or phone. The benefits of recording yourself while reading are significant. You will be able to review yourself and hear the new pronunciation, thus improving your differentiation skills. You will also be able to identify errors and read along as you listen to yourself speak. Reviewing recordings provides you with visual and audio cues to practice with, and I highly recommend doing this regularly.

When moving to conversation level, a good sub-step is to read a sentence but put it in memory. This way, you do not have any visual cues to help you with your pronunciation. Say the sentence as if you are speaking to a friend. Focus on finding the "th" sounds as you recite.

Conversation:
So, you've learned how to hear the new sound, and you've learned how to feel when you're pronouncing your new sound correctly in isolation, syllables, words, phrases, and sentences. You have even practiced and reviewed yourself while reading out loud. These are all necessary steps towards clear pronunciation in conversation. But, unless you actually use your new pronunciation in real-life conversations, your feeling of naturalness and familiarity using the new sound will not occur. You must begin to incorporate your new pronunciation into daily conversations. At first, this will feel extremely uncomfortable. You might even feel as if you are acting or trying to imitate a native speaker. In essence, yes, that's what you're doing, but the feeling of making it your own is what happens with time and practice. You must be aware that this "awkward" feeling is necessary for the process, and you must become habituated to the new movements to speak comfortably.

You might also notice that your speech becomes slower as you focus intentionally on using your new pronunciation skills. You might begin by speaking slowly as you become familiar with how to adapt your pronunciation in speech. In time, your speed will increase, and you will feel more natural. This phase in practice will often result in many self-corrections while speaking, meaning you might repeat words over as you hear yourself pronounce a sound your old way, and you work to repeat and correct the sound. It will essentially feel as though your fluency is being impacted. This is normal and expected. As you are processing and focusing on pronunciation, it won't be easy at first to catch the sounds before you say them. Again, as you practice, your processing speed will increase. You will begin to notice the target sounds just before saying them, thus reducing your need to repeat your words. It's a process, and it takes practice, but don't give up! It's a phase, and the results of pushing through this discomfort are well worth it.

The last thing I would like to say about conversation is that it often requires a supportive speaking partner. If you have a friend or spouse who is supportive of your goal to improve the clarity of your English pronunciation and understands your goals, you are far more likely to practice freely with them. If, on the other hand, you experience judgments or others do not understand your goals, you may not have the benefit of feeling vulnerable enough to practice around them. Find people in your life who care about your goals, and explain to them that you are working through improving your pronunciation. My clients find it often really helpful to find other English language learners through other social circles or social media groups with whom to practice. You may find there to be less pressure with unfamiliar people.

If you find yourself in a situation where you have no consistent practice partner, fear not! You do not need one to improve. You can be your own partner. Yes, this may sound weird, but hear me out! I have often recommended clients record themselves telling themselves about a funny dream they had last night or a story from their childhood. Using a recording tool, you can talk freely using your new speech patterns. A bonus is that you can review how you sound. It's the next best thing to a real-life conversation and has great benefits.

Tips For Practicing In Conversation

First, I just want to point out that bulk practice, i.e., practicing all at once, is not as effective as sprinkling your new pronunciation throughout the day in conversation. It is far better to practice for 5-10 minutes multiple times throughout the day than to do one hour of practice in the evening.

To generalize your skills, it is important to use your new pronunciation in different environments by talking about various topics, with new communication partners, at different times of the day. These variables help to carry over your skills into your daily life. I often encourage my clients to set multiple timers throughout the day as reminders to use their new skills in the next 5 minutes that they speak.

Early in the conversation practice phase, you will likely forget to use your new clear sounds and go back to fast speaking with your old pronunciation. Do not be hard on yourself. Just wait for your next timer reminder, and focus on clear speech again. If you found yourself speaking quickly with a friend, for example, and didn't think about your pronunciation, then you can likely assume that you went back to your old pronunciation habits. The early phase of conversation practice requires intention. It requires significant focus. So, if you find you're in a group chatting and you haven't thought about your speech sounds, chances are you forgot. Again, that's expected. When you catch yourself, go back to focused, intentional speaking, and do this as much as you can in your day. With practice and intention, your pronunciation will change over time.

Chapter 4: /v/: Bite Your Lip In Anticipation!

/v/ is a commonly mispronounced sound in English. Similar to "th," this sound does not exist in many languages around the world, and as a result, is a target for mispronunciation in English second language learners.

Description:
The /v/ is pronounced by lightly biting the bottom lip with your top front teeth. The amount of lip that you make contact with the teeth is minimal. The general rule of thumb is to place the inside 1/3 of your lower lip past the top teeth. More than this and your pronunciation of /v/ will not only feel awkward, but it will also look too intentional. Keeping the /v/ natural is the goal here!

The second element of the /v/ involves airflow. We want to blow air, just like in a /f/ sound, so that the air flows between the teeth and the lower lip that you're "biting." You must feel the air, either by sensing it on your lower lip or just by ensuring you hear the blowing of the air. Suppose you neglect the airflow element of this sound. In that case, you will end up with a flat vowel-like pronunciation that will be very unnatural and noticeably different than the General North American English pronunciation of /v/.

The third element of the /v/ is voicing. The /v/ sound is voiced, meaning you must turn your voice on. Your vocal folds must vibrate together to produce voice. So, either feel the buzz on your throat with your hand, or you may get away with just feeling that "buzz" sensation on your lower lip as you say the sound.

Common Differences:
Some of the most common mispronunciations include substituting a /b/ for the /v/ sound. For example, "never" becomes "neber." Another substitute often uses a /w/ sound, so "very" becomes "wery." Some people also devoice the /v/ to /f/ so "have" turns to "half."

/v/ vs. /f/:
Often, the /v/ is erroneously devoiced, so it sounds like a /f/. This devoicing commonly occurs in the word "of." The spelling of this word is often what creates

confusion. The /f/ in this word is pronounced as a voiced /v/, so the IPA transcription of "of" is /^v/. When the /v/ in "of" is devoiced, it will sound very similar to "off," thus causing issues with non-native English speakers understanding the meaning. The voiced /v/ is important, and you must be aware of the voicing element to ensure others understand you. Let's compare the /f/ and the /v/ sound in the words below. Feel how the /v/ is different since you are adding your voiced "buzz."

F vs. V Minimal Pairs

fail	veil	ferry	very	half	halve/have
fan	van	fie	vie	leaf	leave
fast	vast	file	vile	life	live
fat	vat	fine	vine	off	of
fault	vault	foist	voiced	proof	prove
fear	veer	foul	vowel	safe	save
fee	V	belief	believe	skiff	skiv
feel	veal	duff	dove	strife	strive
feign	vain	gif	give	surf	serve
fender	vendor	grief	grieve	waif	waive

/b/ vs. /v/:
If we compare /b/ and /v/, we must look at a few more notable differences. /b/ is a bilabial sound, meaning we use both lips. The /b/ is produced with both the upper lip and lower lip making contact. The /b/ is voiced as well. The /v/, on the other hand, is different since we must slightly "bite" of the lower lip. Compare the pronunciation of the words below.

B vs. V minimal pairs

bale	veil	bile	vile	dribble	drivel
ban	van	boat	vote	dub	dove
bane	vein	bolt	volt	fibre	fiver
bat	vat	bow	vow	gibbon	given
beer	veer	bowel	vowel	lobes	loaves
bent	vent	bowl	vole	rebel	revel
berry	very	broom	vroom	verb	verve
best	vest	bury	very		
bet	vet	curb	curve		

/v/ vs. /w/:
/w/ and /v/ are oftentimes confused. The /w/ is produced when the lips are in a rounded position, similar to "oooo." The /v/, on the other hand, includes biting the lower lip. Both are voiced. Try to compare the difference in pronunciation between

these sounds in the words below. Look in the mirror to see how the shape of your lips for /w/ is round and how your upper teeth should be visible for the /v/ sound.

/v/ vs. /w/ minimal Pairs:

V	we	versed	worst	vine	wine/whine
vary	wary	vest	west	volley	Wally
veil	whale	vet	wet	vow	wow
vein	wane	Vicks	wicks	V's	wheeze
vent	went	vie	why		
verse	worse	vile	while		

/v/ vs. /w/ Sentences:

You should be very wary of the shadows

We need a second letter "v" to spell the word savvy

This veil makes me look as big as a whale

The blood pressure in my vein is beginning to wane

I went to look at the vent on the floor

That verse was worse than the first verse

She was well versed in making up the worst type of insults

When I went out west, I always wore a vest

The vet got wet in the rain

The wicks of these candles smell like Vicks Vaporub

I will vie for your attention, although I don't know why

The smell was so vile while the window was shut

The grapes of the vine create the most wonderful wine

Wally was great at volleyball

My vows are going to wow her

Everyone will join in singing the worst verse

Whenever you play the violin, I smile

Would you like to try my very wonderful vitamin water?

West Virginia is where I'd love to travel the most

I wonder if this wave of violence will be over soon

Whatever you want to do, I'll join you

We will invent new software

Where is the Volkswagen now?

You did very wonderful work today, Ivan.

Spelling:

63

Spelling here is not too difficult. The "v" spelled in words is always pronounced as /v/. There are no silent /v/s. The term "of" is an exception and must always be pronounced with a voiced /v/ sound, "uv."

Hear it!
Compare your most common substitution sound with the /v/ sound. Hear the vibration. Hear the difference in the sound first. Ensure that in the lists above, you can actually hear how the words sound different. Differentiating this is an essential step towards clearer, more accurate pronunciations of /v/.

Feel it!
There are three things to feel for /v/. First, you must feel that your upper teeth are slightly biting your lower lip. Feel that only the inner 1/3 of the lip is in contact with your teeth. Feel that the bite is truly just a slight contact, not a tight hard bite at all. You can also use a mirror to ensure you are in the proper position.

Second, you must feel the airflow. Feel the stream of air that exits your mouth near your bottom lip. Feel the hot air if that helps you identify the airflow.

Third, you must feel that you have turned your voice on. Place your hand on your throat to feel the buzz of the vibration of your vocal folds. If you can feel the buzz on your lips, then you can use that feeling to ensure you know that your voice is turned on. You should hear that the sound has a deeper voiced quality.

Do it!
Okay, so now that you can hear the difference and differentiate the /v/ from your previous substitution, you're ready to dig deeper into /v/ production. Let's do this!

Isolation:
Hold the /v/: vvvvv, vvvvv, vvvvv, vvvvv, vvvvv

Syllables:
va, ve, vi, vo, vu
av, eev, iv, ov, uv
ava, evee, ivi, ovo, uvu

V Words:
Beginning
vacation   vacuum   vague

64

vain	van	vault
valentine	vandalism	veal
valet	vanilla	veer
valiant	vanish	vegan
valid	vanity	vegetable
valley	vapor	very
value	variety	void
valve	varnish	
vampire	vase	

Middle

avid	evil	never
avoid	fever	oval
bravo	given	oven
cover	gravy	over
devil	heavy	pivot
elves	ivory	river
even	liver	seven
event	lover	wives
ever	movie	
every	navy	

End

above	have	rave
brave	hive	save
carve	leave	serve
cave	live	shave
dive	love	shove
drive	move	slave
five	nerve	solve
give	of	stove
glove	olive	valve
grave	pave	wave

Phrases:

Beginning

vain vampire	very big vase	very warm vacation
vapid vapor	variety of vegetables	valuable vacuum

Middle

over the river

olive lover

never ever

evil elves

seven movies

movie fever

End

leave the grave

five alive

drive the wave

above the hive

have a stove

move the glove

Sentences:

Beginning

She took a vacation in the vacant house

The vase was very valuable to the vendor

The house has a very nice view of the village

The vapor was leaking from the very big vat of hot water

Vegetarians don't eat veal; they eat a variety of vegetables

The weather was very warm during my vacation in the valley

Middle

That movie will forever be my favorite

Seven ovals covered the artist's painting

I was too heavy for the pool cover to hold me

The avengers avenged the very evil villain

We need to do severe edits on our renovation videos

I have never been an olive lover, but olive oil is used on everything

All of the guest's wives got a fever after eating the questionable liver dish

End

Don't move my glove

Five Alive is my favorite drink

I have one of those to give away

I gave the hive a kick to turn it over

Move my glove away from the stove

You should never shave while you drive

The shark dove into the underwater cave

He is one of five people who are still alive

There is a scratch on the other half of the stove

Reading:

Choose a favorite book, newspaper, blog, or even your work emails to practice your new pronunciation of /v/. If the reading is digital, you can highlight all of the /v/sounds to help you as you read along by pressing the "Ctrl +F" keys (or use the 'Find' function) and entering in "v." Record yourself while reading, either on your computer, laptop, or phone.

<u>Conversation:</u>

Remember, at first, using this new sound will feel highly uncomfortable. You might feel as if you are acting or trying to imitate a native speaker. You already know that this "awkward" feeling is necessary in the process, and you must become habituated to the new movements to speak comfortably. You must begin by speaking slowly as you become familiar with how to adapt your pronunciation. In time, your speed will increase, and you will feel more natural. As you are processing and focusing on pronunciation, it won't be easy at first to catch the sounds before you say them. Again, as you practice, your processing speed will increase, and you will begin to notice the target sounds just before saying them, thus reducing your need to repeat your words.

Set reminders for yourself throughout the day. Each time the timer goes off, it will remind you to speak intentionally with your new sounds. After 5 minutes, you will likely forget as you talk quickly with friends and colleagues. Over time, however, you will slowly become habituated to the new pattern, and you will feel much more fluent. Frequent timers or reminders are a great strategy to get you used to using this new sound in different environments, with different people, and talking about various topics. Variability is important to carry over your skills into your daily life.

Chapter 5: /p/ /t/ /k/ Airflow: Get Out Those Tissues Now!

Description:
The three sounds in English that are pronounced slightly different from the rest are the /p/ /t/ and /k/ sounds. These three sounds differ in one very special way; they differ in how we "aspirate" or allow air to flow during the sound. Think of it as blowing. The /p/ /t/ and /k/ sounds have a special airflow that is especially noticeable at the beginning of words and stressed syllables.

If you take the words "pot, top, and cop," for instance, and place your hand in front of your mouth, the General North American pronunciation would include a strong puff of air or "aspiration" at the first sound of each of those words.

One way many people pronounce these three sounds differently is by not releasing any air. When you don't release the puff of air, it is called "de-aspiration." In many languages, the /p/ /t/ and /k/ sounds typically produced are not made with any blowing puff of air. I like to think of aspiration on a sliding scale of blowing from 0 to 10. On the one end of the scale, you have no blowing (unaspirated or 0/10), and on the other end, the /p/ /t/ or /k/ is entirely aspirated (or 10/10). You could think of the air as being strong enough to blow out a candle as 10/10, or like you're spitting the sound at someone! If your first language is more like a 0/10 with air blowing (aspiration), we will want to increase the airflow. This is especially important at the beginning of words and stressed syllables. We want to increase the airflow release to a natural level, so somewhere like a 4 or 5 /10.

So, the words "pot, top, and cop" should all have a little puff of air at the beginning of words and stressed syllables. The word "pot" could be thought of as "phhhhhhot." If you see these three sounds at the start of a stressed syllable, you must release that puff of air with some aspiration or blowing. So, you could think of an aspirated /t/ as being like a 5/10 on my imaginary-blowing scale. So the word "toe" would have more aspiration or blowing puff of air than a /t/ in the middle of a word like "photo."

The /p/ /t/ and /k/ sounds at the ends of words in English are also released, and this is particularly noticeable when these sounds are the final sound in a phrase or sentence. By released, I mean that the air in the mouth will be let out rather than being held in the mouth. These sounds at the ends of words and syllables are not "aspirated" but rather just released. In my imaginary blowing scale, I would rate the aspiration level at the ends of words to be like a 1 or 2/10....the point here is that it should not be a 0/10!

Common Differences:
The most likely issue people face with these three sounds is lack of airflow or aspiration. The fix here is to increase the airflow at the beginning of words and stressed syllables and to also allow the air to release at the ends of words. You can physically see aspiration if you use a tissue by your mouth during speech. The tissue would not really move if you said the word "pot" with no released air. If you add aspiration to a scale of 5/10, you should see the tissue move when you say "phhhhot." The same would occur for /t/ and /k/ words.

There are no minimal pairs to demonstrate as examples since the lips, tongue, and jaw are placed in exactly the same positions to produce each variety of sound. The small difference between accents is the aspiration, so truly, it is just a variant of the same sound. Changing the aspiration element of the /p/ /t/ and /k/ sound will not result in greater intelligibility, meaning there will be no change in word meaning or misunderstandings due to a change of aspiration. By changing the aspiration of these sounds, you are merely creating a closer match of pronunciation to the General North American accent.

Spelling:
For each of these sounds, the /p/ at the beginning and ends of words is spelled with a "p," the /t/ is spelled with a "t." The /k/ is spelled with a "ck" as in words like "kick, snack, and track," "ke" as in words like "hike, bake, and take," as well as "che" as in words like "ache."

Hear it!
Practice each of the /p/ /t/ and /k/ sounds with an additional "hhhh" airflow after them. Listen to how it sounds vastly different from when you do not add any airflow. Practice each sound with a greater aspiration at the beginning of words and stressed syllables and slightly less aspiration (but some) at the ends of words. Record yourself and listen to the differences until it is crystal clear to you the difference that aspiration makes in the sound.

Feel it!

Get those tissues out! Take some time to focus on adding a puff of air or "h" after each /p/ /t/ and /k/sound. Watch as the tissue flies up to indicate that you have added aspiration to the sound. If you don't see the tissue move, try to purposefully add the 'h' sound after the consonant and see if that helps. If you don't have a tissue, use your hand to feel the hot air hit your palm after the sound.

Do it!
Okay, so now let's work at differentiating the /p/ /t/ and /k/s from your typical pronunciation. Let's do this!

Isolation:
Say the /p /: p, p, p, p, p

Syllables:
pa, pe, pi, po, pu
ap, eep, ip, op, up

/p/ Words:
Beginning

package	parent	pencil
painful	parking	put
painted	parrot	people
pancake	passing	pizza
paper	password	pocket
parade	peanut	pot

Ending

asleep	escape	roundup
backup	flip flop	shortstop
bus stop	ketchup	soap
chip	makeup	soup
cup	mop	tip
doorstop	mousetrap	top
drop	rope	up

/p/ Phrases
Beginning

pink paint	pair of pants	pack of peaches
pancake pan	play at the park	pot of peanuts

pointy pear

pizza pie

pop the popcorn

pen and pencil

Porky Pig

pour the pennies

pocket patch

Ending

coffee cup

up the rope

sweep up

loop and hoop

top of the ship

maple syrup

wipe the lamp

shop for a stamp

sticky tape

dirty mop

hand soap

drop the trap

metal pipe

chip in my soup

can of pop

hop and stop

/p/ Sentences:

Beginning

I bought a pack of peaches

I had to patch up my pocket

I'll wear this pair of pants today

She plays at the park once a week

She ate the whole pot of peanuts

Pour the pennies on the ground

Porky Pig was lying in the pig pen

Pop the popcorn in the popcorn pot

You'll need a pen or a pencil to write with

The pancake looks really good on the pan

There are many pink paints to choose from

Ending

Climb up the rope

Don't hop, please stop

I dropped a chip in my soup

I have to sweep up the mess

You can't fix a pipe with tape

I cleaned the syrup up with soap

You should wipe the lamp

The captain stood at the top of the ship

I need to go to the shop to buy a stamp

The wolf decided to creep up to the sheep

I have to mop up the mess from the trap that I dropped

I sewed a loop in the material and a hoop for the button

Say the /t /: t, t, t, t, t

Syllables:
ta, te, ti, to, tu, at, eet, it, ot, ut

A note about /t/. There are 3 types of "t" sounds in English. In future chapters, the three "t's" will be discussed in detail. Once you have mastered the true aspirated /t/, I would recommend reading the chapter on /t/ to become aware of a few things native speakers do with "t."

/t/ Words:

Beginning

table	tiger	toothpaste
taco	time	tornado
take	tired	tortilla
talk	tissue	touch
tall	toad	towel
taste	toast	toy
teacher	toe	tub
team	tongue	turkey
teeth	tool	turtle
tennis	tooth	two

In the Middle of words when the syllable is stressed:

anticipate	guitar	retain
attack	hotel	return
attain	nineteen	spectator
attention	potato	uptight
baton	pretend	

Ending

bat	flashlight	kite
boat	foot	late
boot	fruit	not
cat	get	parrot
chocolate	goat	peanut
coat	hat	pit
cut	hot	quiet
eat	Jacket	right

sit

wait

wet

white

/t/ Phrases
Beginning

table for two	tennis teacher	toy turkey
taco Tuesdays	tired turtle	take the tissue
takes two to talk	touch my tooth	totally true
tasty toast	tea time	take the test

Ending

cat in the hat	sit and wait	got the flashlight
late night	get the boot	wet fruit
get my coat	hot chocolate	white goat
eat the peanut	cut the light	

/t/ Sentences:
Beginning

It's time to hit the tub

Her teeth are tinted yellow

Take the tennis balls away

Tony had two tacos today

The tiger hunted near the tree

Terry was seated at a tiny table

That's the tenth teacher so far

Do you prefer tacos or tortillas?

Try to tell the tiger to stay away

The tree is too tall for the doorway

She took all the tissues to the trailer

Put toothpaste on your toothbrush

The tornado totally trashed our town

Ted traded ten towels for twenty dollars

Try to keep your tongue near your teeth

My team lost the final tournament today

She worked so tirelessly that she is truly tired

In the Middle of words when the syllable is stressed:

Hand over the baton

I'd love to learn guitar

Hold the potatoes, please

I hope to attain that degree

I'm staying at this hotel too

I look uptight in this outfit

I will pretend to be surprised

His colleague was on the attack

He didn't anticipate that reaction

Can I get your attention, please?

Don't pretend you don't have a hat

He'll be turning nineteen this summer

Look at all of the spectators at the stadium

I'll need to return the pants I ordered online

I'll practice so I can retain all of this information

Ending

I love that coat

Why is that hat so flat?

The bat ate all of the fruit

He went out to sail on his boat

The kite flew to a new height

I put the pit in my pocket for a bit

The cat loves to sleep in that big boot

Why doesn't the boat float in the moat?

The elephant would only eat one peanut

I can't believe that cute rabbit bit his foot

It is so dark even the flashlight won't work

She brought a coat and a jacket on the trip

I tried with all my might to turn on the light

The parrot and the rat are afraid of the cat

I walked(t) on the mat to be as quiet as possible

When I wait, I like to sit and chat with strangers

Isolation:

Say the /k /: k, k, k, k, k

Syllables:

ka, ke, ki, ko, ku

ak, eek, ik, ok, uk

/k/ Words:

Beginning

cake	cave	corn
can	coat	cow
candy	coin	cub
car	cold	cut
card	color	key
carrot	comb	kid
cart	cone	kite
cat	cool	
catch	cop	

/k/ In the Middle of words when the syllable is stressed:

because	accountable	recording
vacation	application	accounting
persecution	economy	peculiar
medication	justification	
academy	amplification	

Ending

back	hook	rock
bike	leak	shake
book	lick	sick
check	lock	snack
cheek	music	stick
cook	neck	truck
duck	pack	walk
hawk	pick	
hike	rake	

/k/ Phrases

Beginning

cold cabbage	Christmas candle	covered cave
cottage cabin	candy corn	collared coat
cut the cactus	cool car	cop car
carrot cake	cold carrots	computer keyboard
coffee can	cat call	

Ending

back of the neck	sick peacock	lick the cupcake
bike lock	walk on a hike	duck neck

sick stomach   rock and stick   milkshake for a snack

/k/ Sentences:

Beginning

He is a cute kid

I love carrot cake

That's such a cool car

The cat crawled away

The cop worked a case

I never eat cold cabbage

Nobody likes candy corn

Watch out for the cop car

I bought a new collared coat

Is a cottage the same as a cabin?

I need a new computer keyboard

Take out the special Christmas candle

Grab the cold carrots from the fridge

The large cat entered the covered cave

I like the smell of coffee grinds from a can

If you cut the cactus, you can drink its fluid

/k/ In the Middle of words when the syllable is stressed:

That's a peculiar shirt

The vacation was amazing

Don't stand for persecution

I submitted my application

I have no justification for it

You are great at accounting

It's because you told me to do it

The medication helped me immensely

The economy is improving every year

I was accepted to the royal academy

You need to be accountable at work

I copied the recording for my own records

Ending

Look at his bike lock

76

I lost my music book
I want to lick that cupcake
That's a very sick peacock
Look at the back of my neck
I had a milkshake for a snack
Don't smack my cheek
She is too sick to go to work
Want to go for a walk or a hike?
Give me back my rock and stick
I will walk by the truck for good luck every day
A peacock neck is longer than the neck of a duck
He has back pain, a headache, and a sick stomach

Reading:

Spend time daily recording yourself reading magazines, emails, and books. Listen to yourself as you read and follow along to pay extra attention to the words. As you are able to speed up and add aspiration and release the airflow in reading passages, you will move towards readiness for using this sound in conversation.

Conversation:

When practicing in conversation, take it slow. I often like to think of conversation practice as reading the words as they come from your mouth. If you are a visual learner, you can imagine that the string of words you are saying is written out and flowing out of your mouth like a string as you speak. You can slowly find the target sounds as they flow from your lips. Your intention when speaking must be high, meaning; you must focus on how you are speaking and make an effort to be intentional when pronouncing your goal sounds. You must allow yourself to make lots of mistakes as you practice! Remember, this is a journey, so each self-correction you do is a step closer to your goal. Keep up the practice!

Chapter 6: /n/: Right On The Nose!

Description:
The /n/ is a nasal sound. This means that sound is produced by the air that flows out of the nose. /n/ is a voiced sound, so the vocal folds will be vibrating to turn the voice on. If you feel your throat with your hand, you should feel a vibration when you make this sound. The tongue tip will rise up to the roof on the "bump" behind the front top teeth, called the alveolar ridge. Place your tongue tip just behind your top front teeth. You will notice not only the tip of your tongue goes up to the roof but also parts of the side of your tongue as well. The tongue contact must happen because we are essentially creating a blockage to keep the air from escaping out the mouth so that it can go out of the nose instead.

Common Differences:
The most common pronunciation issue I see with my clients is the deletion of this sound altogether in their speech. Many languages do not have such a sound in their first language sound repertoire, so this is an entirely new motor movement to learn. When we delete the /n/, words like "down" will sound like "dow," and "men" will sound like "meh." As you can imagine, dropping this sound will wreak havoc on your ability to be understood, as there are so many words that will change in meaning without the /n/.

Another common pronunciation substitution I often see with my clients is using a form of "ng" for the /n/. So, instead of using the tip of their tongue to produce the sound, they use the back of their tongue to get an approximately similar sound. So the word "John" might sound like "Jong." Determine for yourself which sound change you make in your speech by listening and feeling your tongue position when pronouncing it.

Lastly, another mispronunciation of /n/ is to produce an "L" instead. In this case, the tongue position is correct, but the airflow is still coming out of the mouth. To fix this, breathe out the nose and begin to compare air coming out the mouth vs. the nose. Once the airflow difference becomes obvious, add the sound while producing the /n/, ensuring the air flows out the nose. You may want to close the airway out the mouth more by making more of the tongue contact the roof of the mouth to keep the opening closed. If using a mirror under your nostrils helps you see the /n/

steam up the glass, do it. Any cue that enables you to identify how to get nasal airflow, you should use until you get the hang of the sound.

Spelling:

The /n/ sound is represented in spelling by an "n," thank goodness! Well, not so fast. This /n/ sound does come with it a few little tricks as well. The "kn" is also pronounced as /n/since the "k" is silent. So, words like "knife, knee, know" are all pronounced with an initial /n/ sound. There are words with silent /n/ as well. Silent n's tend to come at the ends of words and after "m." See a list of silent /n/ words below:

Autumn	It's usually cool in autumn
Condemn	The judge had to condemn the man to a life sentence
Column	You can't support a building with just one column
Solemn	The mood was solemn
Hymn	We stood to sing the hymn
Damn	He didn't do a damn thing

Hear it!

Make the /n/ sound really long, so you are sure to hear the sound. You should actually hear how the sound is coming from your nose...cool, right?

Feel it!

For /n/, the best way to feel the sound is to block the air from coming out of your nose. Plug those nostrils and say /n/; the sound will only continue for as long as the little bit of air in your vocal tract can pass through your vocal folds. Once the air no longer has anywhere to go, you can't make your voice, and the resonance out of your nose can't occur. The sound stops. So if you want to be sure you're saying the sound right, plug your nose for a second. If the sound stops, the air is coming out of your nose. Remember, you are using the tip of your tongue for this sound. The tip of your tongue will touch the roof of your mouth. Feel how the tip of your tongue rests near the top front teeth. Use this sensation to help you identify when you are producing this sound accurately.

Do it!

Okay, are you ready?

Isolation:

Hold the sound: /nnnnn/, /nnnnn/, /nnnnn/, /nnnnn/, /nnnnn/

<u>Syllables:</u>

na, ne, ni, no, new, ny

ana, eenie, ini, ono, unu, aynay

ann, een, ine, own, oon, ain

<u>Words:</u>
Beginning

knee	nectarine	no
knife	needle	noodles
nachos	neighbor	nose
nail	new	notebook
nail polish	newspaper	now
napkin	night	nurse
necklace	nine	nuts

Middle

animals	doughnuts	pepperoni
banana	enough	piano
blonde	funny	sunny
brownie	honey	tennis
bunny	lemonade	tuna
dinner	onions	vanilla
dinosaur	peanuts	zucchini

End

afternoon	on	garden
again	an	man
airplane	begin	lion
alone	between	magazine
attention	chicken	then
bacon	emotion	raccoon
in	fireman	telephone

<u>N Phrases:</u>
Beginning

nosey nurse	napkin on your knee	ninety-nine noodles
new nail polish	no nuts in the nachos	new neighbors

Middle

tuna for dinner	onions and zucchinis	piano symphony
honey brownies	funny bunny	earning money

End

brown crayon	man on the moon	run to the man
chicken pen	fun in the sun	mountain rain

N Sentences:

Beginning

Nelly knelt on her knees.

I left a note for the nice nurse.

He was napping on his napkin.

I never knew you had a new nickel.

I'll be there around nine at night.

I never learned how to knit napkins.

The nice little necklace fell off of her neck.

I knocked nine nails in a new piece of wood.

The bird made a new nest in the neighbor's tree.

I never know where I put all my notes and notebooks.

Middle

Lightning hit the ground.

I couldn't find the blender.

He loves to drink lemonade.

Annie's bunny was running away.

Is she naturally blonde or brunette?

He enjoys running in the morning.

Bennie canoed on a windy morning.

Money can be like sand in your hand.

I eat vanilla ice cream when it's sunny outside.

I want brownies, bananas, and doughnuts for dinner.

End

The moon looked golden in the sky.

The lion was hungry for a fine meal.

She likes her bacon thin and crunchy.

Give me a phone call in nine minutes.
I ran the whole marathon in eleven hours.
I need to sew a brown button onto my shirt.
The chicken coop had a strong chain link fence.
The fireman climbed the mountain ten times.
We flew in an airplane, not in a hot air balloon.
She scratched a thin line on her phone by accident.

Words with "On":
Some people struggle specifically with words that end in "on." For example,
"crayon" and "nylon." This combination can be difficult because the tongue is forced
to move from a really low position in /a/ "ah," then moves up to the roof. There is a
greater range of movement, and therefore there is a greater struggle to ensure that
the tongue tip actually does make full contact with the roof for /n/. If this
combination of sounds is difficult for you, try to practice the words and sentences
below. Focus on your jaw moving from open to closed as your tongue tip moves up
to the roof.

"ON" Words

nylon	blonde	rayon
on	consult	salon
argon	honest	tonic
neuron	honor	wander
coupon	ironic	non
pylon	online	
python	onward	

"ON" Sentences:
I bought a nylon pylon online
I decided to go blonde at the salon
The price is on the coupon
I'm honored to be considered the most honest of the bunch
She served me tonic water
My favourite animal is the python
This shirt is made out of nylon and rayon

<u>Reading:</u>

Find a favourite song or poem. Read it out loud, with a focus on the /n/ sound. Feel and hear the /n/ as you read the words. Try to repeat the sentences over and over again, faster and faster each time. Remember, it's quality and accuracy you must focus on; the speed will come with practice.

<u>Conversation:</u>

Now go out and test your new clear pronunciation of /n/! Go to the grocery store and ask a clerk where you might find all the green bananas. Find as many different environments to use your speech sounds and with as many people as possible. If you find it easier to use your new sounds with strangers, then strike up a conversation. You'll likely never see them again, and as a bonus, they never knew how you pronounced your words before, so there's no chance of others noticing a change. Remember, though, regular daily practice is key to forming a habit. It takes time, and that's okay. Just keep practicing. Try it out!

Chapter 7: "Ng" or /ŋ/: An Exercise Of The Tongue Like No Other!

Description:
The "ng" is a frequently mispronounced sound in English. This sound is somewhat of a mystery to many non-native English speakers, and due to its nature, it isn't easy to hear the nuances of exactly what we do to make this sound. But fear not! That's why you're here and reading this. So let's unveil precisely what's going on with this sound and what makes it so difficult to pronounce.
The "ng" is the sound heard in words like "king," "wrong," and "going."

This sound is nasal, meaning the air is coming out of our noses. To call this a strictly nasal sound, in my opinion, is a bit misleading, as there is an oral component where air switches out of the mouth afterward.

Remember how we talked about the parts of our tongue? Remember the "back" of the tongue? Well, this is the part of the tongue that we use for the "ng" sound. The IPA symbol for this sound, by the way, is /ŋ/. The back of our tongue goes way up to touch the roof of our mouth, much like the /k/ and /g/ sounds; only for "ng" we let the air come out of our nose to make a sound. If you try to make this sound, it should stop once you plug your nose. Now, THERE'S a party trick for you (yes, the lamest party trick ever). There is more to this sound, though! A critical element of this sound is that the back of the tongue drops down off the roof after the nasal sound. This "drop" is very quiet, almost imperceptible. This drop can sort of sound like a little pop of air. If you relax your tongue and just let it "fall" off the roof, that is the sound we are going for. We want to avoid adding an "uh" sound afterward, so it does not sound like "kinguuuuh." The "ng" should be a short and quiet sound with a soft drop of the back of your tongue.

"ng" Common Differences:

Since this is not a typical sound in many other languages, the "ng" is changed in so many ways. Remember, we use the closest sound that we can pronounce in our first language to mimic this sound. Here are the most common differences of the sound/ŋ/:

Replacing /ŋ/ with a plain old /n/

One of the most common ways speakers mispronounce the /ŋ/ sound is to reduce the sound to just the /n/. So the word "ring" turns to "rin," or "wing" turns to "win." Native English speakers often reduce "ing" to "in" in their speech, although it is commonly restricted to very casual speech and generally just for "ing" verbs. It is always highly recommended that you learn how to pronounce your sounds precisely and clearly before you start reducing speech in English. Getting the foundations of accuracy in pronunciation is important to know what to do, and you will not get into trouble with misunderstandings that way. If you decide you have mastered the proper form and would like to practice the reduced form for "ing" verbs, then great! But, remember, this is for very casual and informal speaking situations. All of the other "ing" words will be pronounced with the true /ŋ/ sound.

Adding a strong /k/ after the /ŋ/

Often, a common change of the /ŋ/ sound will include adding a /k/ sound at the end. An example of this would be to say "goink" instead of "going." For some, the /k/ is a soft addition; for others, this /k/ is a strong and loud plosive sound at the end of the /ŋ/.

Adding a strong /g/ after the /ŋ/

Another prevalent difference in the /ŋ/ sound production is adding a hard /g/ sound at the end. So the word "long" /Laŋ/ for example, turns into "lonGuh" /Laŋgə/. For many non-native English speakers, spelling influences how they pronounce the "ing" words. Thus this hard /g/ persists. I commonly hear from clients who explain that they were explicitly taught to make the /g/ sound as it is spelled, and therefore they had no idea that there was any other way of saying it. This is a great example of why your instructor matters!

Deleting the /ŋ/ altogether

Finally, an extremely common change to the /ŋ/ sound is when the final element of the sound is deleted entirely, leaving words like "laughing" /LæfIŋ/ to sound like "laughih" /LæfI/.

Spelling:
The /ŋ/ is spelled with the letters "ng" in words that have "ong" and "ing."

It is important to note that English vocabulary also includes words with the "ng" in the middle position, so you must be careful! The "ng" words in the middle position WILL include the strong hard /g/ sound. The "ng" at the ends of words, however, will not! We will practice and differentiate between the various pronunciations when "ng" is pronounced with the hard /g/ and when it is not.

Hear it!
Compare the words below. If you struggle with accidentally adding the /k/ or /g/ in "ing" words, say the "ng" words with and without a hard /g/ or /k/ at the end. Be sure that you can hear the difference.

N vs. ŋ Minimal Pairs: No hard /g/

ban	bang	go in	going	season	seizing
bun	bung	gone	gong	sin	sing
chin	ching	hun	hung	stun	stung
clan	clang	kin	king	sun	sung
coffin	coughing	lion	lying	taken	taking
din	ding	pan	pang	tan	tang
Don	dong	pin	ping	thin	thing
done	dung	raisin	raising	tin	ting
fan	fang	ran	rang	ton	tongue
garden	guarding	run	wrung	win	wing

Minimal Pairs Sentences:
I was going to go in
It is not a sin to sing
She sang about the rising sun
The king takes care of his kin
The lion was lying in the pasture
The pans made a pang on the floor
I'm raising children who love raisins
She ran away as she rang the alarm
I will be seizing that seasoning
Have you hung the clothes to dry, hun?
The fang of the wolf hung near the fan
The gardener was guarding the garden
That is a really thin little thing
The tin can made a ting sound
She wags her tongue a ton!
The bird with the broken wing didn't win

The worker was done shoveling the animal dung at the zoo
The gong was gone, and no one knew who had taken it

He decided to run after the bully wru<u>ng</u> the rag in anger
The community decided to ban all noises and bangi<u>ng</u> sounds after 7 pm
I was stunned when I learned that I had been stu<u>ng</u>

Feel it!
Feeling the difference between the accurate "ng" and your general "ng" difference will be your greatest tool! Feel the back of your tongue go up to the roof when you make the nasal portion of this sound. Feel the air come out of your nose. Again, this is a nasal sound, so check by plugging your nose that air is, in fact, coming out of your nose. After the nasal sound is produced, FEEL that the back of your tongue lightly drops off the roof almost silently. You should feel a true tongue-drop. No real sound has to come out while you drop the back of the tongue. The tongue drop will be a nearly silent element of the sound; however, there is an auditory component when your tongue falls automatically, so don't do anything purposefully to add a sound during the "drop."

Do it!

Isolation: "ng, ng, ng, ng, ng."

Syllables: ang, ong, ing, eeng, ung

Words:
Pronounce the /ŋ/ **WITHOUT** the hard /g/ in these words:

aging	coping	eating
along	coupling	enduring
annoying	cracking	evening
being	crashing	exacting
bleeding	creeping	feeling
blessing	crying	filing
blinking	dangling	flashing
blooming	diagnosing	fleeting
bouncing	doing	fling
breeding	drafting	flooring
briefing	drinking	glancing
bring	dripping	going
caring	during	greeting
cling	dwelling	grinning
coloring	dying	grouping

grueling	printing	string
haunting	rating	stuffing
hiking	retiring	swelling
hoping	ring	swing
icing	rinsing	tackling
imposing	ruining	tempting
incoming	ruling	thing
informing	saving	thinking
insisting	shocking	towering
investing	sing	trimming
inviting	singer	tumbling
king	sinking	tying
knitting	sling	understanding
linking	smashing	upcoming
losing	something	uprising
loving	sounding	wearing
lying	speeding	wing
meeting	spelling	winking
morning	spinning	wrapping
nothing	spring	writing
outgoing	sting	yearning
playing	stirring	yielding
pleading	stocking	young

Pronounce the /ŋ/ **WITH** the hard /g/ in these words:

anger	fungus	strongest
angle	hunger	tangled
bangle	jingle	tango
bongo	jungle	tingle
bungalow	kangaroo	untangle
elongate	linger	wrangle
English	longer	younger
finger	mingle	youngest
flamingo	stronger	

Phrases: with NO hard /g/:

acting out	bee sting	biting my nails
aging man	being strong	boing boing
airing it out	billing your invoice	booking the gig

boring lesson
bowling ball
boxing and fighting
bring that thing
broken wiring
caring and sharing
casting call
cling clang
coming along
crown molding
crying out loud
cutting the edging
ding dong
doing nothing
doing something
during the evening
dying wish
facing the music
fading to grey
feeling young
filing cabinet
fitting in
fling the sling
flying birds
going along
going nowhere
going tubing
golden ring
good rating
good timing
honorable king

hoping and wishing
lasting impressions
laying around
leasing agreement
lining the pockets
living for today
loading the song
long ending
long swing
losing battle
lovely outing
loving every minute
lying through your teeth
mailing the letter
making it better
mapping it out
marking your work
mining for gold
mixing drinks
morning and evening
moving things
my darling
new earring
packing and moving
paving the way
paying attention
piling the chores
Ping Pong
piping the icing
prying eyes
raging mad

resting place
rising sun
sailing along
saying something
seating plan
seeing is believing
sewing machine
sing along
singing singer
soaring high
spring fling
staging the play
String Theory
strong awning
strong ranking
strong swing
strong wing
taking care
tapping to the song
the King's ring
touring Egypt
trying anything
tying the knot
using it
very amusing
wasting no time
white siding
wring the rag
wrong song
young thing

Sentences:
Be careful. Some words have the hard /g/ (middle of words) while others will not (ends of words).
Sing a song about the jungle
The bell goes cling clang ding dong
I was going to hang the hanger with the dress, but it was too long
I lost my ring playing ping pong

I swung on the swing wrong and tangled the ropes

I'm going to mingle a bit longer and linger over here

The kangaroo and the flamingo were playing together

Are you leaving now?

What time are you going?

When will you be coming back?

I'm going now, see you this evening

I'm going to be doing a lot of work today

What are you going to do in the morning?

Will you bring me something back when you get home?

"Ong"

Many people struggle specifically with "ong" rather than "ing" words. This can be because the tongue must move farther from /a/ "ah" to the /ŋ/ sound. If this is you, you might benefit from specific practice opening your mouth for the /a/ "ah" and transitioning the back of your tongue to contact the palate for the /ŋ/ sound. Go through the words and sentences below and feel your jaw and tongue position change.

"ONG" Words:

along	lifelong	song
belong	livelong	strong
billabong	long	tagalong
bong	monophthong	throng
dingdong	oblong	tong
diphthong	pong	weeklong
dong	prolong	wrong
folksong	prong	yearlong
gong	sarong	
headstrong	singalong	

"ONG" Sentences:

The headstrong man didn't go along with the plan

Playing professional ping pong is a lifelong goal of mine

I only use a <u>long</u> <u>tong</u> for my salads

I wear a sar<u>ong</u> and th<u>ong</u> sandals at the beach

I sing s<u>ong</u>s all the livel<u>ong</u> day

My muscles get str<u>ong</u> when I prol<u>ong</u> my exercises

Syllabic /n/

The /n/ can be pronounced as an entire syllable, deleting the vowel altogether. Using the /n/ as a syllable is termed the syllabic /n/. The syllabic /n/ can occur when the /n/ is in an unstressed syllable. Notice how the vowels before each /n/ in the words below are deleted altogether. We produce the /n/ AS the syllable. This knowledge will help you avoid over-pronouncing vowels that get dropped in the connected speech of native English speakers. Practice with these words:

Often	"ahh f<u>n</u>"
Person	"per s<u>n</u>"
Human	"hyoo m<u>n</u>"
Common	"cah mm<u>n</u>"
Happen	"haa pp<u>n</u>"
Taken	"tay k<u>n</u>"
Suddenly	"sud<u>n</u> lee"
Garden	"gar d<u>n</u>"
Region	"ree j<u>n</u>"
Student	"stoo d<u>nt</u>"
Absence	"ab s<u>n</u>se"
Listen	"lih s<u>n</u>"
Efficiency	"uh fish <u>n</u> see"
Written	"wri t<u>n</u>"
Medicine	"meh duh s<u>n</u>"

Reading:

Spend some time looking over an email. To highlight all of the sounds you're looking for, type CTRL+F (or use the 'Find' function), and type in which sound you would like to highlight. If you use this trick, you can save lots of time. You can even use this to highlight your goal sounds in any written documents you might want to read. I recommend looking up Ted Talks on the internet because you can listen to the speaker and read the transcript of what the speaker is saying at the same time. Reading the transcript can help you focus on your goal sound and help highlight the stress and intonation patterns (the music of language) of English. We will discuss stress and intonation in later chapters.

Conversation:

First, begin to listen for the "ng" in other native speakers' conversations. Attune your ears to listen for it on television, movies, and listening to people around you. Begin to model the "ng" as you speak as well. Set reminders throughout the day to remind yourself to use the sound regularly. Choose two or three "ng" words that you will focus on throughout the day so that whenever these words come up, you will use your new pronunciation.

Chapter 8: "Sh": Get Ready To Pucker Up!

Description:
The "sh" symbol in IPA is /ʃ/. The "sh" is the sound we usually make to remind someone to be quiet, "shhhhhhh." This sound is made by rounding your lips. The jaw is in a neutral closed position, and we pull the tongue back. The sides of the tongue are pressed up to the roof of the mouth on each side. You can feel that the tongue on each side touches the side teeth. The middle of the tongue is down, almost like a tunnel or pathway for the air to pass through. The air should flow out the center of the mouth. The "sh" is a voiceless sound, so the voice should be off, and you should feel no vibration on your throat.

Common Differences:
The most common substitution sound for "sh" that I see in my practice is the /s/. This substitution makes sense since the /s/ and "sh" are very alike. The difference between a /s/ and "sh" includes the lip position (/s/ is spread, like a smile), and tongue position (/s/ is more forward). If you were to make an /s/ sound and hold it, then slowly slide your tongue back, it should eventually sound more and more like a "sh." That's because as you slide your tongue back, the tip moves away from the alveolar ridge (that bump on the roof of your mouth behind the front top teeth). Slowly the sides of your tongue come closer to the sides of the roof of the mouth. The thing to do now is round your lips, and voila! You have a "sh."

Spelling:
/ʃ/ in English is relatively straightforward in spelling, represented by the "sh" letters. There are always a few exceptions in English because, well… it's English. So, the /ʃ/ is spelled with "c" and "ch" in words like:

ocean	champagne	machine
parachute	chalet	brochure
chauffeur	chic	chute

The /ʃ/ is also pronounced when words have "tion" and "ci/ce" words, like in:

action	nation	mention

attention		musician		licorice	
section		delicious		groceries	
information		special			
motion		facial			

We also have the "sh" sound in the word "sugar" even though it starts with an "s."

Hear it!
Try to pronounce the word list of minimal pairs below. Listen to the sound difference between the /s/ and the /ʃ/ sounds. Listen to how the sound changes as you smile for /s/ vs. rounding your lips and pulling your tongue back for "sh."

/s/ vs /ʃ/ minimal pairs

sack	shack	see	she	sue	shoe
sag	shag	sell	shell	ass	ash
said	shed	sew	show	bass	bash
sale	shale	sift	shift	crass	crash
sake	shake	sigh	shy	crust	crushed
same	shame	sign	shine	fist	fished
sank	shank	sin	shin	gas	gash
save	shave	single	shingle	sass	sash
scene	sheen	sip	ship	gust	gushed
seal	she'll	sit	shit (yup!)	mass	mash
seat	sheet	so	show	mess	mesh
seed	she'd	sock	shock	moss	mosh
seek	chic	son	shun	plus	plush
seen	sheen	sop	shop	puss	push
seep	sheep	sore	shore	rust	rushed
seer	sheer	sort	short		
seize	she's	suck	shuck		

Feel it!
Besides hearing the difference in sounds, how else will you know if you pronounce this sound correctly? You must feel it! Feeling the difference is especially important if hearing or differentiating the difference is difficult for you. Remember how our ears can trick us?

To feel the /ʃ/ sound, you must feel that your lips are in a circle shape. Slide your tongue back from a /s/ if this helps you to pull your tongue back. Feel how the tip of the tongue is not touching anything. However, you will feel that the sides of your tongue are now touching the roof near your upper molars.

A great trick I use to elicit the /ʃ/ sound is to have my client say a long 'eeeeeeee' sound as in "meeeeeeeeee." If you hold this position, then blow an 'h' sound, you will hear a slight /ʃ/. Now add the rounded lips and voila, the perfect /ʃ/! The reason this works is that when we make the /i/ or "eeeee" sound, the sides of our tongue go up to the roof, and the tip pulls back, exactly like the "sh" sound. The only difference is your lip position. Try and feel for yourself.

Do it!
Okay, so let's practice!

Isolation:
Hold the /ʃ/ sound: "shh, shh, shh, shh, shh,"

Syllables:
Get used to blending the sound into the surrounding vowels. You should not hear a space or pause between the /ʃ/ and the vowel. Try it for yourself.

sha, she, shy, show, shoe, shay
ash, eesh, ish, owsh, oosh
asha, eeshee, ishi, osho, ushu

Words:
Beginning

chef	shave	shiny
shack	shawl	ship
shade	she	shirt
shady	shear	shit
shaft	shed	shock
shag	sheen	shoe
shake	sheep	shook
shaky	sheer	shoot
shall	sheet	shop
sham	shelf	shore
shape	shell	short
share	shift	shot
shark	shin	shout
sharp	shine	shove

show	shrub	shut
shown	shrug	shwa
showy	shun	shy

Middle
addition	fishing	reshape
airship	flagship	roadshow
ashamed	flashing	seashore
ashore	flashlight	sideshow
ashtray	flashy	slasher
bashful	fleshy	slashing
bishop	freshen	slushy
bookshop	freshman	smashed
brushed	gunshot	smashing
bullshit	hardship	starship
bushel	kingship	sunshine
bushes	kinship	thrasher
cashew	kosher	tissue
cashier	lordship	toothbrushes
crashing	lotion	township
crushed	machine	trashed
cushion	marshal	unshaven
dashing	milkshake	unwashed
directions	mushroom	upshot
dished	nutshell	warship
dishes	ocean	washable
earshot	offshoot	washer
eggshell	offshore	washing
enshrine	outshine	washout
eyelashes	overshot	washroom
fashion	pet shop	wishbone
finished	polished	wishful
fishbowl	pusher	workshop
fisher	pushing	worship
fishery	pushover	

Ending
| ambush | blush | brush |
| banish | boyish | bush |

cash	hush	rush
clash	Josh	sash
crash	lash	slash
crush	lavish	slosh
Danish	leash	slush
dash	licorice	smash
dish	lush	smoosh
eyelash	marsh	splash
famish	mash	squash
finish	mesh	squish
fish	mush	stash
flash	perish	swish
fresh	plush	thrush
frosh	posh	ticklish
gash	punish	trash
gnash	push	vanish
gosh	radish	wash
gush	rash	wish
harsh	ravish	
hash	relish	

Phrases:

Beginning

shake the shampoo

the chef showed off

show the sheep

sharp shoes

short ship

shut the shop

Middle

motion in the bushes

mushrooms on the seashore

fishing in the ocean

one additional cushion

washing machine

sunshine on my lashes

End

dish of mu<u>sh</u>

ca<u>sh</u> in the tra<u>sh</u>

I wi<u>sh</u> for licori<u>c</u>e

spla<u>sh</u> the fi<u>sh</u>

musta<u>ch</u>e ra<u>sh</u>

wa<u>sh</u> the toothbru<u>sh</u>

<u>Sentences:</u>

Beginning

<u>Sh</u>e gets hungry when <u>sh</u>e <u>sh</u>ops for groceries

You must <u>sh</u>are the <u>sh</u>ip with the mighty ocean

The <u>sh</u>eep got a <u>sh</u>oulder wound from a <u>sh</u>arp <u>sh</u>ovel

The <u>ch</u>ef likes to <u>sh</u>ake the <u>s</u>ugar on everything <u>sh</u>e bakes

<u>Sh</u>e wore a nice <u>sh</u>irt and <u>sh</u>iny new <u>sh</u>oes to her interview

It's good to use <u>sh</u>ampoo in the <u>sh</u>ower and <u>sh</u>ave in the morning

Middle

The wa<u>sh</u>ing ma<u>ch</u>ine is shot

The musi<u>c</u>ian loved the sounds of the o<u>c</u>ean

The ca<u>sh</u>ier didn't get paid to wash the di<u>sh</u>es

You don't need to use a fla<u>sh</u>light in the sun<u>sh</u>ine

The chef showed the staff how he ma<u>sh</u>ed the potatoes

I never want to try a mu<u>sh</u>room milk<u>sh</u>ake

End

The starfi<u>sh</u> never made a spla<u>sh</u>

Mouthwa<u>sh</u> can cost you a lot of ca<u>sh</u>

Throw your old toothbru<u>sh</u> in the tra<u>sh</u>

I'm going to wa<u>sh</u> my paintbru<u>sh</u> in a fla<u>sh</u>

It was difficult to pu<u>sh</u> the car after the car cra<u>sh</u>

His musta<u>ch</u>e caused a ra<u>sh</u> he wished would go away

I wi<u>sh</u> my licori<u>c</u>e hadn't fallen in that bu<u>sh</u> and turned to mu<u>sh</u>

<u>Reading:</u>

Now go check out your emails. Read them aloud. You can use everyday tasks to practice pronunciation; it doesn't always have to take extra time out of your day. Use items you would already be reading in your day; just read them aloud! Use this time to find your difficult sounds and practice your new skills. Try to push yourself to find the sounds faster and faster so that your reading becomes quick and fluent.

<u>Conversation:</u>

So now is the real test. Can you use this sound in a real-life conversation with others? At first, this will be very a difficult task. Not only will you find it hard to focus on what you're saying and HOW you're saying the words simultaneously, but catching your own errors takes a lot of intention and focus (at first). As with all things, if you practice, you will get better. Getting over the fact that you will sound different is something my clients struggle with at the onset of their instruction, and sometimes this can be a big issue for them. Remember, your old pronunciation will always be there; you can use that way of speaking whenever you like! The new pronunciation you are learning is only a tool, so get good at it to serve you.

Chapter 9: "Ch": Get Ready To Pucker Up Even More!

Description:
The "ch" sound is an affricate, meaning two sounds are pronounced one after the other. The first is a stop /t/ sound. The second is the "Sh" sound we learned previously, which is a fricative. When you place these two sounds one after the other together quickly, you have "tsh," which is the "ch" sound. The IPA symbol for "ch" is /tʃ/, which makes sense when you think about how there are two sounds together.

The trick here is to ensure you don't put any space or pause between the sounds. First, place the tip of your tongue up on the roof behind your front teeth. This bump is called the alveolar ridge. Make a quick /t/ here. After the tongue releases the /t/ it slides IMMEDIATELY back to the "sh" sound (see the "sh" description in the previous chapter). We actually round the lips for the whole production from beginning to end. The /tʃ/ is also a voiceless sound since /t/ and "sh" are both voiceless, so you should not turn your voice on for this sound.

Common Differences:
The "ch" is commonly mispronounced as "sh." An example of this substitution would be to substitute the word "share" for "chair," or "wash" for "watch," or even "mashing" for "matching." The fix here is to add the /t/ first and blend it into the "sh."

Here are a few minimal pairs to compare "sh" /ʃ/ and "ch" /tʃ/:

Beginning
"sh" /ʃ/ vs. "ch" /tʃ/:

share /chair	she's /cheese	sheep /cheap
shatter /chatter	shin /chin	ship /chip
sheaf /chief	shilling /chilling	shore /chore
sheet /cheat	shoe /chew	
sherry /cherry	shop /chop	

End

bash	/batch	hash	/hatch	wish	/which, witch
cash	/catch	mash	/match		
dish	/ditch	wash	/watch		

Another common substitution of the "ch" sound is to drop the fricative "sh" portion, which sounds like a /t/. In this case, the word "watch" would sound like "wat," and "chicken" would sound like "ticken."

Here are some minimal pairs to compare the /tʃ/ with the /t/:

/tʃ/ vs. /t/:

chair	/tear	chest	/test	chip	/tip
chap	/tap	chew	/two/to/too	choose	/two's
char	/tar	chick	/tick	chop	/ top
chart	/tart	child	/tiled	chose	/toes
cheat	/teat	chill	/till	chubby	/tubby
cheek	/teak	chime	/time	chug	/tug
cheese	/ tease	chin	/tin	churn	/turn

End

arch	/art	hitch	/hit	peach	/peat
batch	/ bat	hunch	/hunt	pitch	/pit
beach	/beat	hutch	/hut	porch	/port
belch	/belt	itch	/it	pouch	/pout
bench	/bent	march	/mart	roach	/wrote
bitch	/bit	match	/mat	starch	/start
botch	/bot	much	/mutt	teach	/teat
catch	/cat	notch	/not	twitch	/twit
coach	/coat	ouch	/out	watch	/what
each	/eat	parch	/part	which	/wit
hatch	/hat	patch	/pat	wrench	/rent

Spelling:

The /tʃ/ sound is typically spelled with a "ch," but not all "ch" spellings are pronounced as /tʃ/. How confusing is that (see the spelling examples in the "sh" chapter)! We also pronounce words with the /tʃ/ sound ending in "tu" with a "ch" sound. So "ture" and "tune," would sound like "cher" and "chune." Such words like "picture, nature, capture, statue, and fortune" are examples of this. Most of the time, when you see the "ch" spelled, you will produce the /tʃ/, but there are some words, as we have already discussed, which can be pronounced as /ʃ/. Here are a few examples:

/ʃ/

parachute	chalet	brochure
chauffeur	chic	chute
champagne	machine	

"ch" can also be pronounced like the /k/ sound in these words:

chemical	chorus	technical
chemist	Christmas	
chord	school	

Being aware of these spelling anomalies will go a long way in weeding out the exceptions.

Hear it!

Compare the "sh" and "ch" minimal pair words below. Say them out loud and hear how the "sh" is a softer, more subtle sound, and the "Ch" has a strong stop /t/ sound at the beginning.

Feel it!

What you should be feeling when pronouncing the "ch" is the little /t/ at the beginning. Make a few tiny quick t's first. T, t, t, t, t, t, t. Then blend into a "sh" sound after. Try to pronounce them closer and closer until they are almost produced as one sound. FEEL the tongue tip touch the bump on the roof of your mouth, and then feel how your tongue pulls back after the /t/. Feel how you round your lips the whole time. You can use a mirror to help you ensure you are fully rounding your lips for this sound.

Do it!

Okay, so now that you can differentiate the "ch" from your old production and feel when you pronounce the "ch" correctly. Let's get practicing!

Isolation:

Repeat the sound: "chhhhh, chhhhh, chhhhh, chhhhh, chhhhh"

Syllables:

cha, che, chi, cho, chew
ach, each, iche, oche, uch

acha, eachy, ichi, ocho, uchu

Words:
Beginning

chair	checked	chiller
chamber	checker	chime
channel	checkup	chimney
chap	cheek	chin
chapter	cheer	chip
char	cheerio	chipper
charger	cheese	chocolate
chariot	cheeseburger	choking
charity	cheetah	choose
Charlie	cherish	chop
charmer	cherry	chopper
chart	chess	chose
charter	chest	chowder
chase	chew	chubby
chatter	chick	chuckle
cheap	chicken	chug
cheapen	child	church
cheat	children	churchy
check	chill	churn

Middle

achieve	gotcha	patchy
arched	grandchild	peaches
archer	hatchet	picture
archery	hatching	pitcher
archway	inches	preachy
beach ball	itching	rancher
butcher	itchy	rancho
catcher	ketchup	ratchet
catchy	kitchen	raunchy
crunchy	macho	reaching
crutches	marching	riches
duchess	matches	satchel
etching	matchup	sketchy
furniture	orchard	starchy

statue
teacher
temperature

touched
touchy
urchin

voucher
watcher
witches

Ending

arch
batch
beach
belch
bench
birch
bitch
botch
branch
bunch
catch
coach
couch
ditch
each
etch
fetch
finch
hatch
hitch
hunch
hutch

inch
itch
latch
leach
lunch
lurch
march
match
mooch
much
mulch
munch
notch
ostrich
ouch
parch
patch
peach
perch
pinch
pitch
poach

pooch
porch
pouch
punch
ranch
reach
rich
roach
speech
stretch
such
switch
teach
torch
touch
vouch
watch
which
witch
zilch

<u>Phrases:</u>

Beginning Phrases

a <u>ch</u>ipmunk's <u>ch</u>in
baby <u>ch</u>ick
<u>ch</u>amber bed
<u>ch</u>apter book
<u>ch</u>ariot awaits
<u>Ch</u>arlie <u>Ch</u>aplin
<u>ch</u>arred <u>ch</u>ips
<u>Ch</u>arter rights
<u>ch</u>ase the <u>ch</u>icken
<u>ch</u>atter with friends
<u>ch</u>eap item
<u>ch</u>eapen the pile

<u>ch</u>eat sheet
<u>ch</u>eck the book
<u>ch</u>eck your <u>ch</u>air
<u>ch</u>ecked the list
<u>ch</u>eek to <u>ch</u>eek
<u>ch</u>eer the team
<u>ch</u>eerios for breakfast
<u>ch</u>eese and crackers
<u>ch</u>eesy <u>ch</u>oice
<u>ch</u>erish the moment
<u>ch</u>erry flavored <u>ch</u>ocolates
<u>ch</u>erry pie

<u>ch</u>ess tournament
<u>ch</u>est of drawers
<u>ch</u>ew your <u>ch</u>eeseburger
<u>ch</u>ewing gum
<u>ch</u>ild of mine
<u>ch</u>ild's <u>ch</u>air
<u>ch</u>ill the drink
<u>ch</u>ime the bells
<u>ch</u>in-up
<u>ch</u>ips and dip
<u>ch</u>ocolate <u>ch</u>ip cookie
<u>ch</u>oking hazard

choose me

chop the piece

choose to stay

chubby chicken

chuckle at the joke

chug your drink

churchy sermon

churn the butter

clam chowder

down the chimney

favourite channel

finished the chart

get in the chopper

give to charity

go to church

good chap

got a checkup

happy children

huge cheeseburger

in the chiller

phone charger

play checkers

running cheetah

spicy chicken

what a charmer

wood chipper

Middle Phrases

achieve a lot

apple orchard

arched bow

beach ball game

bite is itching

bronze statue

catchy phrase

clean furniture

cold temperature

crunchy peanut

dangerous matches

etching the glass

farm rancher

five inches

friendly butcher

funny teacher

ghosts and witches

great catcher

hatching the eggs

he's the catcher

I gotcha

I love ketchup

in her satchel

in the kitchen

itching knee

itchy mosquito bite

ketchup and fries

ketchup in the kitchen

lost my crutches

macho man

marble archway

marching band

matches and lighters

matching statues

math teacher

nachos in your lunchbox

new furniture

oldest grandchild

patchy spots

peaches and cream

pears and peaches

picture this

pitcher of lemonade

pitcher of water

preachy preacher

rags to riches

reaching far

reaching out

scenic picture

sea urchin

sharp hatchet

sketchy alleyway

solid statue

talented archer

teacher in crutches

ten inches

the egg is hatching

the skill of archery

touched by an angel

touchy subject

walk with crutches

warm temperature

what a ratchet

where's my voucher

witches and ghosts

wonderful grandchild

End Phrases

birch tree

bitch is a bad word

botch the job

bunch of grapes

catch the ball

clear speech

coach said so

couch potato

each of you

etch in glass

fetch the ball

golden finch

hatch the egg

hitch a ride

I have a hunch

in the ditch

in the hutch

lunch is soon

march to the beat

match the cards

mooch off your parents

never belch

notch in your belt

on a ranch

on the bench

ostrich feather

patch of grass

peach cobbler

pinch me

pitch the idea

poach the egg

reach out to me

rich or poor

stretch your vowels

such a pity

switch places

teach a lesson

too much

tree branch

vouch for me

warm beach

watch the game

which is it?

bench on the beach

coach can catch

ostrich on the couch

stretch after you march

watch my lunch

reach the branch

Sentences:

Beginning Sentences

I always choose cheese for a snack

The church gave to charity

The happy children are playing checkers

Chad changed his order to a cheeseburger

The good chap got a checkup at the doctor

Charlie needs to check his chair for chalk marks

Please chew your cheeseburger quietly at lunch

I chased the waiter so he could check my receipt

I dropped chocolate on the chapter book I was reading

Chuck, the dog, chose a big squeaky cheese for a chew toy

Don't Chug your drink before you finish your clam chowder

I learned how to churn butter from watching my favourite channel

I need to finish the chart, but my phone is still charging

I still need to chop up the chicken and chill the drinks before the party

I'll cherish the moment I win the chess tournament

No child of mine will walk around with chewing gum in their hair

The best chocolate chip cookies have the most amount of chocolate chips

Your child's chair is beside the chest of drawers

Can you chill the drink before we bring out the cherry-flavored chocolate, please?

Chop it up into little pieces, so it doesn't pose a choking hazard

I chose to chuckle at his jokes even though they weren't funny

When offered chips, I always choose the cheesiest ones

Chew your cheeseburger well, and we can have some cherry pie afterward

I raised my chin when the bells chimed

Middle Sentences

I asked Archie to put some nachos in his lunchbox

Those peaches feel so itchy on my chin. It's torture!

Please check if there is any ketchup left in the kitchen

The teacher slipped on ketchup, so now he's in crutches

The coach insisted that the marching band statue be taken down

I always grab a pitcher of iced tea when the temperature reaches 30 degrees

They only erect a bronze statue for a person who achieves a lot

Let's go to the apple orchard after the beach ball game

The man was too macho to admit that he had lost his crutches in the archway

The entire marching band wore matching itchy uniforms

The butcher will get angry if he catches anyone putting ketchup in his kitchen

End Sentences

Which month do you prefer; March or April?

We must teach the rich to reach out to the poor

I like to stretch out on the couch and eat ranch chips

Fetch me the ladder so I can reach that branch

I asked Blanch to watch my lunch

I saw a bunch of benches on the beach

The farmer wants to watch the egg before it will hatch

It's such a pity that the peach cobbler is gone

His weight was too much for the tree branch to bear

Be sure that the coach doesn't catch you stretching after your march

There's an ostrich on the couch

Reading:

Now that you understand how the "ch" is spelled, how it sounds, how to feel when you are producing it correctly, and have practiced enough to feel comfortable, let's move on to reading more complex tasks. Choose anything you like, a favorite book, blog, magazine, whatever, and start to practice! Work on finding your sound as you read and feel the sound as you say it. Work to increase your speed and fluency over time. Practice daily!

Conversation:

Using the sound in conversation is your next challenge. Use this new sound with a new person in your life (or even a stranger!) every day. Keep in mind that if you are speaking effortlessly and very quickly at the beginning stages, it's almost certain that your focus is not strong enough that you are actually correcting your sounds. You must start with focus and intention. It does take effort to feel for every "ch" as you speak. It will almost certainly mean speaking slightly slower at first to give your articulators (tongue/lips/jaw) the time you need to produce this new sound accurately. Give yourself some slack, and go with the flow. Let yourself mess up because it is going to happen. A lot. That's okay, just keep at it, and don't give up. You got this!

Chapter 10: "J": We're Not Done With Puckering Quite Yet!

Description:

The "J" sound is transcribed in IPA as the symbol /dʒ/. Notice that there are two signs here; the /d/, a stop sound, and the /ʒ/, a fricative, air-flowing sound. The two together are called an affricate. We produce this sound by making a /d/ with the tongue tip up on the alveolar ridge just behind the front teeth. Turn your voice ON for /d/. Then slide your tongue back, so the sides of your tongue touch the sides of the roof of the mouth, but the tongue tip no longer touches the alveolar ridge. Your lips should be in a slightly rounded position, just like you would do with the "sh" and "ch" sounds. There is airflow blowing, so ensure you are blowing just like you would for the "sh" and "ch" sounds. The "ch" and "sh" are similar sounds to "j"; only you will add your voice for the "j" sound. So, this is a voiced sound since both parts of the sound are voiced. If you feel your throat, you should feel a vibration to help you identify that your voice is on. If you have a tricky time adding your voice, think of it as "humming" while making the "j" or making it "loud." You will need to round your lips for this sound as well.

Common Differences:

The first common change non-native English speakers make with the /dʒ/ sound is to leave the voice off. Leaving off the voice is common since many languages that do not have this sound have a close sister sound, the "ch" or /tʃ/. So, if you turn your voice off for /dʒ/ or "j," it will sound like a "ch." The word "jip" would sound like "chip." The tongue and lip positions are exactly the same for both sounds. The only difference is the voice is off for "ch." To adjust the /dʒ/ sound, your sole focus should be adding your voice and feeling the vibration on your throat.

Now, let's look at some minimal pairs to see how vocabulary and intelligibility can be significantly impacted if you are not producing your "j" with the voice ON.

"ch" vs. "j" minimal pairs

char	/jar	cherry	/jerry	choke	/joke
cheap	/jeep	chest	/jest	chug	/jug
cheer	/jeer	chin	/gin	chump	/jump
cheese	/jeez	chalk	/jock	chunk	/junk

h	/age	larch	/large	rich	/ridge
batch	/badge	march	/marge	search	/surge
britches	/bridges	perch	/purge		

The second common change made to the /dʒ/ sound is to drop the /d/ at the beginning, resulting in the /ʒ/ sound. We make this /ʒ/ sound by saying "sh" and adding your voice, like in the word "beige" /beʒ/. To produce the /dʒ/ sound correctly, you must add the voiced /d/ at the beginning and transition quickly to the /ʒ/afterward.

The third common change non-native English speakers make with the /dʒ/ sound is to use the "y" sound. So, a word like "joker" would sound like "yoker." Again, the reasons for this change depend on the first language you speak. Speakers choose the most similar sound from their first language to insert into new language production. The "y" lacks the airflow and the /d/ at the beginning, but other similarities make this a common substitution. The IPA symbol for the "y," funny enough, is /j/. Now don't tell me that doesn't add to the confusion!

So, to correct this difference, we need to do two things; first, add the /d/ before, and during the sound, add airflow or blowing. Let's practice with some minimal pairs to get a sense of how different these sounds are and just how much this can impact your ability to be understood by others.
Here are a few minimal pairs to compare the two sounds:

"y" vs. /dʒ/ "J" Minimal Pairs

you'll	/jewel	use	/juice	yip	/gip
yam	/jam	yell	/gel	yak	/Jack
year	/jeer	yin	/gin	yolk	/joke
yet	/jet	yoke	/joke		

Spelling:
We spell the "j" or /dʒ/ sound in a few different ways. The typical spelling is "j." However, we sometimes refer to this sound as the "soft g," so in words that have "ge," "dge," "gy," and "gi" the /dʒ/ is pronounced. Look at the word list below to see the various word spelling for /dʒ/. The letter "j" is only spelled at the beginning and middle of words, but you will likely never see a "j" at the ends of words; the ends of words are typically when you see the "ge" and "dge" spelling. There is also a strange spelling in the word "soldier," as we pronounce this word with the /dʒ/: /soldʒɚ/.

See the /dʒ/ examples below with various spellings:

GE

gel	budget	challenge
gentle	emergency	huge
gem	danger	age
general	angel	large

GI

giant	allergic	fragile
gist	engineer	imagination
giraffe	apologize	logic
gigantic	engine	original

GY

gym	allergy	trilogy
gymnastic	energy	prodigy
Egypt	edgy	neurology

Hear it!

Go through the minimal pairs list above that best match your most common substitution, and read them aloud. Attune your ears to hear the difference. Once you are sure this difference is evident to you, you can feel the difference between the two sounds.

To recap, for the differences below, this is what you will need to change:

/tʃ/ "ch" vs /dʒ/ "j": add your voice

/ʒ/ "zh" vs. /dʒ/ "j": add the /d/ at the beginning

/j/ "y" vs. /dʒ/ "J": add the /d/ at the beginning, as well as add blowing airflow to the sound

Feel it!

Similar to hearing the difference and improving your differentiation, it is extremely important also to feel the difference between these pronunciations. Your ears will likely deceive you. You are trying to overcome years and years of the habitual practice of a sound, and it is difficult to surpass this motor muscle memory. Keep at it!

If "ch" or /tʃ/ is your common substitution, you will need to feel the vibration of your voice turning on. To do this, place your hand on your throat. Remember, this is where your vocal folds are, and when you turn your voice on, you can feel the vibration here. You may also be able to feel a deeper vibration sensation when your voice is turned on in your face or on your tongue and lips. Decide for yourself what sensation will help you best identify that your voice is on. If you are having trouble turning your voice on, try to "hum" loudly with your lips apart while attempting this sound. You could also think of it as making a really loud version of "ch"; not with your airflow but with your voice.

If your substitution is a "y" /j/ sound, you will need to feel a few things. Since your voice is on for "y" already, you will only need to focus on your tongue's position. First, make the /d/ and feel how the tip of your tongue touches that bump, the alveolar ridge on the roof of your mouth. Then you need to feel yourself pulling your tongue back. The sides of your tongue touch the sides of the top of your mouth. If this is difficult, you can try to do the "ch" and then add your voice to the sound to make this process a bit simpler.

Here's an overview based on whichever change you make:
/tʃ/ vs. /dʒ/: Place your hand on your throat to feel your vocal folds vibrate when you add your voice
/ʒ/ vs. /dʒ/: Add a /d/ before transitioning to the /ʒ/.
/j/ vs. /dʒ/: Add a /d/ and feel as you blow air, similar to how you would with a "ch." You can use a tissue to see the airflow as it moves the tissue around.

Do it!
If you have gone through the minimal pairs list successfully, and you feel confident that you can hear and feel the difference in your typical old pronunciation versus the General North American English pronunciation of /dʒ/, then you are ready to move on!

Isolation:
Hold the /dʒ/ sound: "jjjjj" "jjjjj" "jjjjj" "jjjjj" "jjjjj"

Syllables:
ja, je, ji, jo, ju
aj, eej, ije, oje, uj
aja, eje, iji, ojo, uju

Words:

Beginning

germs	jelly	joke
giant	jerk	jolt
gym	Jess	Josh
jab	jest	jot
Jack	jet	journal
Jade	jig	joy
jail	Jill	jug
Jake	jilt	juggle
jam	jinx	juice
James	jive	juke
Jane	job	jump
jar	jock	jungle
jaw	Joe	junk
jay	Joey	jury
jazz	jog	just
jean	John	
jeep	join	

Middle

agent	enjoy	nudged
apologize	fidget	object
badger	fudged	oxygen
badges	gadget	pages
banjo	hedged	pajamas
budged	imagine	pigeon
budges	inject	project
budget	injury	register
cadged	intelligent	reject
cadges	judged	rejoin
cages	ledger	ridged
cajole	lockjaw	ridges
carjack	lodged	skyjack
conjoin	longitude	soldier
dodged	magic	subject
edges	major	suggestion
eject	manager	unjust

| urgent | wedged | widget |
| vegetables | wedges | |

Ending

acknowledge	edge	nudge
age	fridge	package
badge	fudge	page
begrudge	garbage	partridge
bridge	grudge	pledge
budge	hedge	porridge
cabbage	hodgepodge	postage
cage	huge	ridge
cartridge	image	sausage
college	judge	sludge
courage	knowledge	smudge
damage	language	stage
dislodge	ledge	storage
dodge	lodge	wage
drawbridge	marriage	wedge
drudge	misjudge	

Phrases:

Beginning

blue jay	jade stone	John's jeans
common germs	Jake and Jim	jet jump
cool your jets	jam and jelly	joyful jog
do a jig	James's germs	juggle and joke
George of the Jungle	Japanese journal	juggle and jump
giant genie	jar of jam	jumping jacks
giant jar	jar of pickles	jungle gym
giraffe jaw	jaws of life	just juice
great job	jazz band	magic genie
gym rat	jeans and a jacket	on a jet
he got jilted	jeans and a t-shirt	shark jaw
it's a jinx	Jeep Cherokee	strawberry jam
Jack and Jill	Jerry's jacket	what a jerk

Middle

| aged object | badger cages | badges of honor |

114

banjo from Egypt
bridges in Egypt
caged animal
caged pigeon
college project
conjoined twins
courageous soldier
crazy badger
damaged agent
dangerous blue jay
dodged a bullet
edges of pages
edges of the paper
eject the pilot
enjoy a seat
fidget in your chair
fudged the numbers
garbage banjo

he budged
hedged my bets
hold the object
hugest badger
I apologize
imagine that
inject the medicine
intelligent argument
judge the agent
judged by a judge
largest group of judges
latitude and longitude
lodged in my tooth
magic show
magical stages
major improvement
new manager
new project

nudged him to do it
object on the pages
on a budget
oxygen is essential
pajamas to bed
pigeon in the street
played with the gadget
register to be joined
reject that position
rejected angel
rejected marriage proposal
secret agent
storage and lodging
storage cages
trimmed the hedges
turn the pages

Ending

acknowledge your ideas
age of innocence
bridge over water
budge on it
cage damage
chocolate fudge
clear image
cold fridge
college garbage
college student
dirty sludge
dodge a bullet
drudge up the past
earned a badge
edge of bridge
edge of the sword
fudge in the garbage
got a nudge
have courage

hedge your bets
hodgepodge of stuff
hold a grudge
huge plan
in a lodge
in the garbage
ink cartridge
the judge held a grudge
knowledge is power
language of marriage
large beverage
large cabbage
large fudge
damage the luggage
marriage proposal
message from the judge
message of knowledge
misjudge a person
on a ledge

package ridge
partridge in a pear tree
pledge my allegiance
porridge in a bowl
postage on the package
postage stamp
received a package
sausage and a beverage
sausage and potatoes
smudge on the glass
speak a language
stage fright
stoney ridge
storage container
storage package
sustained damage
turn the page
village filled with cabbage
village stage

wage a war   we<u>dge</u> between us
<u>S</u>entences:

Beginning Sentences

<u>J</u>erry <u>j</u>umps away from germs

I <u>j</u>ust want some <u>j</u>uice for breakfast

The <u>g</u>iant went for a <u>j</u>oyful <u>j</u>og

I have <u>j</u>et lag from my trip to <u>J</u>apan

<u>J</u>im forgot his <u>j</u>acket in the <u>j</u>ungle-gym

<u>J</u>ordan couldn't open the <u>g</u>iant <u>j</u>ar of <u>j</u>am

<u>J</u>essica didn't want to <u>j</u>ump out of the <u>j</u>et

<u>G</u>iraffes are not known to have a large <u>j</u>aw

Little <u>J</u>oshua wants to go to the <u>j</u>ungle gym

<u>J</u>ohn's <u>j</u>aw dropped when he read <u>J</u>en's <u>j</u>ournal entry

I wear <u>j</u>eans and a <u>j</u>acket when it's cold outside

I have never <u>j</u>uggled, <u>j</u>umped, or <u>j</u>ogged on my way to work

The magic <u>g</u>enie granted <u>J</u>erry's wish for new <u>j</u>eans

Middle Sentences

Those are dama<u>g</u>ed ob<u>j</u>ects

I in<u>j</u>ured my hand playing the banjo

The blue <u>j</u>ay landed on the ba<u>dg</u>er cages

The ink stained the e<u>dg</u>es of the aged pages

The coura<u>g</u>eous sol<u>di</u>er became a secret a<u>g</u>ent

I put my ob<u>j</u>ects in storage and found nearby lo<u>dg</u>ing

Angie did her college pro<u>j</u>ect about the bri<u>dg</u>es in Egypt

The sol<u>di</u>er felt de<u>j</u>ected when he failed the high <u>j</u>ump test

I wrote about all of the re<u>j</u>ected ob<u>j</u>ects in the pages of my book

The <u>J</u>udge sentenced the secret a<u>g</u>ent to jail for his undercover pro<u>j</u>ect

End Sentences

With age comes knowle<u>dge</u>

He received a ba<u>dge</u> on stage

Was the cage under the bridge?

I found the message in the garbage can

The Ju<u>dge</u> was known to harbor a gru<u>dge</u>

Who would ever throw fu<u>dge</u> in the garbage?

A large block of fu<u>dge</u> tastes better than cabbage

A large range of new images surged on the internet

I got a message from the Ju<u>dge</u> while I was at College

The village view is gorgeous at the edge of the bridge

The marriage rates are low in the village on the ridge

She arrived at her cottage with her large luggage in hand

In my luggage, there is a package and some postage stamps

I would like a sausage and a beverage, but no cabbage, thank you.

The man lunged away from the animal in the cage to avoid any damage

If you speak the language of love, you won't damage your marriage

Reading:

Once you have a good feel for the /dʒ/ sound in sentences, it's essential to move up the ladder of complexity. Begin to find more difficult reading passages to practice with your new /dʒ/ pronunciation. I find that reading emails aloud can be an excellent way to practice. The goal is to identify and pronounce your new sound faster and faster, so your processing is so quick that you are prepared for conversation-level practice. Record yourself reading, and listen to your pronunciation to hear and see how accurate you are.

Conversation:

Now you're ready to begin to use your new sound with others when you speak. As with all sounds, it will be uncomfortable at the onset. This discomfort will reduce with time as you realize that native English listeners anticipate hearing your new pronunciation of "j." Really, it is your old way of pronouncing the /dʒ/ differently that would increase your listeners' attention to how you are speaking. You will find that others will rarely notice when you use your new sound, and others will understand you more. Try for yourself, and set up a reminder schedule to remember to use your new pronunciation many times throughout the day. The only way to make this habitual is to use it more than your old pronunciation, so get on it. You can do this!

Chapter 11: All About "R": Tongue Tip Gymnastics

Description:

The /r/ is among the most commonly mispronounced sounds in English. This sound is complex to articulate, and it simply does not exist in many languages. The /r/ is considered a "liquid". A liquid means that the sound changes slightly depending on the sounds that exist around it. The /r/ tends to take on elements of the vowels around it. In IPA, the transcription of "r" is /r/, but be careful because the Capitalized /R/ stands for a different sound, the trilled /r/. We will dig deeper into what this means exactly later, but be aware that a true /r/ in English is the small /r/ in IPA transcription.

The /r/ is produced with the teeth nearly closed and together. The lips are rounded slightly, almost like a large circle. Be sure to avoid a small tight rounded lip, much like the /w/ sound. If you round your lips too small, the /r/ will begin to sound like a /w/. The whole tongue is generally pulled back and "bunched." The sides of the tongue push up against the roof of the mouth near the molars. The tip of the tongue can do a couple of things. Because everyone's oral cavity is slightly different, the /r/ can be produced slightly differently for each person. The tongue tip should be pulled back and pointed or curled slightly back. The tongue tip should NOT touch the roof but rather curl back into the open space below the roof. The back of the tongue presses tightly up against the top back molars. The /r/ is a voiced sound, so you need to ensure that your voice is turned on. Some people produce what we call a "retroflex" /r/and will curl their tongue back significantly more to produce a /r/. Both are acceptable and will create the typical /r/ sound in the North American English accent. Try for yourself and feel what you do with your tongue to create this sound.

Common Substitutions:

There are a few common sound substitutions that non-native English speakers will insert in place of the /r/. The first common substitution is a /w/ or a more rounded lip pronunciation that sounds more like a /w/ than a /r/. An example of this type of substitution would be to say "wed" for "red." One of the elements of this sound that you will need to focus on is your lip position. The lip position for /r/ is a large, almost square-like protrusion of the lips, rather than a small rounding like in "w."

Here are some good examples of /r/ vs /w/ words.

R vs. W Minimal Pairs:

rack	/whack	reared	/weird	rink	/wink
rag	/wag	red	/wed	rip	/whip
rage	/wage	reed	/weed	ripe	/wipe
rail	/wail/whale	reek	/week	rise	/wise
rake	/wake	rent	/went	risk	/whisk
ram	/wham	rest	/West	roar	/war
rare	/wear/where	rich	/which/witch	roared	/ward
rate	/wait/weight	ride	/wide	rock	/wok
rave	/wave	rig	/wig	room	/womb
ray	/way/weigh	right	/white	run	/one/ won
reap	/weep	rim	/whim	rye	/why/Y
rear	/we're	ring	/wing		

R vs. W Sentences:

Ron whacked the rack by accident

Ted wagged a rag in the air to signal to his friend to come

I felt rage when my wage was significantly decreased

I have to stay awake to get to the store to buy a rake

Where is the rare diamond?

He always raves about the waves at that beach

Ray decided to weigh himself today

We're near the rear of the theatre

She reared a very weird child

You'll have to walk through the weeds and reeds to get there

I went to grab the rent check

The rest of the family moved west

Which artist became rich?

I want to ride in a wide boat

You were right about the white paint

The girl winked at him at the skating rink

I ripped the Cool Whip lid by accident

The peach was so ripe I had to wipe the drips off my mouth

The lion will roar when he's ready for war

There isn't much room for the fetus in her womb

I'll be back from my run at one o'clock

Another common substitution of /r/ is to produce an "L." So the word "red" would sound more like "led." With a substitution like this, we must focus mainly on the tongue position. For "L," the tongue tip must touch the roof of the mouth, where for /r/, the tongue tip is curled and bunched back slightly and never touches the roof of the mouth. For /r/, the tongue tip will go near the roof but never actually makes contact.

R vs. L Minimal Pairs:

race	/lace	rental	/ lentil	rocket	/ locket
rack	/lack	rice	/lice	wrong	/ long
rake	/lake	Rick	/ lick	room	/ loom
ram	/ lamb	rid	/ lid	root	/ loot
ramp	/ lamp	rise	/ lies	rot	/ lot
rain	/ lane	right	/ light	royal	/ loyal
wrap	/ lap	writer	/ lighter	rump	/ lump
rash	/ lash	rhyme	/ lime	rung	/ lung
rate	/ late	rink	/ link	rush	/ lush
rather	/ lather	rip	/ lip	rust	/ lust
raw	/ law	wrist	/ list	pirate	/ pilot
ray	/ lay	road	/ load	arrive	/ alive
read	/ lead	robe	/ lobe	berry	/ belly
red	/ led	rock	/ lock	correct	/ collect

R vs. L Sentences:

The girls raced to be first to choose the best lace

The gym lacked racks for the equipment

Someone threw a rake in the lake

A ram and a lamb are very different animals

She walked through the rain in the lane to get home

I dropped my chicken wrap all over my lap

Always remove your makeup at night to avoid a rash on your eyelashes

If you pay the bill late, your rate will increase

I'd rather lather on liquid soap than use a bar of soap

Ray decided to lay down

If you're the leader of the group, you'll have to be a good reader

She led me to a red car

The rental smelled like lentil soup

Rick licked his ice cream cone

He stood right in the light

The <u>wr</u>iter decided to take a <u>l</u>ighter approach in his <u>wr</u>iting

The boy fell and felt a small <u>r</u>ip on his <u>l</u>ip

Someone dropped a <u>l</u>oad of their groceries on the <u>r</u>oad by accident

If you're <u>wr</u>ong, don't take too <u>l</u>ong to admit it

My grandmother never used that <u>l</u>oom in the sewing <u>r</u>oom

Throw the apples out, or they'll <u>r</u>ot a <u>l</u>ot more than they already have

Wear a seatbelt so you can be sure to a<u>rr</u>ive a<u>l</u>ive

You are co<u>rr</u>ect to co<u>ll</u>ect your belongings after the flight

R Blend vs. L Blend Minimal Pairs:

brew	blew/blue	crown	clown	grow	glow
bruise	blues	free	flea/flee	pray	play
brush	blush	freeze	fleas	sprint	splint
crash	clash	grand	gland		

R Blend vs. L Blend Sentences:

My <u>br</u>uise turned different shades of <u>bl</u>ues and purples

I need a new <u>bl</u>ush <u>br</u>ush

A <u>cl</u>own should absolutely never wear a <u>cr</u>own

I set the <u>fl</u>ea <u>fr</u>ee when I opened the door

If I accidentally let a few <u>fl</u>eas in the <u>fr</u>eezer, will they <u>fr</u>eeze?

The plant will <u>gr</u>ow if it's allowed to bask in the <u>gl</u>ow of the sun

I <u>pr</u>ay that the kids won't <u>pl</u>ay too harshly today

I had to get a <u>spl</u>int on my shin from that <u>spr</u>int I did yesterday

My homemade beer <u>br</u>ew <u>bl</u>ew up in the garage

The officers had a <u>cl</u>ash of opinions after witnessing the <u>cr</u>ash

The third type of common change to the general North American English /r/ is the "trilled" /R/. The trilled /R/ is also referred to as the "rolling" /R/ because it is produced with a long rolling sound. The tongue tip flicks against the roof of the mouth at the alveolar ridge extremely quickly. In some cases, this "flicking" contact is repeated rapidly and produces the trilled /R/. Again, to make a clear /r/, we will need to focus on the tongue tip and what it is doing. The trilled /R/ can sound like a quick /d/, making the word "friend" sound like "fdend," or "girls" sound like "geddulz." To change this pronunciation, we will need to pull the tongue tip back and down so it does not touch the roof but rather sits in the oral cavity space, making no contact whatsoever.

The final sound change made to the /r/ is to delete it altogether. The /r/ is deleted in the last syllable position in many languages and other dialects of English. It is deleted in British English and some dialects of North American English, like the well-known "Boston accent." The word "car" may sound more like "ca." In the General North American English accent, however, the true /r/ is always produced. There are no exceptions here. So the change to make, if you commonly drop the /r/, is actually to produce every /r/ in every word. No biggie, right? (Awkward cough).

Spelling:
Luckily, spelling is really simple. When you see a /r/, you say the /r/. No tricks here! Finally!

Hear it!
Go over the list of minimal pairs above. Pay attention to see and hear if you substitute your /r/ with either an "L" or a "w" sound. If you find that you either delete or trill your /r/, go through only the /r/ word columns. Say the /r/ your typical old way, and then say it with intention by curling your tongue tip and bunching your tongue back, so it does not touch the roof of your mouth. Compare each word both ways; begin to hear how they are different.

Feel it!
To feel the pronunciation of /r/ will take you a lot further than just listening for the difference since, as we know, the ability to hear sounds not typical in our first language can be difficult. For /r/, you will want to focus on your lip position first. Feel that your lips are only slightly rounded in a large circle. Use a mirror to see what it looks like and compare it to a small rounded lip position like in /w/. Next, you will want to feel for the tongue position. The tip of your tongue should be pointing up and curled slightly back. Your tongue sides will press up against the top teeth or the sides of the roof of your mouth. The tip of your tongue should not, I repeat, should NOT touch the roof of your mouth at any point for this sound. The /r/ is a voiced sound, so turn that voice on!

Do it!
Let's practice!

Isolation:
Hold the /r/ sound: "rrrrrr, rrrrrr, rrrrrr, rrrrrr, rrrrrr"

Syllables:

Get used to blending the sound into the surrounding vowels. Try it for yourself.

ra, re, ry, row, roo, ray
ar, ear, ire, or, oor
ara, eeree, iri, oro, ooroo

Beginning /r/ words

rabbit	reasonable	relief
race	rebel	relies
radar	recall	religion
radio	receive	reload
rag	recent	rely
rain	recently	remain
raise	recess	remember
raised	recession	remote
raisin	recognize	remove
rake	recommend	repeat
rally	record	report
ran	recording	represent
ranch	recovery	rest
random	red	result
range	reduce	return
rapid	reduction	rhythm
rare	reference	ribbon
rarely	referendum	rice
rat	referring	rich
rate	reflect	ride
rather	reform	right
ratio	regardless	ring
reach	regime	rip
reaction	region	rise
read	register	river
reader	regular	road
ready	regulation	rock
real	relationship	rocket
reality	relatively	rolled
really	release	room
rear	relevant	root
reason	reliable	rope

rose	run	written
round	wrap	wrong
row	wrist	wrote
rug	writhe	
rule	write	

Middle /r/ words

Africa	factors	park
already	fairy	part
America	farm	party
area	fingers	pattern
arm	first	perhaps
barn	flowers	person
bird	force	pirate
camera	forest	record
carefully	fork	scissors
carrot	form	several
carry	four	shirt
century	general	short
children	giraffe	start
circle	government	story
corn	hard	surface
correct	heard	surprise
course	heart	syrup
covered	horse	temperature
dark	hours	third
dictionary	important	toward
different	interest	turn
direction	iron	turtle
discovered	large	understand
during	learn	verb
early	lizard	very
earring	mark	walrus
earth	material	warm
energy	morning	work
Europe	natural	world
every	north	worm
everything	nurse	zero
exercise	paragraph	

Ending /r/ words

air	door	jar
alligator	ear	ladder
are	everywhere	letter
bear	father	mother
beaver	feather	or
car	flower	other
chair	for	pear
deer	four	tear
dinosaur	hair	there
doctor	hammer	tire
dollar	here	

Beginning /r/ Phrases:

far reach	rat race	reduction rate
faster reader	rather happy	referring physician
good reaction	read a book	reflect the light
Northern region	ready to go	regardless of this
on my radar	reality-tv	regional director
point of reference	really great	register early
quick recovery	rear mirror	regular admission
race a car	reason to believe	regulatory body
radio silence	reasonable argument	relatively easy
rain or shine	rebel without a cause	release the prisoner
raise it up	recall the idea	reliable friend
raised a child	receive a present	remain calm
rally in line	recent activity	remember to practice
ran a race	recently moved	rip in the rug
random thoughts	recommend my services	rock and roll
range of motion	record a video	romantic relationship
rapid rate	red ribbon	rug rat
rare occurrence	red robin	wrap the rice
rarely there	reduce and reuse	

Middle /r/ Phrases:

already there	arms up	around the world

125

around this area
beautiful children
bird brain
birds in flight
carefully processed
carry it out
circle of care
corn syrup
covered in confetti
crazy pattern
dark circles
during the day
early riser
every person
everything matters
exercise caution
factors to consider
farmers market
fingers crossed
first one there

first paragraph
flowers in a vase
force of nature
forest fire
fork the broccoli
form and function
four or more
fourteen earrings
full of energy
general store
government funding
hard bargain
heard the sound
horse power
horse's trot
hours of service
important plans
iron armor
large parlor
learn to break dance

mark my words
material witness
morning glory
natural progression
north to south
of course
out of Africa
perhaps I might
person to person
record the record
short story
start there
starts with a plan
surface water
surprise present
the current century
warm temperature
what a difference
wrong direction
zero words

Ending /r/ Phrases:

air purifier
alligator jaw
are there
bear claw
beaver dam
brother and father
car tire
clear mirror
dollar store
door to door
feather pillow
flower in her hair

for her
four more
four square
hair loss
her car
her ear
her hammer
here and there
here or there
jar of jam
large dinosaur
long ladder

more flour
mother and daughter
other than her
pear core
scare the deer
screwdriver and hammer
there and everywhere
there they are
tire fire
write a letter
your chair
your doctor

<u>Sentences:</u>
Beginning
<u>R</u>andy <u>r</u>ushed as he drove down the <u>r</u>oad
<u>R</u>emember to <u>r</u>aise the <u>r</u>evenue predictions

I'm not ready to retire from the ranch just yet

His remark indicated that he resisted her ideas

I require rather red rocks to create my refined jewelry

He wrote about a rocket that raced through the universe

Robert is working on not being so rigid in his relationships

Middle

The area's tourist industry is improving

The juniors love to party during spring break

You can improve your health through nutrients and hydration

Only a courageous hero could have saved that horse in the park

Harry had to hurry around the corner to get to the store before it closed

Ending

There are more over there

Where did you put the pear jar?

I swear the bear is still over there

Your four-door car needs more care

I got a tear on my ear from that earring you pulled last year

Remember to add color to the mural for tomorrow's show

That bear has been sniffing around here, there, and everywhere!

My father likes flowers more than my mother and sister

Vocalic /r/

Before we get onto more practice with /r/, I want to point out how /r/ can change slightly depending on the vowels around it. When a /r/ comes directly after a vowel, we call it a vocalic /r/. The /r/ portion itself is pronounced precisely as described above, but you will need to focus on whether you pronounce the vowel before it accurately. We will go into detail in later chapters about the specifics of vowels, but I want you to be aware of how open your jaw must be for many vowels that exist before /r/s. So let's dig into vocalic /r/s.

"er"
Spelling: er, ir, or, ur, ear

Description: Keep your jaw in a near closed position before the /r/:

Words:

after	hers	publisher
alert	inner	refer
alter	jerk	rider
Amber	laser	river
anger	later	rover
answer	layer	ruler
baker	lever	runner
berg	lighter	serve
boxer	liner	sewer
butler	liver	sharper
clerk	loser	smoother
cover	lover	sober
dancer	lower	stern
daughter	manager	super
deliver	mercy	swimmer
derby	merge	teacher
driver	meter	terror
elder	mixer	there
enter	nerve	tiger
error	never	timer
ever	offer	tower
faster	order	under
fern	other	upper
fever	over	utter
fiber	overt	verb
flyer	paper	verbal
fur	perm	verse
germ	peter	voter
helicopter	piper	water
herb	powder	were
herd	power	writer

Phrases:

accounting clerk	answer the question	butler's pantry
after hours	baker's dozen	butter popcorn
alter boy	ballerina dancer	classroom teacher
amber alert	big purse	cover to cover
anger management	big spider	cute girl
another brother	boxer glove	deliver her meal

128

dirty germs
elder advice
enter here
ever after
family dinner
faster and faster
first place
he's a jerk
helicopter blade
her driver
herbal tea
herd of sheep
hers and his
hit a nerve
hurt finger
inner circle

laser focus
later alligator
layer the cake
learn math
lover not a fighter
lower and lower
male turkey
manager directions
mercy on my soul
merge with the company
meter reader
never ever
offer assistance
older daughter
order a burger
over and over

overt and covert
paper shredder
Peter Piper
poodle fur
power couple
roller derby
severe lawyer
shovel dirt
stir around
tall ladder
whisper softly
white paper
white skirt
winners and losers

Sentences:

We were at work early
Never forget your first turn
The earthworm lives in the dirt
If I were you, I'd burn those furs
I heard a bird chirp for his dinner
The nurse found the thermometer
Bert is closing the firm early today
The firm will merge next Thursday
The clerk doesn't earn much money
Vern hurt his finger on his surfboard
That fern looks thirsty, she whispered
The clergy rode in the hearse with her
The water was frozen after the blizzard
Your pronunciation is easier to understand
Kurt is in charge of urban development
She loves to be showered with humor
The bird searched for a worm in the dirt
The government-run factories won't survive
It takes a lot of nerve to drive over that curb
Herb is such a jerk for dropping butter on my shirt
The first word of the verse is blurred on this paper
Irma spilled perfume in her purse, and now it's dirty
She was on the verge of giving birth for the first time

129

The girl works at a German church, stirring the soup

I'll grab a ladder to get the bird down from that perch

The teacher was searching for a spider on the birch tree

Can you confirm that you'll return on the first?

I'm eager to stop working and enter early retirement

I don't normally want to go for food after a rollercoaster

I never understood the other transportation systems

I've already ordered my hamburger from the other waiter

It's the girl's birthday on Thursday the thirteenth

My teacher permitted me to retake the midterm exam

She felt awkward when the boy presented the flowers to her

The purpose of the research is to publish in a journal

The sound of the crowd turned to an outburst of laughter

The first "R" words are more difficult than the final "R" words

"ar"

Spelling:

Ar- car, far

Ear- heart

Description: Open your jaw wide before the /r/:

Words:

alarm	barber	carving
apart	bark	charge
arbor	barley	charm
arc	barn	chart
arcade	Barney	dark
archer	barred	darn
arctic	bizarre	dart
are	car	depart
argue	carb	embark
arm	carbon	far
armor	card	farce
army	cargo	farm
arson	Carl	farmer
art	carp	farther
artery	carpet	garbage
artist	cart	garden
artwork	cartoon	garland
bar	carve	garlic

130

garment
garner
garth
guard
guarded
guitar
harbor
hard
hardly
hardy
harm
harness
harp
harsh
heart
hearth
hearty
jaguar
jar
jargon
karma
lard
large

lark
larva
marble
march
margin
mark
marked
marker
market
marsh
mart
martial
marvel
monarch
parcel
pardon
park
part
parted
parting
partly
party
radar

regard
remark
scar
scarf
scarlet
shark
sharp
sharper
smart
spark
sparkle
sparse
star
stark
start
tar
target
tarp
tart
yard
yarn

Phrases:

alarm clock
Arcade Fire
arctic star
are you there?
arm wrestle
army battalion
army marshal
army squad
art show
artist work
bar hopping
barbershop
barley soup
barnyard
Barney and Friends
big yard
bizarre events
car parked
carbon taxes

charged with arson
dark night
don't argue
farmers market
fast car
fell apart
flower arbor
funny remark
give my regards
glass marble
green marker
large arm
large parcel
large scar
long scarf
loud alarm
loud bark
march on
margin of error

marked car
martial arts
metal armor
museum art
old farm
old garbage
on a lark
on my radar
pardon me
park yard
part of the park
parted ways
partly to blame
party girl
play the harp
red heart
royal monarch
scarlet letter
security guard

shark bite
sharp knife
shiny star
shuffle cards
smart child
soggy marsh
spark a fire

sparkle and shine
Star Trek
start running
start the race
sweet-tart
target practice
tarred and feathered

veins and arteries
white garlic
wool yarn
yard work
yarn basket

Sentences:

It's starting to get dark

I hear barking in the yard

Are you going to park the car?

We parked far from the park

Let's have a party in our apartment

The sharp tool left a mark on my arm

Don't throw the paper star in the garbage

She made a card for Barney in the shape of a heart

The army squad heard the alarm to start their drills

She put all of her art in her car in the dark of the night

My grandfather stored his old harp in the farmyard barn

The dog started to bark in the yard when he saw the squirrel

The security guard didn't get far running after the car on foot

"or"

Spelling:

or –storm, more, fork
oor – door, floor, poor
ar – war, warm
our – course, four, pour
oar – boar, roar, oar

Description: round your lips with your jaw open moderately "oh", then transition to the /r/afterward "ohwer."

Words:

abort	chord	corpse
acorn	chore	course
adore	coral	court
adorn	cord	decor
aorta	core	door
board	cork	dork
bore	corn	dorm
born	corny	floor

flora	moral	snore
foray	more	snort
force	morning	sore
ford	morph	sorry
forest	mourn	sort
forge	norm	source
forgo	north	sport
fork	oral	store
form	orange	stork
fort	orbit	storm
forth	orca	story
forty	order	sword
forum	organ	swore
four	poor	sworn
fours	popcorn	thorn
fourth	porch	torch
glory	pore	tore
gore	pork	torn
gorge	port	tornado
gory	pour	torso
gourd	poured	wore
horde	pours	worn
horn	score	wort
horse	scorn	your
horseshoe	shore	yours
lord	short	
lore	shorts	

Phrases:

ad<u>ore</u> you	d<u>oor</u> to d<u>oor</u>	gl<u>or</u>y days
b<u>or</u>ed student	d<u>or</u>m fl<u>oor</u>	g<u>or</u>y st<u>or</u>y
b<u>orn</u> to fly	fast h<u>or</u>se	guts and g<u>ore</u>
butter popc<u>orn</u>	fl<u>oor</u>b<u>oar</u>d	h<u>or</u>de the candy
buy sh<u>or</u>ts	F<u>or</u>d sedan	h<u>or</u>se carriage
church ch<u>or</u>us	f<u>or</u>ge steel	h<u>or</u>seshoe game
clean fl<u>oor</u>	f<u>or</u>k and knife	it's the n<u>or</u>m
clothing st<u>ore</u>	f<u>or</u>m-fitting	loud h<u>or</u>n
c<u>or</u>al reef	f<u>or</u>ty-f<u>our</u>	modern dec<u>or</u>
c<u>ore</u> belief	f<u>our</u> cars	m<u>or</u>al of the st<u>or</u>y
c<u>or</u>kscrew	f<u>our</u> c<u>our</u>ses	m<u>ore</u> and m<u>ore</u>
c<u>orn</u> on the cob	f<u>our</u> m<u>ore</u>	m<u>or</u>ning gl<u>or</u>y
c<u>or</u>ny joke	f<u>our</u>th estate	m<u>our</u>n his death
c<u>our</u>t jester	front d<u>oor</u>	n<u>or</u>th and south
doing ch<u>or</u>es	fun st<u>or</u>y	ocean sh<u>ore</u>

on all fours
oral cavity
orange juice
orbit in space
orca whale
order a drink
organ donor
peeled orange

play sports
poor and alone
popcorn kernel
pour water
pumpkin gourd
rainstorm
scary tornado
strong force

such a dork
thick forest
tiny acorn
vocal chord
wood floor
yellow corn

Sentences:

Get more iron ore

Pour the coarse flour

We haven't had world war four

We need more forks on the table

A horse will never eat an orange

The landlord can't afford new floors

This cord is too short to reach the floor

The forest floor was covered in thorns

I finished everything on my chore board

I'm going to knock on three more doors

The chorus sang beautifully with the organ

I read her a story during the lightning storm

She was bored doing her chores all morning

Let's shop at more stores around the corner

There are four more storms on the north shore

There are three or four more reports over here

I want to open a store by the seashore up North

The corn from the store was even tastier than before

Another four more stories were heard before that one

Let's eat popcorn during the movie, and I'll pour you more to drink

Four more pairs of shorts had stains on them after the boys played sports

There's more rain coming in the storm

Put your fork away

The poor girl was sitting on the floor

They declared war in the warm summer season

I have to finish four more courses

The oar of the boat was caught in even more seaweed than before

"air"

Spelling:

air – air, chair, stair

ear – wear, bear, pear

are – share, care, aware

ar – contrary, vocabulary, ordinary

er- sheriff, cherry

Description: This is a diphthong vowel, so you must begin by opening the mouth wide with your lips smiling "eh," transition to closed mouth, and pull your tongue up to the "eee" sound ("eh ee"), then produce the /r/. It should sound like "eh eee rrr" or/eIr/. Be sure to make two distinct vowel sounds before the /r/ and transition smoothly, so there are no pauses or spaces.

Words:

affair	dairy	mohair
air	dare	pair
airbag	eclair	parachute
airbus	fair	parents
airing	fairly	parrot
airway	fairy	repair
airy	flair	share
arrow	hair	sheriff
asparagus	hairdo	square
barefoot	haired	stair
care	hairy	staring
caring	impair	stereo
chair	lair	unfair
chairs	marathon	where
cherry	married	
	midair	

Phrases:

airplane chair	dairy cow	impaired driver
airing it out	dare you to go there	long hair
airy space	eclair for dessert	marathon runner
asparagus bunch	fair is fair	married couple
asparagus for dinner	fairly hairy	mohair sweater
barefoot bear	fairy dust	new sheriff
beware of dog	great hair	nice to share
blocked airway	hairy bear	one arrow
bow and arrow	happy parents	open parachute
care for my hair	his chair	pair of pants
caring and sharing	hungry bear	parachute drop
cherry pie		parents rules

135

parrot chatter
repair my shoes
ride the airbus
romantic affair
run a marathon
sad nightmare
safe airbag

share the pie
sheriff in town
square block
square shape
staring back
state fair
stereo speakers
talking parrot

tasty pear
tear paper
unfair share
up the stairs
where are they
wooden chair

Sentences:
Where is the fair?
I will compare airfares
He had barely prepared
Careful on the tall stairs!
Matthew didn't care to share
Do you care if I eat your pear?
She got her rare watch repaired
The hairy bear was hunting for food
I had a nightmare about a scary parrot
Be careful what you share at daycare
Don't take more than your fair share, Terry!
I can't help but stare at her long, pretty hair
The Sheriff didn't know where to put his chair
We shot arrows at the fair and won the cherry pie contest
It's not fair that the marathon is only for barefoot runners
Her parents told her to beware when using a bow and arrow
The married couple made a dare to see who would share the most marshmallows

"ear"
Spelling:
er- hero, zero
eer – beer, engineer, volunteer
ear – weary, beard, clear
ere – here, we're, mere
ei – weird
ir – irritate, irresponsible
ier- pier, pierce
yr- pyramid

Description: Keep your jaw nearly closed and your lips spread to a smile "ee". Pull the sides of your tongue up to the roof for the "eee" sound, then produce the /r/ "eeeee rrrrr" or/ir/.

Words:

adhere
beard
beer
cafeteria
career
cashier
cereal
chandelier
cheer
cheerful
cheering
cheerios
cheery
coherent
dear
deer
disappear
domineer
eerie

engineer
fear
feared
gear
hear
hearing
hereby
hero
mere
merely
mirror
mutineer
near
peer
period
pioneer
profiteer
puppeteer
pyramid

racketeer
rear
reindeer
revere
severe
shear
sincere
souvenir
sphere
steer
telomere
ulterior
veered
veneer
volunteer
weird
year

Phrases:

amazing career
bought a souvenir
bowl of cereal
bushy beard
cheap souvenir
cheer for the team
cheerful friend
cheering me on
cheery disposition
clear ocean
coherent argument
crystal chandelier
cut the beard
dear John
don't domineer
eating cheerios
eerie lights
fear no evil

feared by everyone
find an engineer
free beer
grocery store cashier
he's a hero
hear the good news
hearing aids
here and there
hereby declare
hospital cafeteria
keys always disappear
long pier
long spear
loud cheer
merely avoided it
metal shears
mirror reflection
must adhere

near each other
near the window
new cafeteria
new year
nice cashier
peer through the window
period piece
pioneer equipment
reindeer sighting
revered by everyone
saw a deer
severe reactions
side view mirror
sincere belief
small hearing aid
soggy cereal
sphere objects
steer clear

switch gears	ulterior motive	volunteer here
tall pyramid	veered that way	weird hat
the greatest year	veneer on the furniture	weird science
the rear of the theatre	visit the pyramids	

Sentences:

He was weary of drinking beer

The engineer moved here this year

The volunteer feared his fierce peers

My career is clearly in high gear this year

I had a fear that his beard looked weird

I could hear them cheer in the stadium

Where did my pruning shears disappear?

The cashier in the cafeteria is friendly this year

I could hear the crystal chandelier crash near me

I'm going to learn how to throw a spear this year

If you walk to the end of the pier, the water is clear

He puts a hearing aid in his ear so he can hear properly

He has a lot of fear about cutting his beard without a mirror

The mere thought of another dreary day made him irritable

It was better for my ears to wear earplugs before going to work

The pioneer was a hero for steering the group to safety with all of their gear

"ire"

Spelling: ir, ire, ur, ier, iar, oir, yer, igher

Description: This is a diphthong, so there are two vowel sounds before the /r/. Start with your jaw open for the "ah" sound and transition to closed jaw with a smile for the "eee." Keep your jaw nearly closed, and your lips spread to smile. Pull the sides of your tongue up to the roof for the "eee" sound, then produce the /r/ "ah eee rrr."

Words:

acquire	campfire	enquire
admire	choir	entire
aspire	choirs	esquire
attire	desire	expire
bonfire	dire	fire
briar	dryer	firefly
buyer	empire	fireman

gunfire
haywire
higher
inquire
inspire
Ireland
ironing
liar
pliers

require
retire
retired
rewire
sapphire
satire
sire
siren
spire

squire
tire
tired
umpire
vampire
wire
wired
wiretap

Phrases:

acquire the design
admire her
admired friend
aspire to be a leader
barb wire
beautiful attire
big liar
blind umpire
briar bush
buy a wire
buyer beware
call the fireman
campfire food
choir song
church choir
clothes dryer
desire to connect
dire situation
dryer sheets
empire of the century
Empire State Building

enquire about it
entire meal
expire this year
firefly lane
fireman courage
flat tire
found a wiretap
get the pliers
going haywire
going to Ireland
heard gunfire
higher shelf
hire new staff
home buyer
inspire a new idea
ironing board
lost and found flier
metal pliers
new hire
not a liar
on fire

require an answer
retire this year
retired salesman
rewire the switch
roaring fire
sapphire jewel
sapphire ring
scary vampire
see Ireland
set the campfire
sire a son
siren call
so tired
spire of the castle
sung by the choirs
thirsty vampire
tired of the boredom
watchful umpire
wired brain
wonderful bonfire

Sentences:

The liar retired
Cut the wire with pliers
The boy admired the umpire
Her entire jug of milk expired
He was tired after the campfire
The plane flew higher over Ireland

I'd like to inquire about the tragic fire
The fireman is tired of putting out fires
Never get too tired to inspire your students
The Empire State Building is higher than I thought
They got a first-time buyers discount on the pliers
The choir performed in the Ireland folk music competition
She put the clothes into the dryer before she ironed them
She wants to hire a new worker because the old employee was a liar
They were tired after they posted a lost and found flyer to find their dog

R-Blends

I want to provide you with a specific section on R-blends since R's blended with other consonants can be particularly tricky. Many instructors do not overtly discuss the pronunciation of blends, but it is important to do so since blends are often a particularly difficult group of sounds to master. A blend is when two or even three consonants are produced directly after one another. For example, "spr" in "spring" is a consonant cluster or blend. Pronouncing multiple consonants after one another creates a complex requirement for your tongue. For /r/ in a blend, you really don't need to do anything differently in terms of your pronunciation. However, I find it helpful to direct my clients to elongate the /r/ in blends a millisecond longer to give your tongue the time it needs to make the sound accurately. If you do not give yourself this extra time for /r/, you may find that your old pronunciation starts popping out again. Difficulty with /r/ blends often occurs if you typically produce your /r's/ as a trilled /R/. Practice these words and phrases by elongating the /r/ slightly in the blend, ensuring you still feel the curled tongue tip position.

PR
Words

princess	press	prawn
pretty	printer	prison
pray	price	principal
pretzel	prince	present

Sentences
Prancer pricked his hoof

The prawn was an excellent price
The pretty princess eats pretzels all day
I pray that the printer will print my papers
The principal went to prison for stealing a present

BR
Words

bread	brick	braces
bridge	breakfast	break
broom	bracelet	broccoli
brush	brother	breeze

Sentences

I ate brown bread for breakfast
I can smell broccoli in the breeze
She left the broken broom under the bridge
The bracelet and the hairbrush were brown
His brother fell onto a brick and broke his braces

TR
Words

train	trampoline	tree
trim	trophy	tray
troll	trash	tractor
triangle	trumpet	truck

Sentences

Someone put my trumpet on a dirty tray
The troll lived in the trash under the big tree
Trim the bushes and trees in a triangular shape
The train was faster than the tractor and the truck
It's true, I won a trophy for trampoline jumping

DR
Words

drum	dryer	dream
dragon	drawer	dry
draw	drive	drink
dress	drill	drip

Sentences

I drove to the store to get my dream dress

The dreary dresser needed a drastic change

I've dreamed of getting a drum set all my life

I dried the drink I spilled on my shirt in the dryer

I put my drawing of a drill in the bottom drawer

FR

Words

frog	frying pan	freeway
frie	fridge	freezer
fruit	frame	frost
Frisbee	friend	front

Sentences

The fridge and the freezer are frosty

I was looking at the front of the picture frame

Francis loves French fries for some reason, but not fruit

My friend took the rest of the meal from the frying pan

Fred loves the feeling of freedom when he's on the freeway

KR

Words

Crab	creek	cricket
crown	cry	crack
cream	crib	crocodile
crayons	crow	crawl

Sentences

The baby cried in his crib

The king had a crooked crown

I cringe whenever I see a crocodile

The crowd went crazy over the band

The crow grabbed the cricket from the creek

Why are there never any cream-colored crayons in the box?

GR

Words

grasshopper	grow	grandma

grandpa	grass	grill
grater	group	green beans
grab	grapes	grave

Sentences

A group of grapes always taste great

You're a great group of grape growers

The grub laid on the newly-grown grass

I use a grater to process my wheatgrass juice

Grandma and Grandpa always grow the greatest green beans

Words With Multiple R's!

gingerbread	Gingerbread is very delicious
Robert	Robert Redford is an actor
reporter	Ron is a serious court reporter
roller	Roller coasters terrify my friend
roar	I want to hear that leopard roar
rover	I have never driven a Range Rover
restaurant	Red Robin is my favorite restaurant
rare	That Beatles vinyl record is really rare
river	The stream turned into a roaring river
writer	I read a book by a best-selling writer
rider	Ron is a Harley-Davidson motorcycle rider
grasshopper	The green grasshopper hopped in the river
farmer	The farmer's market has the best produce
ranger	The forest ranger was rendered unconscious
racer	The NASCAR racer prefers high-speed races
rear	I love to relax in the rear of the movie theatre
quarter	My team won in the fourth quarter of the game
railroad	You should ride the railroads across the country
rooster	The red rooster crows really loudly in the early morning
carpenter	The carpenter raised the barn roof to make more room for the roosters
caterpillar	The caterpillar rollercoaster was the fastest rollercoaster in the park

R + L

Practice transitioning from an /r/ with a curled tongue tip to the /L/, placing your tongue tip on the roof of the mouth.

When attempting this difficult combination of consonants in a one-syllable word like "world," I have a great trick to help make this easier. When a word has an /r/ followed shortly by an /L/, you can add a slight quick vowel sound between them. Think of it as an "uh" sound as in uh-oh. So, the word "girl" might sound more like "ger uhl." This applies to one syllable words. The other words, you just have to transition from an /r/ to an /L/ by not adding a vowel. Give it a try.

Words:

airless	furlough	overly
airlift	garland	parlor
airline	garlic	pearl
barley	girl	poorly
Berlin	gnarl	scarlet
burlap	gnarly	snarl
burley	hairless	starlet
Carl	harlot	surly
Charlie	heirloom	swirl
clearly	hourly	tearless
curl	hurl	twirl
curling	hurled	utterly
curly	hurling	warlock
darling	majorly	waterlog
dearly	merlot	whirl
Earl	miserly	world
earlobe	motherly	worldly
early	nearly	yearling
elderly	orderly	yearly
fairly	overlap	
fatherly	overlord	

Phrases:

airless tires	burley man	curl your tongue
airline pilot	Carl won the race	curling champion
barley soup	Charlie Chaplin	curly hair
Berlin City	Christmas garland	darling girl
burlap bag	clearly see it	dearly beloved

144

Earl was home
early riser
elderly man
fairly easy
fatherly advice
garlic bread
girl in the shop
gnarled edges
hairless cat
hourly work
hurl the ball
hurled it along
hurling it over
hurt your earlobe

in the parlor
majorly disappointed
merlot or riesling
miserly old brute
motherly advice
nearly over
orderly group
overlap in answers
overly opinionated
pearl necklace
poorly completed
priceless heirloom
Scarlet O'Hara
snarling dog

starlet to be
surly man
swirl the drink
tearless shampoo
twirl your skirt
utterly obnoxious
warlock lord
waterlogged fingers
whirl it around
world order
worldly beings
yearly plan

Sentences:
The girl twirled her curls
Earl hurled the ball
Carl arrived early to the yearly conference
Surely, the burlap is utterly useless in this situation
It's the best thing in this whole wide world
Swirl the pearl in the ocean water
I left the bottle of Merlot in the parlor
I bought this barley in Berlin
He nearly dropped all of the garlic on the floor
That debate was dealt with poorly
Charlie helped the elderly in his neighborhood
Scarlet is so worldly. She knows nearly every band
Fatherly and motherly love is so valuable
The hairless overlord was sure to hold on to his family heirloom

R + W

Words:
afterward
airwaves
airway
carwash
dinnerware
doorway
earwax
earwig

fairway
forward
narwhal
otherwise
overwhelm
paperwork
silverware
stairway

stairwell
underway
underwear
underwent
waterway
waterworks

Sentences:
The Na<u>rwh</u>al is a mighty mammal
We need to hit the ca<u>rw</u>ash today to get rid of the mud on our car
Clear the doo<u>rw</u>ay for the crowd
The outcome is unde<u>rw</u>ay
I'll fo<u>rw</u>ard that email to you today
The stai<u>rw</u>ell was packed with boxes
I have a lot of pape<u>rw</u>ork to complete tonight
The silve<u>rw</u>are hasn't been polished in years
I moved all of the dinne<u>rw</u>are to the other cupboard
It's important to speak clearly; othe<u>rw</u>ise, your meaning will be lost
Every time I see an ea<u>rw</u>ig, my skin crawls
I completed my report early so I wouldn't get ove<u>rw</u>helmed tomorrow
Once one tear fell, the wate<u>rw</u>orks were sure to follow

Reading:
Find the /r/ wherever you go. Notice them in signs, the newspaper, magazines, and emails. Anywhere. Read out loud and get used to your new tongue position for /r/. Keep at it, and over time it will begin to feel natural and fluent.

Conversation:
This sound, in particular, causes many people to feel a kind of "imposter syndrome." Because this sound is notoriously "North American," it can stand out as a sound that feels like you're mimicking someone else. The /r/ is one sound that you should be aware of might make you feel slightly strange when you start to use it with others. Don't let that stand in your way, though! It might come as a shock to hear your pronunciation change so dramatically, especially for people who already know you well. Prepare yourself for some reactions. Hopefully, you have loved ones who are supportive, and this will not interfere with your goals. Speak with strangers who have no preconceived notion of what you typically sound like to try this sound out. You will gain confidence as you begin to implement this sound into your daily life.

Chapter 12: All About "L": <u>L</u>ikely Not Your Favourite Sound In This Si<u>ll</u>y O<u>l</u>d Wor<u>l</u>d!

Description:

We pronounce the "L" or /L/ by placing the tip of the tongue up to the roof of the mouth, just behind the upper front top teeth. Placement varies slightly from individual to individual, but overall, as long as the tip of your tongue is somewhere between your front teeth and the alveolar ridge on the roof of the mouth, then you're good. Be careful to keep your tongue tip from going too far back or anywhere BEHIND the alveolar ridge. As you may recall, the alveolar ridge is that bony ridge on the roof of your mouth. You might be able to feel that behind the alveolar ridge, the palate goes up into a vaulting arch, so keep your tongue tip out of this region and closer to your front teeth.

Common /L/ difficulties:

One of the main issues that non-native English speakers face with /L/ is tongue position. For many, the /L/ that they produce involves no actual physical contact of the tongue tip and the roof of the mouth. The lack of contact is what can often be perceived as a dropped /L/. If the tongue does not physically touch the roof AND you find that your lips are slightly rounded, the result is a sound similar to the /w/ sound. It is typically more noticeable at the ends of words like in words "will" and "bell," which would sound more like "wiw" and "bew."

Practice comparing how the tongue feels when it touches the roof for /L/ versus making no contact for /w/ words.

/w/ vs. /L/ Minimal Pairs:

whoa	low	way	lay	war	lore
why	lie	wet	let	womb	loom
wham	lamb	wed	led	wire	liar
wax	lax	weak	leek	white	light
wag	lag	work	lurk	walk	lock
whip	lip	where	lair	wimp	limp
wit	lit	wick	lick	wean	lean

west	lest	wink	link	Rio	reel
wide	lied	wait	late	toe	toll
whim	limb	wine	line	mayo	mail
went	lent	wife	life	go	goal
weep	leap	ow	owl	camo	camel
ward	lord	ew	ill	meadow/medal	

/w/ vs. /L/ Sentences:

<u>Wh</u>oa, that plane flew <u>l</u>ow

<u>Wh</u>y must you <u>l</u>ie?

That elastic band <u>wh</u>ipped my <u>l</u>ip

Your <u>w</u>it and charm <u>l</u>it up the room

That is the best <u>w</u>ay to <u>l</u>ay on a couch

<u>L</u>et the <u>w</u>et clothes dry

That <u>l</u>eek soup smells quite <u>w</u>eak compared to the onion soup

The boss always <u>l</u>urks around when I <u>w</u>ork

<u>Wh</u>ere is your secret <u>l</u>air?

Never <u>l</u>ick a candle <u>w</u>ick

The <u>l</u>ight is so bright and <u>wh</u>ite

I can't <u>w</u>ait for you when you're <u>l</u>ate

I <u>w</u>aited in <u>l</u>ine to buy the <u>w</u>ine

My <u>w</u>ife makes my <u>l</u>ife so much better

It took a to<u>ll</u> on me when I stubbed my t<u>oe</u>

There's a may<u>o</u> coupon in the mai<u>l</u>

G<u>o</u>, team. Get that goa<u>l</u>!

Another common issue with /L/ is to confuse the /n/ sound with /L/. This will make the word "low" sound like "no." Practice the word list below to feel how the /L/ words need to involve your tongue tip touching the roof, making an oral sound. The /n/ words are nasal, so feel the air coming out of your nose.

/n/ vs. /L/ Minimal Pairs:

no	low	nine	line	bin	bill
name	lame	nip	lip	bone	bowl
nap	lap	knife	life	bun	bull
neigh	lay	knock	lock	chin	chill
net	let	knot	lot	coin	coil
nice	lice	barren	barrel	con	call
night	light	Ben	bell	cone	coal

dean	deal	inn	ill	sane	sail
dawn	doll	Jane	jail	sewn	soul
done	dull	Jen	jell	sin	sill
earn	Earl	keen	keel	ten	tell
even	evil	main	mail	tin	till
fin	fill	mean	meal	tone	toll
fun	full	nun	null	tune	tool
gin	Jill	on	all	vein	veil
gun	gull	pan	pal	when	well
hen	hell	pin	pill	win	will
hun	hull	rain	rail		

Sentences

There is no way I will go that low

I wish I didn't have such a lame name

My dog took a nap on my lap

Let the net do the work

There is nothing nice about lice

Turn on the night light

There are nine people in line

This knife saved my life

Knock on the door. It's locked.

I do not know a lot about knots

Dawn lost her doll

Earl earns a lot of money

Even evil people have basic rights

I am done dressing in dull colors

Jill will only drink gin and tonic

Everyone at the inn was ill

Jane went to jail for three years

Just put the mail in the main mailbox

Put all of the reports on the desk

Tell me ten stories

When you do it well, you will know

We will win the next championship

Another issue with tongue placement can be how far back your tongue makes contact with the roof of the mouth. The location you place your tongue will result in a very different sound. Typically the North American English pronunciation will be

149

just behind the front teeth. If you find that your tongue is farther back and even further back beyond the alveolar ridge, then focus on placing your tongue tip more forward near the front top teeth.

Clear vs. Dark "L"

Many clients come to me having already watched lots of online videos about the "L" and then became really fixated on the clear vs. dark pronunciation. I'll explain the difference here, but likely, your issue is not so much the slight differentiation of clear vs. dark /L/, but the fact that you ELIMINATE the /L/ altogether. I tell my clients to focus on actually ensuring a /L/ exists, and we can perfect the dark /L/ afterward. So if this is you, focus on ensuring that the tip of your tongue actually touches the roof as your first priority.

The clear "L" is the "L" I described above, with the tongue tip touching the roof, and the middle and sides of the tongue generally fall lower in a relaxed position. We produce the clear /L/ at the beginning of syllables in English, like in "let, like, and lifejacket." The dark /L/ is produced with even MORE of the tongue raised up towards the roof of the mouth. The sides of the tongue go up as well. The middle of the tongue is also raised in a tense position. It should feel like you are pushing the first third of the tongue up against the roof of the mouth. The dark /L/ is produced at the end of syllables and in /L/ blends, so words like "girl, pull, mail, and please."

Common Differences:
The most prevalent issue that non-native English speakers have with /L/ is the lack of actual contact with the tongue tip and the roof of the mouth. Without the tongue tip touching the roof, it essentially sounds like the /L/ is deleted altogether. It may sound more like a vowel than an "L." Another change in this sound I often hear from clients' assessments is what I call an "almost" /L/ production, meaning the tongue tip almost touched the roof but stopped short of actually making contact. The result of these changes to /L/ makes words sound similar to a /w/. So, the word "seal" might sound more like "seaw."

Spelling:
The /L/ spelling is quite simple. /L/ is spelled with an "L." There are, however, some words that exist in English where the "L" is silent. The only way to know when to

pronounce the /L/ and when it is silent is to memorize the silent /L/ word list. Once you have the silent "L" words memorized, all others can be safe to pronounce. Sorry, I know memorization is no fun task! Unfortunately, there is no other way to get around it. Below are the silent /L/ words you should know.

Silent "L" Words and Sentences

calm	The Sea was calm
balm	That's the best lip balm ever
palm	The palm tree swayed in the breeze
salmon	Salmon is a healthy food
half	I practice my pronunciation for half an hour each day
calf	One of our cows recently had a calf
chalk	These boards are covered with chalk
talk	Don't talk with your mouth full
walk	Let's walk home through the park
stalk	Jack and the bean stalk is a very old story
folk	Folk music is popular with these students
yolk	The egg yolk is yellow
could	We could hear the palm leaves swaying
would	Would you like some chocolate cake?
should	You should put on a warm sweater today

Hear it!

Listen to the difference in the words below. Notice how each word sounds different when it is produced with the tongue tip touching the roof versus no contact.

Compare the /L/ and /w/ in this minimal pairs list:

Beginning of words:

lead	/weed	link	/wink	lip	/whip
lock	/walk	lead	/wed	line	/wine/whine
lick	/wick	let	/wet	leak	/week/weak
light	/white	late	/wait	lay	/weigh/way
liar	/wire	leap	/weep		
lake	/wake	life	/wife		

Ends of words:

gull	/go	all	/ow	ill	/ew

mull	/mow	dull	/dough	renal	/Reno
howl	/how	haul	/how	chill	/chew
veal	/view	goal	/go	excel	/xo
null	/no	full	/foe	medal	/meadow
reel	/Rio	wall	/wow	camel	/camo
hull	/hoe	call	/caw	natal	/NATO
bull	/bow	hall	/how	brawl	/brow
duel	/duo	roll	/row	local	/loco
pal	/pow	bowl	/bow	metal	/meadow
lull	/low	soul	/sew/so	thrill	/throw
yell	/yo	toll	/toe	radial	/radio
doll	/Dow	sell	/sew		
wool	/whoah	real	/Rio		

Feel it!

To ensure that you are producing this sound correctly, you must physically feel the tip of your tongue touch the roof of your mouth just behind your front teeth. You can think of it as "licking" the roof of your mouth but holding your tongue in that position. Feel the bumpy alveolar ridge with the tip of your tongue, and then turn on your voice. Feel the vibration created when you turn your voice on with your vocal folds with your hand on your throat.

Do it!

Okay, so let's practice!

Isolation:

Hold the /L/ sound: "LLLLL" "LLLLL" "LLLLL" LLLLL" "LLLLL"

Syllables:

Get used to blending the sound into the surrounding vowels. You should not hear any space or pause between the /L/ and the vowel. Try it for yourself.

la, le, li, low, lu, lay
al, eel, isle, owl, ool
ala, eelee, ili, olo, ulu

Words:

You may notice that words are particularly easy in one position but especially hard to produce in other positions. Pay attention to this, as you can hone in on your problem areas. Typically the /L/ at the ends of words proves to be most difficult, but for others, any and all /L/s in words are difficult.

Beginning

lace	lefty	lock
lack	leg	loft
lady	lemon	log
ladybug	lend	logo
laid	less	lone
lair	let	long
lake	liar	look
lama	lice	loom
lamb	lick	loop
lame	lied	loopy
lamp	lieu	loot
land	life	lord
lane	lift	lose
lard	light	loss
lark	like	lost
lash	lily	loud
lass	limb	love
last	lime	low
late	limp	lube
lathe	line	luck
laugh	link	lull
lava	lion	lump
lawn	lips	lunch
lazy	list	lung
lead	listen	lure
leaf	little	lurk
leak	live	lush
lean	load	lust
leap	loaf	lynx
leek	loan	
left	lobe	

Middle

alarm	almost	always
alive	alone	apply
allow	along	balloon

153

belief	health	select
belly	island	shoelace
below	itself	silly
build	jelly	silver
built	killed	simply
calendar	likely	solid
child	mainly	solve
daily	merely	split
delay	mostly	supply
dollar	myself	truly
early	nearly	twelve
easily	newly	unless
elbow	olive	unlike
eleven	online	valley
failed	pillow	value
fairly	pilot	volume
false	police	wallet
family	policy	wallpaper
fault	public	wealth
fellow	really	weekly
field	relate	wholly
follow	relief	world
fully	result	yellow
golden	sailing	yield
hardly	salad	

Ending

actual	bowl	coral
aerial	brutal	crawl
all	burial	cruel
angel	call	denial
animal	canal	dental
annual	cancel	detail
appeal	carol	devil
awful	casual	diesel
ball	cereal	drill
barrel	chapel	enroll
basil	chill	entail
bowel	civil	equal

excel	medal	seal
facial	mental	sequel
fall	metal	serial
fatal	modal	shell
fetal	moral	shovel
final	mortal	signal
fiscal	muscle	skill
floral	mutual	skull
focal	nail	small
formal	neural	smell
fossil	nickel	social
frail	normal	spell
fungal	novel	spill
funnel	ordeal	spinal
girl	owl	spiral
global	panel	stall
gospel	pastel	steal
gravel	patrol	still
grill	pearl	stool
hazel	pencil	stroll
heel	pixel	swell
herbal	plural	symbol
hill	pool	tail
hotel	portal	tall
ideal	postal	thrill
jewel	primal	tool
joyful	pupil	total
kernel	racial	towel
label	radial	trail
lawful	rebel	travel
legal	recall	trial
lethal	rental	tribal
level	retail	tunnel
local	reveal	until
loyal	ritual	unveil
mail	rival	uphill
mammal	royal	useful
manual	rural	usual
marvel	school	verbal

vinyl
viral
visual

vital
vocal
whale

wheel
yell

Phrases:

Beginning

long letter
lucky ladybug
lazy lizard

Logan's lunch
little lamb
lamb's leg

locked and loaded
love a little
long lost loves

Middle

all by itself
all over
almond salad
brave police
field of dreams
follow your dreams
fully tested
golden apple
hardly believe it
healed elbow
health is priority
island breeze

jelly belly
jelly sandwich
killed the flower
likely alive
mainly believers
mellow fellow
merely a dream
mostly frozen
my fault
nearly over
need a little relief
newlyweds

old pilot
old policy
older policeman
olive garden
police alarm
public policy
really old
relate to it
silly shoelaces
yellow pillow

Ending

all the people
build skill
car rental
full bowl
impossible file
movie sequel
nail file
old ritual
old school
retail therapy
reveal the prize
rival enemies
royal decree
rural setting

seal the deal
see the signal
serial number
shell pasta
shovel the snow
small girl
smell the bowl of food
snail mail
social stroll
spell it out
spill the milk
spinal tap
spiral design
still breathing

stroll with me
symbol of love
tall building
tall stool
the right tool
total control
trailblazer
travel alone
trial and tribulation
wet towel
what a thrill
will sell

Sentences:
Beginning

Look and listen for the signs of love

Logan's water pistol was locked and loaded

A ladybug had its lunch on the lemon tree leaf

The lamp wasn't light enough to launch the boat off the land

The leader of the group had a long laugh at the lesson plan

That little letter Lee carried had a long list of lazy people on it

Middle

You must always handle all of the animals gently

I feel an obligation to socialize, especially during the holidays

In the sales world, you need to be totally involved in small talk

My goal is to be healthy, wealthy, and have a lovely personality

I am not very familiar with technology, but I'm sure I'm not alone

The symbolism was especially unclear in his boldly written poetry

A familiar plan is quickly completed, but an unfamiliar plan is usually difficult

Ending

Double trouble

There's a small apple in that bowl

He still has to travel with his pillow

I always work with medical personnel

The girl will feel all the muscles in her heel

This is the first time in my life that I feel old

Financial people are able to build wealth

All the people followed a single rule

If you follow the universal rules, you will get the logical results

Bill will be a logical and practical choice for your legal issues

I have a couple of proposals that have long-overdue deadlines

The hospital had several clinical trials with large sample sizes

Paul, please be social and smile tonight when we're around people

Schedule all of the medical personnel at the same time if possible

Will you be able and available to double all the skilled people in your field?

Several influential people have been successful in producing functional products

"L" Blends At The Beginning of Words

L-blends are words that have another consonant right next to an /L/ in a word. Blends are more challenging to produce since the tongue movements are more complex, and the change must be quick to move from one sound to the other. The rules for /L/ that we talked about earlier in this chapter still apply here. Ensure you can feel that your tongue tip is up against the roof of your mouth and in front of the alveolar ridge. Practice your /L/ sound in the L-blend words and sentences below.

BL

blanket	The blanket blew away
blade	The knife blade was sharp
blocks	I put the blocks on the blanket
blackberries	The blind man loved blackberries
blackbird	The blackbird flew in the blue sky
black sheep	He's the black sheep of the family
blouse	She will only wear that black blouse
blue jeans	Those are my favourite pair of blue jeans
blue ribbon	I won the blue ribbon at the blueberry fair

FL

flag	The flag flew high
floor	The floor was flooded
flashlight	I left my flashlight in Florida
fly	The fly landed on the floor
flamingo	The flamingo has flat feet
flower	The florist arranged the flowers
flat	Florence had a flat tire yesterday
flute	She played the flute in the flower garden

SL

slug	The slug was so slimy
sled	I slid my sled down the hill
slow	The sloth moves very slowly

sleeve	Your sleeve is slightly too long
slide	She slid down the slippery slide
sleeping	The boy was sleeping in his sleeping bag
slippers	The slippers kept the woman from slipping

PL

playing	Please keep playing nicely together
planet	This is the biggest plum on the planet
plant	My plant is growing plenty of tomatoes
plum	She planted the plum tree two years ago
plane	The plane was plummeting to the ground
pliers	I used the pliers to do some plumbing around the house

CL

cloud	The clouds were coming
clear	Clearly, the clip was broken
clap	The crowd clapped for the clown
claw	The bear claw was behind clean glass
class	He dragged clay in the class with his dirty shoes
climb	The climbers climbed the cliff without their climbing gear

GL

glare	Glen glared at his boss
glamorous	Glamorous people are glorified
glow	The lanterns glow brightly at night
glad	Gloria was so glad she passed her exams
glass	The glassblower blew beautiful glass bowls
glue	I used clear glue to glue the pieces together

"L" Blends At The End Of Words

Now that you have your L-blends figured out and you're starting to feel comfortable with them, let's move on to a slightly more difficult blend: the final L-blend. A final L-blend is somewhat more difficult because, in these blends, you will be exercising more of the "dark" /L/ practice. You will have to push up more of the front and sides of your tongue. Begin by tensing the middle and sides of your tongue upwards towards the roof. Give these words a try, and feel how your tongue tip not only needs to go up to the roof but physically push the middle of your tongue upwards to get a "dark" /L/ quality.

Final "L" Blend Words

build	gulp	spilled
child	held	told
cold	helm	wild
crumpled	help	world
emerald	hold	yelp
field	mild	yield
filled	mold	elk
film	old	milk
fold	rolled	silk
gold	shield	
grilled	sold	

Final "L" Blend Sentences

The child wanted to build a fort in the field

I watched an old film about fools gold

She spilled milk all over her silk shirt

I held the sold sign in my hand

She crumpled and rolled the paper as she asked for help

She called all of the animals in the wild

Final "LT" Blends

belt	melt	fault
bolt	molt	guilt
colt	pelt	knelt
cult	salt	quilt
felt	silt	smelt
halt	tilt	difficult
hilt	volt	stilt
jilt	wilt	vault
jolt	adult	revolt
kilt	dealt	insult
malt	dwelt	result

Final L-Blend Sentences:

The insult resulted in a revolt

The belt was difficult for any adult to close

John felt some guilt that he let the ice cream melt

I felt a jolt of cold after eating the milkshake

He felt the material of the kilt to see if it matched the quilt

She knelt down to see the result of the spill on the carpet

The Syllabic "L"

The "L" can be pronounced as an entire syllable. What this means is that we can essentially delete the vowel before the "L" altogether. The syllabic "L" occurs in unstressed syllables. It is helpful to know about syllabic "L" to avoid sounding like you are over-pronouncing words. You pronounce the "L" exactly as you would otherwise; only you do not actually emphasize or pronounce the vowel before it.

So, for example, the word "fuel" would not be pronounced "few **el**" but more like "fe**wl**" /fjuwl/.

The word "bagel" would not be pronounced "beh gel" with the vowel "e" pronounced clearly, but more like "beh gl," with the vowel dropped.

Let's look at some syllabic "L" words below to avoid over-pronouncing the vowel before it:

animal	fuel	model
bagel	hospital	potentially
awful	local	successful
cultural	medical	wonderful
especially	metal	

Reading:

Now is your opportunity to put what you have learned to the test! Read aloud to yourself and record yourself. Then read along as you listen to your speech. Highlight the "L" sounds as you speak and listen carefully as you press your tongue tip up to the roof of your mouth. Find the "L's" that you missed and write them down. Make a silly tongue twister sentence out of the difficult words to practice and repeat them. I like to suggest saying the sentence ten times very quickly. This practice will help you achieve a faster rate and more natural production of this tricky sound.

Conversation:

By now, the "L" sound should feel comfortable, and you should have a significantly better grasp of how it sounds and feels to produce it accurately. Using this sound in conversation is your next step. Focus intentionally when speaking to feel the tongue tip touching the roof. Again, you will need to start slowly. You may find your focus shift when talking to others. Losing your focus and forgetting are expected consequences of pronunciation work. It is a process, so be kind to yourself. Keep at it, practice regularly, and set reminders for yourself to focus on your practice throughout the day. With time, your awareness of the "L" will increase significantly. You will improve your ability to correct yourself, and your speed and naturalness will improve. By producing clearer, more accurate /L/s in English, your clarity and intelligibility when speaking to others improve tremendously.

Chapter 13: The 3 "T's" In English: Yup, 3! Why Not.

Description:

The typical /t/ in English is produced by placing the tip of the tongue on the alveolar ridge or roof of the mouth and releasing it quickly. Now, there is some normal variability between speakers, and some speakers may make their /t/ sound with their tongue tip touching nearer to their top front teeth. Both positions create a clear and accurate /t/ sound. The /t/ is a voiceless sound, so no vocal fold vibration should occur. If you feel your throat when you make the /t/ sound, you should feel no vibration or "buzz" on your throat. The lips are generally spread into a slight smile with the teeth together for the /t/ sound. But, oh, if you thought this was all you needed to know about /t/, then you are sorely mistaken. The /t/ in English is slightly more complicated than that! There are a few different ways that native English speakers pronounce the /t/ sound. For the sake of simplicity (for now), let's talk about the most common problems that people have with the /t/ in English. We'll delve into the more tricky elements of the various types of /t/ afterward.

Common Differences:

People's most common issue with pronouncing the /t/ sound is just plain not saying it! The /t/, in particular at the end of words, is often deleted altogether. Dropping a /t/ can affect the meaning of many words. Words like "can't" and "don't" require that pesky little /t/ to be clear and obvious to the listener. If you drop that /t/, the meaning is lost entirely! Here are a few minimal pairs to compare words that have the /t/ and words that do not. Note how the meaning changes. Comparing these words is a great way to see what would happen if you were to mistakenly drop that oh, so important final /t/!

/t/ minimal pairs:

ate	/a	toot	/two	light	/lie
bite	/bye	tote	/toe	treat	/tree
date	/day	meet	/me	can't	/can
boat	/bow	late	/lay	out	/ow
boot	/boo	fort	/four	eat	/E

Sentences:

I a<u>t</u>e a da<u>t</u>e

I took a bi<u>t</u>e ou<u>t</u> of the radish roo<u>t</u>

I los<u>t</u> my boo<u>t</u> on the boa<u>t</u>

I'll mee<u>t</u> you there, bu<u>t</u> don'<u>t</u> be la<u>t</u>e

You should have a ligh<u>t</u> trea<u>t</u> before we go ou<u>t</u>

I can'<u>t</u> ea<u>t</u> mea<u>t</u>

Aspirated /t/

Another way many people pronounce the /t/ differently is by not releasing any air. When you don't release the little puff of air that follows the /t/ sound, it is called "deaspiration." In many languages, the /t/that is typically produced is not made with any blowing puff of air at all. I like to think of aspiration on a sliding scale of "blowing." On the one end of the scale, you have no blowing (unaspirated /t/ or 0/10), and on the other end, the /t/ is entirely aspirated (or 10/10). You could think of the air as being strong enough to blow out a candle with the /t/ as 10/10, or like you're spitting the /t/ at someone! If your first language is more like a 0/10 with air blowing (aspiration), you will want to increase the airflow. This is especially important at the beginning of words. We want to increase the airflow release to a natural level, so somewhere like a 5 or 6 /10.

So, the word "top" should have a little puff of air released after the /t/. The word "top" could be thought of as "thhhhhhop" (not like the "th" sound, just an "h" or blowing after the /t/). In English, the /t/s at the beginning of stressed syllables are aspirated when followed by a vowel. This means that if you see a /t/ at the start of a syllable, you must release that puff of air with some aspiration or blowing. So, you could think of an aspirated /t/ as being like a 5/10 on my imaginary-blowing scale. So the word "toe" would have more aspiration or blowing puff of air than a /t/ in the middle of a word like "pentagon." The /t's/ at the ends of words in English are also released. By released, I mean that the air in the mouth stopped by the tongue will be let out after rather than being held in the mouth. The /t/ at the ends of words and syllables is not "aspirated" but rather just released. In my imaginary blowing scale, I would rate the aspiration level at the ends of words to be like a 1 or 2/10....the point here is that it should not be a 0/10! Some air should be released.

Spelling:

The /t/ sound is spelled with the letter "t." There are a few words in English where the letter /t/ is silent. Again, it is best to memorize these few words so they don't trip you up!

Silent "T" Words

Silent T Words Ending With -STLE

apostle	hustle	whistle
bustle	nestle	wrestle
castle	rustle	
gristle	thistle	

Silent T Words Ending With -STEN

christen	chasten	moisten
glisten	fasten	
listen	hasten	

Silent T Words With -FT

often

soften

French Words With a Silent T at the End

ballet	gourmet	ricochet
chalet	rapport	

Other Words With Silent T: No rules to explain these crazy rogues!

Chestnut (only the first t is silent)

mortgage

Christmas

The 3 "T's"

As I had mentioned before, English actually has a few different types of /t/s. If you listen carefully, you will notice a few other differences that native English speakers make to /t/ when talking. Usually, native English speakers will use a combination of all of the 3 T's in their speech, depending on the level of casualness in the conversation. The true aspirated /t/ is the most proper pronunciation and is used in extremely formal speech. The lingual flap and glottal stop /t/s (which we will discuss in detail later) are more associated with typical and informal speech. Most native English speakers, however, use all of these in combination, even in formal speaking situations, although often fewer of the flap /t's/ will be present. There is no real rule for how much of one type of /t/ to use in which situation. This is a personal decision, based on how natural or casual you would like to sound. Listen to speakers that you admire and listen closely to the /t/ sounds in their speech. In this chapter, all of the mysteries of the /t/ will be explained to you so there will no longer be any confusion. Now, let's get into the differences between these 3 T's!

The True "T" With & Without Aspiration

The true /t/ is what I described above. The tongue tip touches the roof of the mouth at the alveolar ridge or near the front top teeth. We then release the pressure with a slight puff of air; that puff of air is called aspiration. As I discussed above, the /t/ at the beginning of a syllable would have some airflow, like a 5 or 6/10. We want to keep it natural sounding. An airflow "level" of 10/10 is kind of similar to describing the airflow required to blow out a candle. We don't need this kind of airflow for speech, so be careful to keep it natural.

<u>Hear it!</u>
Go through the examples of the different /t/'s below and listen to how they sound different. It will take some time to get used to the rules here, and yes, it does take

some focus, but once you understand what to do, the mystery is gone! And let's be honest, knowing the difference is half of the difficulty.

<u>Feel it!</u>

Aspirated /t/: The tongue tip must touch the roof. You will focus on feeling the air blow out past your lips.

<u>Do it!</u>

Okay, so let's practice some more!

<u>Aspirated /t/ Isolation:</u>

Repeat the /t/ sound: /t/, /t/, /t/, /t/, /t/

<u>Syllables:</u>

Get used to blending the sound into the surrounding vowels. You should not hear a space or pause between the /t/ and the vowel. Try it for yourself.

ta, te, ti, tow, too

at, eat, it, ot, oot

ata, eetee, iti, oto, utu

<u>Words:</u>

Beginning /t/ words and sentences:

tub	It's time to hit the tub
taco	Tony had two tacos today
tennis	Take the tennis balls away
teeth	My teeth are turning yellow
teacher	That's the tenth teacher so far
tiger	The tiger hunted near the tree
table	Terry was seated at a tiny table
tortilla	Do you prefer tacos or tortillas?
toothpaste	Put toothpaste on your toothbrush
tall	The tree is too tall for the doorway
tissue	She took all the tissues to the trailer
tornado	The tornado totally trashed our town
tongue	Try to keep your tongue near your teeth
towel	Ted traded ten towels for twenty dollars
team	My team lost the final tournament today
tired	She worked tirelessly until she was truly tired

/t/ In the Middle of words when the syllable is <u>stressed</u>: (The stressed syllables are Bold here)

baton	Hand over the ba**ton**
guitar	I'd love to learn gui**tar**
potato	Hold the po_ta_toes, please
uptight	I look up**tight** in this outfit
hotel	I'm staying at this ho**tel** too
attain	I hope to a**ttain** that degree
attack	His colleague was on the a**ttack**
attention	Can I get your a**tten**tion, please?
anticipate	He didn't an_ti_cipate that reaction
pretend	Don't pre**tend** you don't have a hat
nineteen	He'll be turning nine**teen** this summer
return	I'll need to re**turn** the pants I ordered online
retain	I'll practice so I can re**tain** all of this information

Ending /t/ words and sentences:

coat	I love tha_t_ coa_t_
hat	Why is tha_t_ ha_t_ so fla_t_?
fruit	The ba_t_ a_t_e all of the frui_t_
boat	He wen_t_ ou_t_ to sail on his boa_t_
put	I pu_t_ the pi_t_ in my pocke_t_ for a bi_t_
kite	The ki_te_ flew to the highes_t_ heigh_t_
boot	My ca_t_ loves to sleep in tha_t_ big boo_t_
float	Why doesn'_t_ the boa_t_ floa_t_ in the moa_t_?
jacket	Are a coat and a jacket the same thing?
peanut	The elephan_t_ would only ea_t_ one peanu_t_
foot	I can'_t_ believe tha_t_ cu_te_ rabbi_t_ bi_t_ his foo_t_
parrot	The parro_t_ and the ra_t_ are afraid of the ca_t_
flashlight	I_t_ is so dark even the flashligh_t_ won'_t_ work
light	I used all my migh_t_ to turn on the brigh_t_ ligh_t_
quiet	I tiptoed on the ma_t_ to be as quie_t_ as possible
wait	When I wai_t_, I like to si_t_ and cha_t_ with strangers

Glottal Stop "T" /ʔ/ or "Held T"

The glottal /t/ occurs in less than 0.5% of words in English, but practicing the "glottal stop t" can be helpful if your goal is to sound more like native North American English speakers. General North American English pronunciation includes using the glottal /t/ sound by stopping the air in the throat, as you would in the phrase "uh_oh." That stopped feeling in the throat between "uh" and "oh" is the feeling we are discussing. Many people just assume that since they don't hear the /t/ that native speakers are just dropping it altogether. This assumption is wrong. Rather than dropping the /t/, speakers are actually inserting a "glottal sound." If you pause and hold your breath between the "uh" and the "oh," you should feel pressure in your throat. This pressure is actually your glottis stopping the air, hence the term "glottal stop." Essentially the air is not released in the throat. You are blocking the /t/ in the throat before you let the air pop out. You can also try to make the beginning of the "t," but don't let the puff of air release.

Listen to the difference between these phrases:

"great shirt"

If you drop the /t/'s entirely, it will sound like "grey sure."
If you stop the air in your throat for the /t/'s, it will have a different meaning "greaʔ shirʔ."

"colorful plate"

If you drop the /t/, it will sound like "colorful play."
If you stop the air in your throat for the /t/, it will have a different meaning "colorful plaʔe."

We use this crazy sound when the /t/ or /rt/ends a syllable AND when the next sound is a **consonant**. We also use this sound at the end of a line of speaking. That means, if you pause or stop talking, you would use the glottal /t/ there as well. An instance where you might decide not to use a glottal /t/ is when you are making extra emphasis or ensuring extra clarity on a particular word with the /t/. In these cases, the /t/ in an emphasized situation would be produced as a true aspirated /t/. Remember, it is about the sounds we say, not the spelling. So, if there is a silent /e/ that is not pronounced, just ignore that. We are focusing on pronunciation.

The glottal /t/ occurs IN words _and_ BETWEEN them. Here are a few examples of when you would stop the /t/ in the throat:

absent student	cartwheel	cut that
apartment	catsuit	deceitful
artwork	catnap	delightful
assortment	commitment	department
atlas	courtroom	dirtbag
atmosphere	cutbacks	Do it!

169

doubtful
eventful
fitness
flatbed
football
fruitful
guilt-ridden
hate mail
heartbeat
heartburn
heartless
hit them
hotbed
hotdog
hurtful
it was
jet boat
let's start that
meatball
meet me

meltdown
might have
minute by minute
Netflix
network
nightgown
nightlight
nightshade
nighttime
not funny
nutmeg
oatmeal
outbreak
outburst
outdated
outdoor
outfit
outgoing
outlook
outward

paintball
partner
pitfall
platform
quite well
rightly
right now
right side
Scotland
seatbelt
setback
spotlight
straightforward
that thing
treatment
try that
utmost
what a hit
witness

Glottal stop in phrases:

a football game
a fruitful endeavor
a report due
an eventful night
assortment of candies
beautiful artwork
bought new pants
cat suit costume
check the atlas
credit card
cut pieces
did it quite well
diet drink
difficult work
do it right now
doing cartwheels
don't be heartless
don't hit them
don't worry
eat a hotdog
eat your oatmeal
eight legged bug

flat nose
flatbread
flight mode
frat house
go to Scotland
good outlook on life
he was guilt-ridden
horrible heartburn
in the network
in the spotlight
it was an outbreak
it was over here
it's not fair
just do it!
late party
meet me at the park
have to try that
my partner
necessary cutbacks
nice outfit
no more hate mail
not here

not my fault
okay, let's start
on a flatbed
on a jet boat
pet detective
play paintball
quick heartbeat
repeat the words
rightly so
secret note in my journal
security department
she might know
shirt and pants
short stature
shut the door
smog in the atmosphere
so delightful
spaghetti and meatballs
street meat
that could be it
that was hurtful
that was not funny
that was straightforward

that's a commitment
that's doubtful
that's my apartment
that's outdated
the great outdoors
total meltdown

turn on the nightlight
upset her
very outgoing
wear your seatbelt
what a dirt bag
what an outburst

white suitcase
wore my nightgown
write down my address
wrong platform

Glottal Stop with "tly":

"tly" Words:

neatly
partly
bluntly
greatly
tightly
sweetly
overtly

quietly
smartly
nightly
rightly
lightly
shortly
brightly

covertly
devoutly
expertly
secretly
silently
recently

"tly" Sentences:
Rightly so!
I'll be there shortly
The doctor was greatly esteemed
The boss bluntly addressed the crowd
The drawers were all neatly organized
She was partly to blame for the accident
My throat closed tightly when I had an allergic reaction
She whispered the song sweetly and quietly
I was slightly irritated by the nightly dog barking
She expertly played the piano as she lightly touched the keys

Glottal Stop with "tment":

"tment" Words:

allotment
anointment
apartment
appointment
assortment
commitment

compartment
contentment
department
disappointment
enactment
indictment

investment
ointment
recruitment
resentment
treatment

"tment" Sentences:
My apartment is amazing
I have an assortment of candies
You have to show commitment to the team

Grab the pen from the glove compartment
Where's your allotment of scented ointments?
The department was completing recruitment activities
I hope you will avoid disappointment and resentment
You can complete your physio treatment in the clinic
There was a lot of resentment about the employee's treatment
I have an appointment with my banker to discuss my investment

Glottal Stop with the final syllable "n":

The /t/ and /rt/ also become a glottal stop when the final syllable is pronounced /n/ since the vowel is not even produced before the /n/ here. This phenomenon occurs in weak syllables. The syllabic /n/spellings include "tan, tain, ten, tin, and ton." They are all produced with a glottal /t/ and a strong sustained /n/.

So, the word "bitten" would not be pronounced "bih tEn" but rather "bih (t)n." The /t/ is not dropped but stopped in the throat. The vowel is shortened, and the /n/ will be emphasized. Here are a few examples of words ending in a syllabic /n/ that is pronounced with a glottal stop /t/:

batten:	Batten the hatches
beaten:	He was beaten up by bullies
bitten:	I was bitten by the snake
brighten:	This will brighten your day
button:	He pressed the red button
carton:	I bought a carton of milk
certain:	Are you certain about that?
cotton:	This is not made of cotton
curtain:	I have to open that curtain
Dalton:	His name was Dalton
eaten:	I haven't eaten all morning
fatten:	They fattened the cows
flatten:	They can't flatten those boxes
forgotten:	It won't be forgotten
fountain:	Let's meet at the fountain
frighten:	I didn't mean to frighten her
gluten:	It's gluten-free
gotten:	I haven't gotten the deal yet
important:	It's important
kitten:	What a cute kitten
lighten:	She did it to lighten the mood
Manhattan:	I've never been to Manhattan
Martin:	Martin was the leader of the group
mitten:	She lost her mittens

molten:	They saw molten lava
mountain:	I have a mountain of laundry to do
Newton:	I don't know much about Isaac Newton
rotten:	That's a rotten tomato
satin:	I love satin pillows
shorten:	I have to shorten my presentation
straighten:	I straightened my hair today
sultan:	He was the sultan of Broadway
sweeten:	The sugar sweetened the recipe
tartan:	This is my family tartan
threaten:	How dare you threaten me
tighten:	We need to tighten that bottle
whiten:	I whitened my teeth today
written:	Where was this written?

The Flap "T": Sounds like "D"

Since vowels are voiced, it's easier to keep our voice on for the /t/ if it's between two vowels or between a vowel and an "r." We like to avoid switching our voices from on to off to on again to help our speech flow. It's just easier! The reason we keep our voice on for the /t/ is essentially to save time. The voiced version of a /t/ is pronounced just like a very quick, short /d/. The tongue is in the exact same position for both sounds. The only difference between the two sounds is that a /t/ has no voice, and the /d/ does. So, the flap /t/ is just a phenomenon that causes us to turn /t/s into /d/s.

So, the word "butter" will sound more like "budder."
The word "Italy" will sound more like "Idaly."
And, "party" will sound more like "pardy."

The flap /t/ occurs between two vowels or /r's/ in an unstressed syllable (e.g., Vowel /t/ Vowel). For example, "bottom." The flap /t/ does not occur at the beginning of words, however, like in "tooth" because there is no vowel or /r/ before the /t/. Ultimately, what you produce is a very quick soft /d/. The flap /t/ can also occur between a vowel and an /ɚ/ or "r" sound since there is a small vowel before the /r/ in "er." An example of this is in the word "shorter," which would be pronounced as "shorder." An excellent way to practice this sound is to make sure the /d/ sound is very light and rapid.

173

Let's practice:

aorta	forty	political
artichoke	getting	portable
article	hospital	portal
artifact	hotter	potter
artist	hurting	pouting
atom	invited	pretty
auto	Italy	priority
autumn	knitting	putting
batter	later	rotting
beautiful	letter	Saturday
better	lettuce	sensitive
biter	lighter	shortage
boater	literal	sitter
booted	little	sorting
bottom	matter	started
butter	meeting	supporter
celebrated	metal	tartar
circulated	meter	theatre
city	mightier	thirty
commuting	mortal	total
computer	mortified	university
eighty	native	vertical
exciting	noted	waiter
fertilize	notice	water
flirting	party	
floating	photo	

It is important to know that this lingual flap not only occurs within words but in connected speech between words as well! The same rules apply; only the next word would have to begin with a vowel. The flap /t/ should only occur in linked speech or connected words. There would be no real space between the words. So, the examples below will show that two words meld together into one new pronunciation.

What a good idea	"whada good idea"
Whatever	"whadever"
What are you doing?	"whaderyuh doing?"
What is it?	"whadizit?"
A lot of pieces of paper	"uh lahduh pieces of paper"
Get in	"gedin"
Get out of here	"gedouduh here"
Eat out	"eadout"

174

Take it out   "takeidout"
Wait in line   "waidin line"
I heard a lot about it   "I heard uh lodaboudit"
Go to bed   "goduhbed"
From me to you   "from meduhyou"
Go to work   "goduhwork"
It is   "idiz"
It ought to be so   "idoddabeesow"
Say it again   "sayidagain"

Flap /t/ phrases:

art exhibit	hot outside	set our table
at a glance	hurt ourselves	sheet of paper
ate a pie	in the city	shot a movie
beat it	it always has	shut a window
bet I can	late again	sight unseen
bit into an apple	let out a laugh	sort of
but our thoughts are	light up	spit the pit out
court announcement	lot over there	spot on
cut an orange	met over here	suit of armor
date at the movies	Matt arrived	suite eleven
duty awaits	net outcome	title of the book
eight apples	not always true	total amount
fight again	note on my paper	vital information
flat iron	out of the bag	vote again
get away	Peter Piper	wait a minute
go to a party	port of entry	well noted
good data	pot of gold	white apron
got another one	put it down	wrote a book
great idea	quite a scene	yet again
hit a car	rate out of 10	

Now try for yourself in some longer sentences. Remember, when adding a lingual flap /t/, you will link the word to the next with no pauses. There will be sentences where you can also throw in a glottal stop /t/, or you may decide to just do a true /t/. Again, the more glottal and flap /t/s you use, the more casual the pronunciation.

Mixed /t/ Sentences:
That was a flirty article
I'll eat it in a bit
I bought thirty artichokes
Move the portable artifacts
There is a shortage of fertilizer
Could you heat it up first?

She met a nice guy in Seattle
My cat is getting fatter and fatter
She drank a lot of bottles of water
My daughter wore a little sweater
Peter put a letter on the water meter
The pretty British translator had to pick it up

You better not miss the meeting at eight o'clock
I love knitting in autumn for a little indoor activity
We celebrated graduating university with forty burritos
The waiter said he would send me a pot of water later
I told the waiter to bring it a little later since we're not done eating
I bought an automatic automobile for twenty thousand dollars
It doesn't matter what city is prettiest, but it does matter which city is hotter
The boater was very sensitive about losing his thirty fish and started pouting

/t/ in Stressed syllables:

As discussed above, we do not use the flap /t/ for stressed syllables. Below are a few examples of the /t/ between /r/ and vowels, but the /t/ is not a flap here because it is in the stressed word position. Here, the stressed syllable is underlined and bold. In a stressed syllable, the true /t/ is pronounced with a pop of aspiration or air released, NOT a quick /d/ sound.

ar**tis**tic	ho**tel**	po**ten**tial
a**ttack**	insti**tu**tion	pro**tect**
a**ttempt**	mar**ti**ni	pro**tec**tion
a**tten**tion	ma**te**rial	repu**ta**tion
a**ttire**	me**ti**culous	re**tail**
a**ttrac**tive	oppor**tu**nity	re**ta**liate
be**tween**	par**ti**cipate	re**tire**ment
cer**ti**ficate	par**ti**cular	re**turn**
compe**ti**tion	pe**tite**	sani**ta**tion
de**tail**	pe**ti**tion	sensi**ti**vity
de**tailed**	pla**teau**	sta**tis**tical
de**ter**mine	pla**to**nic	
gui**tar**	po**ta**to	

Be aware that as you change a word and add syllables, the use of a flap /t/ will change with it. Below, the stressed syllables are bold and underlined. The /t/ remains a true "popped" /t/ in stressed syllables, but a flap /d/ sound in unstressed syllables.

artist	"AR dist"
ar**tis**tic	"ar TIS dik"
photo	"FOW dow"

176

photograph	"FOW duh graf"
pho**to**grapher	"fow TAH gruh fer"
photo**gra**phic	"fow dow GRA fik"

*See more about stressed syllables in Chapter 32

Practice:

Here is a familiar poem that demonstrates the lingual flap (when /t/ turns to /d/). It's quite fun if you try to do it quickly. Try it for yourself!

Betty Botter is making a cake.
Betty Botter bought some butter, but, she said,
"The butter's bitter."
"If I put it in my batter, it will make my batter bitter."
"But, a bit of better butter will make my batter better."
So, she bought a bit of butter, better than her bitter butter,
and she put it in her batter.
And the batter was not bitter.
So it was better that Betty Botter bought a bit of better butter.

A Note About Spelling

Again, be aware that the differences in the pronunciation of /t/ are about the sounds in SPEECH rather than the spelling. The word itself will not dictate the type of /t/ to use, but what is AROUND that /t/. For instance, the phrase "That ending" will include a flap /t/ or a /d/ sound resulting in "thadending." This very same word followed by a consonant will sound entirely different. "That car" will include a glottal /t/ in the throat because of the consonant after it resulting in this same word sounding more like "thaʔcar."

Similarly, words that start with vowels like "one" truly begins with a consonant sound /w/ "wun." So, if you were thinking of using a flap /t/ for "that one," you would be wrong. In this case, the vowel is pronounced as a /w/, which is a consonant sound. So, in this example, you would use a glottal stop /t/ instead. The same is the case for the "y" sound. Often words spelled with a "u" are actually pronounced as a "y" sound, so they should be treated as a consonant.

Here are a few examples:

righ**t o**ne	" riʔ wun"
bi**t o**nce	"biʔ wuns"
got i**t u**sed	"god iʔ yoozd"
brigh**t u**niform	"briʔ yoo nuh form"
fa**t u**nicorn	"faʔ yoo nuh corn"
a**t u**niversity	"aʔ yoo nuh ver suh dee"

Dropping The "T"

The /t/ can be dropped entirely in English but only in two situations. The first situation is when the /t/ is between two consonants, like in the example "mus**t** be." The /t/ is dropped so that it would sound more like "musbe." The second situation is when /t/ comes after an /n/ like in "nt" and is followed by a vowel in an unstressed syllable. Here are a few good examples of when to drop the /t/ entirely.

Drop the /t/ between consonants with "st" and "ft":

nex(t) week	nexweek	I'm going nex**t** week
jus(t) one	jusone	I'll have jus**t** one more
gues(t) list	gueslist	I'm on the gues**t** list
gif(t) shop	gifshop	Buy one from the gif**t** shop
firs(t) dog	firsdog	I loved my firs**t** dog
lef(t) me	lefme	She lef**t** me at the altar
bes(t) friend	besfriend	You're my bes**t** friend
fas(t) pace	faspace	He's moving at a very fas**t** pace
fis(t) pump	fispump	The fis**t** pump is getting old

Drop the /t/ after /nt/:

wan(t)ed	wan(-)ed	I wan**t**ed that position
pain(t)ed	pain(-)ed	I shouldn't have pain**t**ed it white
ren(t)ed	ren(-)ed	We ren**t**ed for a year
poin(t)ed	poin(-)ed	I poin**t**ed it out to you
slan(t)ed	slan(-)ed	The roof looks slan**t**ed
flaun(t)ed	flaun(-)ed	She flaun**t**ed her good looks
plan(t)ed	plan(-)ed	I plan**t**ed a garden
coun(t)y	coun(-)y	We'll meet in the next coun**t**y
plen(t)y	plen(-)y	There's plen**t**y of leftovers

178

poin(t)y	poin (-)y	Those shoes are pointy
twen(t)y	twen(-)y	I ate twenty Oreo cookies today
in(t)ernet	in(-)ernet	The internet is down again
in(t)erview	in(-)erview	I got the interview
cen(t)re	cen(-)re	They visited the learning centre today
den(t)ist	den(-)ist	My dentist is the best
san(t)a	San(-)a	Santa brought a lot this year
advan(t)age	advan(-)age	I'm going to take advantage of that sale
in(t)eraction	in(-)eraction	I speak clearly in every interaction now
in(t)ernational	in(-)ernational	My book is selling internationally
presiden(t) of	presiden(-)of	He is the president of this company
pain(t) over	pain(-)over	You'll have to paint over that wall again

Here are some words to help you practice your /t/'s. Remember, depending on what is surrounding the /t/, it will be pronounced differently.

Words:

Beginning (aspirated)

table	teeth	tooth
take	tiger	touch
talk	time	towel
tall	toad	toy
taste	toast	turkey
teacher	toe	turtle
team	tongue	two
tear	tool	

Middle (true /t/) *note the /t/ is in the STRESSED syllable

guitar	eighteen	motel
potato	hotel	

*These middle /t/s are not turning to /d/ even though vowels may surround them. Here, the /t/ begins on the stressed syllable, so it will be a true aspirated /t/.

Middle (lingual flap /t/) *Pronounced as a light /d/

beauty	butter	tomato
better	little	biting
city	butterfly	Saturday
water		

179

Middle (glottal stop /t/ before /n/)

cotton	kitten	button
rotten	mitten	

So, to review:

True and aspirated /t/: The tongue tip must touch the roof. You will focus on feeling the air blow out past your lips.

Glottal /t/: Feel the tension in the throat at the glottis, just like in the phrase "uh-oh," that tightness is what you are feeling for. Do not release the air until the next sound occurs.

Lingual Flap /t/: Create a quick /d/ sound instead of the /t/. The flap /t/ is not unlike the /r/ sound produced for those of you whose first language is Spanish. You will feel the tongue tip flick the roof in a quick way, much like a /d/.

When NOT to change the /t/ to a flap or glottal /t/:

If you are trying to show strong emotion or if you really need to express clarity, you should continue to produce the true aspirated /t/. In most cases, except the ones listed above, in words where there are consonants before the /t/ like in "first, kept, fact," you will want to produce the true /t/ clearly with a nice release of air. Again, variations in /t/ are used to simplify speech, so they can be used as much or as little as you desire. If your goal is to produce typical conversational English, it is a good idea to improve your skills and knowledge of the flap and glottal /t/s.

Reading:

Go through a favorite book, or grab a magazine you have lying around. As you read out loud, focus on the T's you see. Record yourself reading out loud, and read along as you listen to your own pronunciation. Listen for the lingual flap /d/sounds between the words and how the glottal /t/ is produced in the throat. Try to listen to native English speakers. You will begin to increase your awareness of the mysteries surrounding the English pronunciation of /t/as you do this.

The more you practice, the better you can attune your ears to hear the differences. You will slowly improve your naturalness and speed and start to integrate these changes into your own speech.

Conversation:

So here is your big homework assignment. Take out your phone and set a few timers for yourself throughout the day. These will serve as reminders to use your new pronunciation as much as possible during your conversations throughout the day. It is important to practice with new conversation partners in new places and environments and varying topics. The more you practice, the easier it will become. Make new habits for yourself. Start small, but set at least five timers per day as a reminder to use your new pronunciation as you speak.

Remember, this is a long process. You are not going to change your habits in a week or two. You will need to work slowly to improve the frequency you are able to change your /t/s. You are going to work towards quicker and more natural speech with your new /t/s every day. Give yourself time and let yourself mess up. You can use these other "t's" when you want and change how you mix up your "t's" as you go. That's what all native English speakers do. Keep at it, and you will see how much this will impact your General North American English pronunciation.

Chapter 14: "D": When Grammar Meets Pronunciation

Description:
The "d" sound in IPA transcription is /d/, easy enough, right? To produce a /d/, place the tip of your tongue on the roof of your mouth near the alveolar ridge. The location should be right behind your front top teeth. The /d/ is a voiced sound, so the vocal folds must vibrate to produce the /d/.

Common Differences:
Typically this is a sound that most people can produce. Generally, the /d/ is most difficult to pronounce at the ends of words as many languages do not distinguish between a voiced /d/ and a voiceless /t/. Many non-native English speakers make one significant difference by devoicing the /d/ at the ends of words. When you devoice a /d/, it will sound like a /t/ since the articulation is exactly the same; only the /t/ is voiceless. Devoicing a /d/ is a problem because in English, doing so means to change the meaning of a word entirely.

Another issue speakers have with /d/ may include tongue position. It is important to know that the tongue tip goes forward or closer to the front teeth. Many speakers tend to place their tongue tip too far back, even behind the alveolar ridge on the roof of the mouth. The fix here is to feel where you are putting your tongue tip and to ensure it is actually touching those front pearly whites! Also, be sure to use the very tip of your tongue. If you find that you are curling your tongue tip so that the underside of the tongue is touching the roof, then your goal is to use the tip.

Let's also look at how important it is to add your voice for /d/ at the ends of words. Below, you will find a comparison of words that end in /t/ vs. the /d/ sound; these are called "Minimal Pairs." Once you realize just how important turning your voice on is, you will see why creating a /d/ properly in English is so essential in order to be understood by others.

T	D				
ant	/and	beat	/bead	blurt	/blurred
at	/add	bent	/bend	bright	/bride
bat	/bad	bet	/bed	but	/bud

cart	/card	hurt	/heard	set	/said
cat	/cad	kit	/kid	sheet	/she'd
clot	/clod	mat	/mad	short	/shored
cot	/cod	meant	/mend	shunt	/shunned
cute	/queued	meet	/mead	site	/sighed
debt	/dead	moat	/mode	skit	/skid
eight	/aid	mount	/mound	slight	/slide
faint	/feigned	neat	/need	slit	/slid
fat	/fad	not	/nod	sought	/sawed
fate	/fade	oat	/owed	spent	/spend
feet	/feed	pat	/pad	spite	/spied
float	/flowed	peat	/peed	spurt	/spurred
font	/fond	plate	/played	state	/stayed
gloat	/glowed	plot	/plod	stunt	/stunned
goat	/goad	port	/poured	tart	/tarred
got	/God	pot	/pod	teat	/teed
grit	/grid	punt	/punned	tent	/tend
hat	/had	quit	/quid	tight	/tied
heart	/hard	route	/rude	tint	/tinned
heat	/heed	sat	/sad	trot	/trod
height	/hide	scant	/scanned	wait	/weighed
hit	/hid	sent	/send	write	/ride

Spelling:
The /d/ sound is spelled with a "d," nice and simple!

Hear it!
Go through the minimal pairs list and hear how the /t/ is a silent sound at the end. Listen and feel for vibration in your throat. Hear a deeper tone in your voice for the /d/ as you turn on your voice.

Feel it!
Place your hand on your throat to feel the vibration of the /d/ sound. You should feel the tongue tip touching the alveolar ridge on the roof of the mouth, then releasing it. It is impossible to hold this sound long. Once the air passes your vocal folds, it can no longer escape. Since your tongue is blocking the passageway, the vibration of your voice must stop. Once your tongue tip releases from the roof, the air can then escape for the /d/.

A Caution!

Often, when people first practice the /d/ sound at the ends of words, there is a bit of exaggeration. The result is an "uh" vowel that is pronounced after the /d/. So, if the word was "had," it would sound like "haduh." You must ensure you do not add any vowel sound after the /d/ and to stop your voice BEFORE you let your mouth open after the /d/. Practice by stopping your voice BEFORE you open your mouth after the /d/ and then compare it with the "uh" sound as you let your voice linger and let your mouth open. E.g., "baduh" vs. "bad." Practice reducing any "uh" sound. Try to hear the difference and do your best to stop your voice earlier to avoid this.

Do it!

Let's look at some more /d/ words and practice this sound in all positions of words.

Isolation:

Practice and repeat /d/, /d/, /d/, /d/, /d/

Syllables:

da, dee, di, do, du

add, eed, ide, ode, ood

ada, edee, idi, odo, udoo

Words:
Beginning

dad	dime	done
dance	dinner	door
dark	dish	dot
date	dive	dove
day	do	down
dear	doctor	duck
dentist	does	dusty
desk	dog	
dig	doll	

Middle

baby doll	Canada	hiding
birthday	daddy	idea
body	feeding	kindergarten
calendar	hidden	ladder

lady	ready	Thursday
louder	riding	Tuesday
medicine	shadow	wedding
radio	speeding	
reading	spider	

Ending

acid	fend	lid
add	feud	lied
aged	find	load
aid	fled	lord
avid	fond	loud
bad	food	mad
bald	ford	maid
band	fund	med
bead	glad	meld
bed	God	mend
bend	gold	mid
bid	good	mild
bind	grade	mind
bird	grid	mold
bold	had	mood
bond	hand	mud
bread	hard	need
bud	head	nod
card	held	odd
cod	herd	old
cold	hid	pad
cord	hide	paid
cried	hold	played
dad	hood	pod
dead	kid	pond
deed	kind	raid
did	lad	read
dud	laid	red
end	land	rid
fad	lead	ride
fed	led	road
feed	lend	rod

sad	sod	ward
said	sold	weed
sand	sped	weld
seed	stud	wild
send	tad	wind
shed	toad	wood
side	told	word
slid	used	yard
slide	wand	

Phrases:

Beginning Phrases:

dancing dad	deep dive	ding the doorbell
dark day	Doctor Dave	damp doughnuts
dentist drill	dry dog	dive down
dot on desk	Daisy's doll	Donald Duck
dig deeper	dusty dish	

Ending Phrases:

a new fad	funny kid	mouse pad
add and subtract	God is good	mud puddle
afraid of sand	good deed	new sod
aid the young	good kid	nod yes
avid reader	good lad	odd job
bad dog	good seed	off the grid
bad mood	had my hand	old bread
bedhead	he's my bud	old fashioned
bend the rules	hid in the shed	old shed
bid goodbye	led the group	open the lid
bread is food	lend a hand	peas in a peapod
caught the cod	lied to his friend	played with dad
cold toad	loud band	pond water
dad said	mad dad	pulled the weed
end of the road	mad man	raid the pantry
family feud	maid of honor	read out loud
fed the group	mend the rip	red bed
fend for yourself	mid jump	red beet salad
fled to safety	mild cold	redhead
fond of the idea	moldy bread	red sand

rid of it	slid down the slide	what a stud
ride and slide	sped away	wizard wand
sad and mad	welded helmet	wood in the mud
sand in my hand	what a dud	

Sentences:

D Beginning Sentences:

My dog chases ducks all day

Dolly loves to dance in a dress

Day in and day out, I do the dishes

My doctor does not do home visits

Dave dove down into the deep water

They have to dig a deep ditch by the driveway

My dad loves to draw dragons and play drums

I don't play with dice when I'm doing desk work

The dentist did some drill work on my dentures

D Ending Sentences:

Hand me the old bread

Could you send it to me?

Where did Brad find that bird?

I need to find a wide round bed

She made the bread in an old wood stove

There was a long pulled thread on my bed

The kid slid down the slide with her friend

My food always tastes weird when it's cold

I ordered a salad, not a hand full of old lettuce

My old friend did a good job and got paid

I'm afraid the red bird is dead in the cold mud

She was mad that her friend was being so loud

My child loves to ride and slide in the playground

My friend said she wanted to have a child in her mid-thirties

There's a weird kind of wild oat bread that my friend likes

I read about a boy who was sad because he knocked his head

The bad dog is not afraid of sand

Dad said he was in a bad mood

I'm such an avid reader, I fell asleep reading and woke up with bed head

They had to bend the rules when they got to the end of the road

I fed the group with bread and food so they didn't have to fend for themselves

The cold toad fled to safety at the end of the pond

The kid was good at catching cod

I was very fond of the good little kid that ended the family feud

She opened the lid and found nothing but an old pea pod

We played with our dad near the pond water

She pulled the weed out of the sand with her hand quite easily

I felt both sad and mad when he got rid of my wizard wand

I thought he was a dud, but my friend thought he was a stud

She grabbed an old rod to take the wood out of the mud

The red-headed girl slid down the slide

"ed" In The Past Tense: A Grammar Lesson

Although this is a pronunciation book, it is important to note that grammar and pronunciation often coincide and affect one another. There are a few pronunciation rules that depend on the grammatical rules that exist. Now, I won't go into any long lesson about grammar, but I want to touch on a common issue that many speakers encounter regarding the /d/ and past-tense "ed" words.

Have you ever noticed that when native English speakers talks, the /d/ at the end of words is sometimes pronounced as a /t/? Well, this is indeed the case with past tense verbs. The word "walked" is pronounced /wakt/ or "wahkt", and "slipped" is pronounced /sLIpt/ or "slihpt". The /d/ is pronounced as a /t/. Let's discuss why and when to pronounce a /t/ versus a /d/ in words that end in "ed."

The general rule of thumb is to look at the sound just BEFORE the "ed."

If the sound before the "ed" is a VOICELESS sound, we keep our voice off and use the voiceless version of /d/, which is a /t/.

So, the words that have the sound /p, k, f, s, "sh," and "ch"/ will have the /t/ produced when the "ed" is present.

If the sound before the "ed" is a VOICED sound, we keep our voice going and use the 1voiced /d/ sound.

So, the words ending with the sound /v, m, n, L, r, "j," g, ð, z, b, ŋ/, and vowels before the "ed" will be pronounced with a /d/.

If the sound before the "ed" is a "t" or a "d," we want to differentiate that sound from the rest of the word clearly, so we add a vowel /ɪd/ to be sure the listener can hear the past tense.

Let's take a look at some examples to show you just how it works:

Pronunciation of –ED pronounced as /t/

When? After <u>VOICELESS</u> sounds.

/p/	typed	hoped	helped
/f/	stuffed	sniffed	laughed
/s/	passed	missed	harassed
"sh"	punished	washed	fished
"ch"	watched	switched	snatched
/k/	baked	snacked	raked

Pronunciation of –ED pronounced as /d/

When? After <u>VOICED</u> sounds.

/v/	lived	waved	arrived
/m/	harmed	confirmed	rammed
/n/	phoned	signed	cleaned
/L/	called	failed	strolled
/r/	preferred	discovered	entered
"j"	changed	judged	aged
/g/	begged	egged	plugged
"th"	bathed	clothed	teethed
/z/	advised	realized	posed
/b/	grabbed	bobbed	robbed
"ng"	banged	belonged	wronged
All vowels	obeyed	shooed	agreed

Pronunciation of –ED pronounced as /ɪd/

When? After <u>/t/ and /d/</u> sounds.

/t/	voted	waited	wanted

| /d/ | minded | sounded | demanded |

Reading:

Now you know what to do! Find a great website, blog, or book, and read it out loud. Look for "d" words and feel how your voice should vibrate. Pay special attention to the past tense words that end in "ed." This is where you might have to stop and think a little bit at first. Trying to figure out which words end in voiced sounds can take a bit of practice. With time, the concept and feeling of the voiced /d/ will become much easier to pronounce. Practice constantly by recording yourself while reading and speaking. You will be amazed at how much you will improve and identify as you listen to your own pronunciation.

Conversation:

Spend time daily using your /d/ in conversation. Feel the vibration and hear the voiced sound as you focus intentionally when you speak. As with all sounds, this is a habit that you will begin to form. You will likely be terrible at this at first! That's okay. The goal is not perfection. Your improvement will take time, and you will slowly work toward your goals with intentional speech and focused self-monitoring.

Chapter 15: "H": Not Just Blowing Hot Air

Description:
The /h/ sound is truly just a breath of air. The sound the air makes as it passes out of your mouth should be slightly audible. Create a /h/ by slightly parting your lips, with your teeth apart in a neutral, open position. The /h/ is a voiceless sound, so no vocal fold vibration should occur. /h/ is a soft sound, not forceful. So, be careful to release the air in a relaxed way.

Common differences:
The issue that most speakers have with /h/is that they pronounce the audible /h/ for the few silent "h" words we have in English. We will review the silent /h/ word list next.

Another issue many speakers have with the /h/ is to produce a vibration or friction sound from the throat. Many languages are widely known for having a louder friction sound for /h/. The friction or vibration sound comes from the back of the throat, near the pharynx. The pharynx is the area at the back wall of your throat. The North American English pronunciation of /h/ is soft, and there is no vibration or friction in the sound. The /h/ is produced by passing air through a relaxed pharynx in a gentle, quiet way. To practice the difference, tighten the back of your throat. Using the back of your tongue, make a sound similar to a soft version of a cough. Then produce the soft /h/ with no contact in the pharynx or the back of your tongue, just an open airway as the air flows by "h."

Spelling:
/h/ is spelled with an "h" as well as some "wh" words as seen in the word "whole." There is no way to know whether a word has a silent "h" or not by spelling alone. It is best if you memorize the silent /h/ words. Can I apologize to you on behalf of English? Memorization is not fun, but it's what you are left with when it comes to this sound. Also, note that in the General North American English pronunciation, /h/ is not pronounced at the ends of words.

Hear it!

Compare the pronunciation of no friction in your throat for "h" and with forced friction. Be sure that you can hear the difference for yourself. Similarly, compare a silent "h" vs. a true /h/ with airflow. Let's take a look at the silent "h" words in English. These words have NO airflow at all. Think of them as having no /h/.

Silent H

<u>H is always silent in:</u>

vehicle "vee uh kull"	honest	vehement
honor	heir	
hour	homage	

<u>You don't say "H" after "g" in:</u>

ghetto "gedow"	ghastly	gherkin
ghost	aghast	

<u>You don't say "h" after "r" in:</u>

rhinoceros	rhyme
rhubarb	rhythm

<u>It's normally silent after "w" in:</u>

What?	When?	white
Which?	Why?	while
Where?	whisper	wheel

<u>BUT "h" IS pronounced in:</u>

Who? "hoo"

"Who'd have thought it?"

<u>And we don't always say it after "ex" :</u>

exhilarating

exhausting

<u>Feel it!</u>

To feel the true /h/ versus a silent /h/, put your hand in front of your mouth and feel your hot breath for the true "h." You should not feel hot breath for the silent "h."

Feel the difference between a North American English /h/ versus a frictional vibratory "h." Feel for the LACK of vibration in your throat. You will feel that the air is just blowing by in a relaxed way, with no tension at the back of your tongue to create any friction. The North American English /h/ is soft, quiet, and relaxed.

<u>Do it!</u>
Let's practice and get great at our new /h/ sound!

<u>Isolation:</u>
Repeat /h/, /h/, /h/, /h/, /h/

<u>Syllables:</u>
ha, ho, he, hi, hoo
aha, oho, ehe, ihi, uhoo

<u>Words:</u>
Beginning

hack	heal	hill
had	health	him
hair	heap	hind
half	hear	hint
hall	heart	hip
halo	heat	hire
halt	heck	his
ham	heel	hiss
hand	height	hit
hang	held	hive
happy	hell	hoax
hard	help	hoe
harm	hem	hog
harp	hemp	hold
hart	hen	hole
has	her	holy
hat	herd	home
hate	here	hood
haul	hero	hoof
have	hers	hook
hawk	hey	hoop
hay	hid	hoot
haze	hide	hop
hazy	high	hope
head	hike	horn

horse
hose
host
hot
house
how
howl
hub

hue
huff
hug
huge
hull
hum
hump
hung

hunk
hunt
hurl
hurt
hush
hut
hymn
hype

Middle

alcoholism
beehive
beforehand
behalf
behave
behavior
birdhouse
coherent
comprehend
doghouse
dollhouse
downhill
fishhook
forehead

grasshopper
greenhouse
groundhog
household
hula hoop
inherent
lighthouse
likelihood
livelihood
motherhood
Ohio
overhead
Pearl Harbor
perhaps

pigeonhole
playhouse
pothole
powerhouse
redhead
rehearsal
reheat
rocking horse
sea horse
sweetheart
uphill
warehouse
White House

Phrases:

Beginning

banquet hall
don't hate
give me a hint
had a chance
hair style
hairy hand
half a glass
halo on her head
halt the operation
ham hock
ham in the oven
hand hygiene
hang on
happy as a clam
happy hamster
hard decision
harm no-one

has to be
haul the ship
have to do it
hawk eye
hay in the barn
hazy day
head over heels
heal the wound
health and happiness
healthy heart
heap of options
hear the news
heart attack
heat the room
heavy hammer
hold your hand
hell of a night

help me
hem my pants
her hanger
her idea
herd mentality
here I am
hey how are you?
hide the candy
hiking hill
his hat
hold my head
horrible headache
hot helmet
house hook
hug the horse
hula hoop

I hid it
it's hers
life hack

Middle

behind the beehive
beware of the beehive
check beforehand
coherent message
comprehend the idea
empty birdhouse
fish on the fishhook
good behavior
Groundhog Day
household chores
I'm a redhead
in the doghouse
in the playhouse
in the warehouse
invited to the White House

over the hill
tell him
to new heights

it's going downhill
it's my livelihood
little grasshopper
look overhead
motherhood is a blessing
my daughter's dollhouse
old lighthouse
on a rocking horse
on my behalf
on my forehead
perhaps you can come
plan for the rehearsal
preheat the oven
rehearsal in the lighthouse
she's a powerhouse

warm hat
what the heck

she's my sweetheart
the groundhog's pothole
the likelihood of
tiny birdhouse
try the hula hoop
uphill and downhill
uphill battle
warm greenhouse
watch for the pothole
White House President
wooden doghouse
you must behave

Sentences:

Beginning

He hit that hammer hard
Her ham hock was horrendous
The horse ran up the hill in a hurry
He has a huge diamond in his hand
That hot helmet gave me a headache
I have to put my hiking hat on a hanger
The hair on his head is hard from his gel
Her heart was filled with happy memories
My happy hamster hurries around in his cage
I'm so happy I have moved to my new house

Middle

Inhale a deep breath of fresh air
He threw a rock behind a beehive
Perhaps the seahorse is unhealthy
That fishhook almost hit my forehead
Going downhill is fast, but uphill is slower
The rehearsal in the lighthouse went well
The groundhog dug a huge hole that turned into a pothole

The girl used the bird_house_ as a doll_house_ for her tiny dolls
Henry never remembers to be_h_ave when he visits the White _H_ouse

Reading:
Read daily while recording yourself. As you listen to your pronunciation of the /h/ sounds, read along and find the sounds as you go. Listening to yourself will help you improve your identification, discrimination, and overall awareness of the /h/ sound.

Conversation:
Get out there and practice as much as possible. Write out a few silly tongue twister sentences with your most challenging words, and have them handy to repeat to yourself when you're doing tasks that don't require conversation. The more practice you get, the more natural and fluent you will sound.

Chapter 16: "W": <u>W</u>histle <u>W</u>hile You <u>W</u>ork!

Description:

The /w/ is produced with the jaw only slightly open. You will need to round your lips into a small tight circle, similar to when you pronounce "oo." Your lips will be somewhat protruded, meaning they will be pulled outwards away from the front teeth. The /w/ is a voiced sound, so you must turn your voice on and feel your vocal folds vibrating in your throat.

Common Differences:

The most typical change non-native English speakers make to /w/ is a close version of a /v/. Often my clients produce what I would call a "combination" of /v/ and /w/, meaning it's not quite a clear /w/ or a clear /v/. The outcome is that the two sounds become morphed into one. I call it the "vw". Since the true /w/ is produced with rounded lips, and the /v/ should be produced by biting the bottom lip with the upper teeth, they should sound and look significantly different. When someone is pronouncing the /vw/, they press their bottom lip against their teeth, as if the inside of the lower lip is creating a /v/ sound. The result is a sound that LOOKS quite similar to /w/ but SOUNDS more like the /v/. The sound is similar to a /v/ because they create a vibration on the bottom lip with their teeth. The fix here is to emphasize your lip protrusion and rounding and to ensure that the lips are not vibrating in any way against the front teeth.

Let's look at some minimal pairs comparing English words that could be confused if you do not accurately round your lips for the /w/ sound. Try these and compare:

/V/ vs. /W/ Minimal Pairs

veil	/whale
vein	/wane
verse	/worse
vest	/west
vet	/wet
vie	/why
vine	/wine
vow	/wow

v's   /wheeze

Spelling:

The /w/ sound is spelled with the /w/. The /w/ can also be spelled with "wh," but be careful, as not all "wh" words are pronounced as /w/! Thanks, English! We also pronounce the /w/ when syllables start with an "o" as in the word "one" /w^n/, which sounds like "wun" or "someone." The /w/ sound also exists in "qu" words, pronounced as /kw/ like in "quiet" or "kwy ut."

The words that begin with "wh" that we do NOT pronounce as /w/, but rather as /h/ are below:

who "hoo"

whom "hoom"

whose "hooz"

Hear it!

Go through the minimal pairs list above for /v/ and /w/. Compare the pronunciation of rounded lips for /w/, ensuring your lips are not pressed against your front teeth but rather protruded slightly outwards. Then compare the /v/ pronunciation, where your top teeth make contact with your bottom lip. As you practice the difference, listen to the difference as well as feel it. Record yourself doing these minimal pairs, listen to yourself, and look at the difference in your lip positions in the mirror. This exercise will heighten your awareness of the differences in these sounds, but it will also increase your differentiation skills overall for listening and pronunciation of /w/.

Feel it!

Aside from distinguishing your typical pronunciation of /w/ versus the new, more rounded protruded version of /w/, it is also very important to FEEL the difference on your lips. Pay attention to how it feels to truly round and protrude your lips. The new lip posture may be a very different position for you, and you may even feel uncomfortable. Now, do your old production of /w/. Feel the difference in your lips. Be aware of just how much you changed your lip rounding and protruding.

Do it!

So let's dig in and get really good at producing this sound!

Isolation:

Hold the /w/ sound for a few seconds; "wwwww" "wwwww" "wwwww" "wwwww" "wwwww"

Use a mirror to see your lip posture and how round and protruded your lips are.

<u>Syllables:</u>
way, wee, why, wo, woo
aw, ew, iw, ow, uw
awa, ewe, iwi, owo, uwu

<u>Words:</u>
Beginning

one	week	why
once	wife	whale
wait	wind	wheat
walk	wings	wheel
want	wish	wheeze
warm	words	while
was	work	whine
wash	world	whip
watch	what	whirl
we	when	whisk
wear	where	whisper
web	which	white
weeds	whether	

Middle

always	homework	reward
awake	housework	school work
award	jaguar	Sea World
awkward	kiwi	seaweed
cakewalk	likewise	sidewalk
cobweb	mouthwash	someone
driveway	pathway	walkway
highway	raceway	worldwide

"Qu" /kw/ Blends

choir	quiet	quit
queen	quilt	liquid
quack	quarter	equal
quick	question	frequent

require

Phrases:

<u>Beginning</u>

once a week	wash with water	windward
what waffles?	white washer	worn window
white wagon	watch the weather	wild wings
workweek	which web?	wide world
worn wallet	white wedding	

Middle

always awake	jaguar on the highway	pathway of seaweed
walkway cobweb	homework and housework	raceway award
Hawaiian sidewalk	kiwi sandwich	

<u>/v/ vs. /w/ Sentences:</u>

You should be <u>v</u>ery <u>w</u>ary of the shado<u>w</u>s

<u>W</u>e need another letter /<u>v</u>/ to spell the <u>w</u>ord sa<u>vv</u>y

This <u>v</u>eil makes me look as big as a <u>w</u>hale

The blood pressure in my <u>v</u>ein is beginning to <u>w</u>ane

I <u>w</u>ent to look at the <u>v</u>ent on the floor

That <u>v</u>erse was <u>w</u>orse than the first <u>v</u>erse

She <u>w</u>as <u>w</u>ell <u>v</u>ersed in making up the <u>w</u>orst type of insults

<u>W</u>hen I <u>w</u>ent out <u>w</u>est, I al<u>w</u>ays <u>w</u>ore a <u>v</u>est

The <u>v</u>et got <u>w</u>et in the rain

The <u>w</u>icks of these candles smell like <u>V</u>icks <u>V</u>aporub

I <u>w</u>ill <u>v</u>ie for your attention, although I don't know <u>w</u>hy

The smell <u>w</u>as so <u>v</u>ile <u>w</u>hile the <u>w</u>indow was shut

The grapes of the <u>v</u>ine create the most <u>w</u>onderful <u>w</u>ine

<u>W</u>ally <u>w</u>as great at <u>v</u>olleyball

My <u>v</u>o<u>w</u> is going to <u>w</u>o<u>w</u> her

Every<u>o</u>ne <u>w</u>ill join in singing the <u>v</u>erse

<u>W</u>hene<u>v</u>er you play the <u>v</u>iolin, I smile

<u>W</u>ould you like to try this <u>v</u>ery <u>w</u>onderful <u>v</u>itamin <u>w</u>ater?

<u>W</u>est <u>V</u>irginia is <u>w</u>here I'd lo<u>v</u>e to tra<u>v</u>el the most

I <u>w</u>as <u>w</u>ondering if this <u>w</u>a<u>v</u>e of <u>v</u>iolence <u>w</u>ill be <u>o</u>ver soon

<u>W</u>hate<u>v</u>er you <u>w</u>ant to do, I'll join you

<u>W</u>e <u>w</u>ill in<u>v</u>ent ne<u>w</u> soft<u>w</u>are

<u>W</u>here is the <u>V</u>olks<u>w</u>agen now?

You did <u>v</u>ery <u>w</u>onderful <u>w</u>ork today, I<u>v</u>an.

Beginning

Wayne waited in the white wagon

He got a watch on his wedding day

He's an award-winning welder

The wide walrus was wide awake

Icy water is wonderful on a warm day

Where do we put the dirty wash water?

He put a wad of money in his white wallet

We drove the white Jaguar on the highway

We could hear the wolf howling in the wind

We washed the wide walrus with warm water

The wagon was painted with white wings on it

I heard that the weather will be cold tomorrow

Walter wondered how his wallet got so worn

Which web was the one that Wendy walked into?

I wish I had an award-winning trophy to show off

They go for a walk when they want to take a break

The wind was so strong it blew my window open

The web swayed between the wayward branches

I did all the housework except for washing the dishes

The cold wind was coming through the old worn window

When the wild bird flew by, you could see his white wings

She's the most wonderful woman in the whole wide world

I wish I could have waffles for breakfast at least once a week

Middle:

I did my homework in the driveway

The Hawaiian sidewalk was free of seaweed

My sandwich got caught in a cobweb on the walkway

A wolf howled in the pathway as it echoed windward

I always lay in bed awake when I hear the cars on the highway

I should get an award for all the homework and housework I do

He stood there wide awake on the driveway, watching the weather

Reading:

As with all sounds that you hope to change in your daily speech, it is essential to move up the ladder of complexity. It is not enough to just know how to produce the sound in simple sentences, but the real skill is acquired when you can use your skills in more complex tasks. Reading is a great middle step before moving to conversation practice. Through reading, you can work up your speed and naturalness without the cognitive functioning required when conversing with someone. Read a favorite book, scan a website, or even just read your emails out loud. Better yet, record yourself reading and review your reading while carefully focusing on the /w/ sound and feeling your rounded lip position. Once you feel you are getting the hang of the change in lip position and are getting faster and more fluent, you can move on to conversation practice.

Conversation:
Now is the time to get out there and practice with others. I recommend starting with strangers. I know that sounds absolutely insane, but my clients actually report it is easier to speak differently with people who have no preconceived notion of what you sounded like before changing your pronunciation. You will often find it easier to ask "where are the walnuts?" at the grocery store than you thought! Of course, it is still very important to use your new skills with your loved ones. It can be a really freeing experience to try your speech sounds with others and gain that confidence! So get out there and practice.

Chapter 17: "Z": You Use This More Than You Think. I Promise You!

Description:

The /z/ sound is the "sister" sound to /s/. We pronounce the /s/ and /z/ sound exactly the same, but we add our voices for /z/. We create the /z/ sound by placing the tip of our tongue up near the roof of the mouth in front of the alveolar ridge (the bumpy area of the palate just behind the front teeth). Some people place their tongue tip closer to the front top teeth, and some even produce the /s/ and /z/ using the tongue tip against the bottom front teeth. These are all normal variations of the /z/ sound. The tongue tip should never be placed outside or past the front teeth enough to be visible; this is called an interdental lisp, and a Speech-Language Pathologist can assist you in correcting this at any age. Your lips should be in a slight smiling position, with your lips spread. The tongue tip is placed close to the roof of the mouth but does not touch; rather, it sits really close, allowing a small pathway of air to pass between the tongue tip and the roof to create the friction heard as /z/. You can feel the airflow coming out on the center of your bottom lip as you produce the /z/ sound. The /z/ is a voiced sound, so you should ensure you have turned on your voice.

Common Differences:

The most typical issue my clients have with /z/ is not turning on their voices. In essence, they produce a /s/ sound instead of a /z/ sound. This slight difference can cause significant difficulty with word meanings in English, as will be described in the minimal pairs below. For most people, the /z/ at the ends of words is where the issue arises most. The fix for this problem usually comes down to understanding some simple grammatical rules. These grammatical rules are not generally taught. However, if these rules are taught, they are even less likely to be explained in terms of pronunciation. I will go into detail about the plural "s" below, but first, I want you to compare the difference in the words that you pronounce with an /s/ sound versus the /z/ sound.

frenzy

frizzy

frozen

fuzzy

gauzy

gazebo

geezer

gizmo

gonzo

guzzle

hazard

hazel

jazzy

kazoo

kwanza

laser

lazy

lizard

losing

mezzo

music

muzzle

nozzle

nuzzle

ozone

physical

piazza

plaza

possess

present

president

proposal

puzzle

raising

raisins

raspberry

razor

reason

refused

results

scissors

scuzzy

season

shazam

sized

sizing

sizzle

sleazy

snazzy

thousand

Thursday

tizzy

Tuesday

unzip

visible

visit

wazoo

Wednesday

wheezy

wizard

woozy

zigzag

End

abuse (verb)

advise (verb)

always

amuse

arise

arose

axes

bans

bases

because

blues

buzz

cabs

cause

cheese

chose

close (verb)

cries

dabs

days

does

dries

ease

eaves

elves

exercise

fizz

flies

fours

fries

fuse

gabs

goes

grams

has

hers

his

hives

hose

house (verb)

is

jazz

lens

lives

lose

muse

needs

news

does it
ma rash
ng woozy
y hair
en water
y bear
le the water
l eyes
gazebo
dessert
frenzy
tizzy
he closet
he plaza
y band
r focus
days
rd in the sand
ng his mind

ays be kind
use me
ause I had to
s beehives
es bands
z goes the bee
eful of spies
ght all of the cabs
se to do it
istmas elves
se the door
s out loud
s on the spot
s quickly
e of use
y does it
rcise your body
y grams

mezzo-soprano
more dessert
music lessons
muzzled dog
nozzle on the faucet
nuzzle in
old dry raisins
old geezer
ozone layer
physical therapy
play the kazoo
possess things
present time
President of the USA
puzzle is complete
raising children
raspberry jam
razor blades
razzle dazzle

flies all around
flower vase
focus the lens
for a good cause
four days ago
French fries
fuse to the metal
get the tongs
good vibes
has he gone yet?
he goes all the time
hit all the bases
hold the reins
house the homeless
in the guise of
Is it hers?
Is that it?
jazz band

reason to live
refused to give in
set it ablaze
sharp scissors
sized up
sizzle on the grill
sleazy plan
snazzy jacket
spring season
thousand islands
Thursday is tomorrow
unzip the zipper
up the wazoo
visible minority
visit family
wedding proposal
what a doozy
wheezy voice
wicked wizard

lives the life
lose your shirt
needs some help
news broadcaster
noise in the street
nose bleed
odds are in your favor
on all fours
ours and yours
pause the movie
phase it out
piles and piles of
please say yes
pose for the camera
propose to marry
raise awareness
reuse and recycle
rise and shine

nibs	reuse	tin	eas
noise	rise	toi	ecz
nose	rose	tri	fee
odds	rouse	us	friz
ours	skies	va	fro
pause	soles	vib	fuz
phase	spies	wa	guz
piles	surprise	wa	ha
please	tales	wh	hig
poise	taxes	wh	ho
pose	taxis	wis	in
propose	tease	wiv	in
raise	these	you	in
reins	those		in
			jaz
			las

<u>Phrases:</u>

Beginning

allowed zones	Zach did zigzags	zipp	liz
do it with zeal	zany friend	zipp	los
he got zilch	zap the bug	zipp	
he's a zealot	zapped my finger	zips	**En**
it has four zeds	zero interest in	zit o	al
school zone	zeroes in on	zits	an
striped zebra	zest for life	zodi	be
the compound zinc	zested the lemon	zom	be
the letter zed	zests in the recipe	zone	blu
the zinnia smells good	zesty seasoning	zoni	bu
tiny zygote	zig around	zoor	ca
trip to the zoo	zigzag design	zuccl	ca
what's your zip code?	zip the zipper		ch
			Ch
			cl

Middle

banzai tree	brazen scolding	daisy	cr
bazaar experience	breezy day	dese	da
benzyl alcohol	business plan	desig	dr
biohazard	busy day	desig	ea
blazon disregard	buzzer sounded	dizzy	ea
blizzard of the century	Cheesecake Factory	do it	e
blue blazer	crazy friend	dozer	fi

Rose of Sharon

rouse to wake

say cheese

she gabs a lot

skies the limit

soles of your feet

surprise present

tales and stories

taxes are due

these are the ones

those are my favourite

throw the axes

tries to achieve

use your head

was it his?

was that true?

water hose

ways to do it

what a whiz

who's got the answer?

wise woman

yellow taxis

yours and mine

The 3 Sounds Of Plural "S"

I could not go on with this chapter without explaining a fundamental set of rules that apply to the letter "s."

You may be like so many of my past clients, who only just realized that "s" is not always pronounced as /s/. As my clients often are, you might be a little frustrated about why your English teachers never mentioned this, never explained any rules, and never corrected you on your pronunciation. The truth of the matter is that English teachers very rarely touch on pronunciation specifically, and when they do, it is with a few obvious sounds. There is such vast information to understand about pronunciation that without a background in speech and language pathology, the specifics of articulation are not something instructors are really proficient in themselves. If you were taught English by a non-native English speaker who also had an accent, it is likely that they, too, did not know the rules of English pronunciation. Whatever the reason, these are not often taught rules and are very important to understand if your goal is to speak English with clarity and confidence. You are not alone!

So, why does the sound of the plural "s" change?

The reason is simple; efficiency. English speakers want to say the most they can in the shortest period of time. The addition of voicing helps speakers do this. Often, we like to simplify things by just keeping our voice on instead of turning it on and off within and between words. Keeping our voice on for multiple sounds that are close together allows the vocal folds to be more efficient, to continue what they are already doing, vibrating.

So, let's dig into the three rules of the plural /s/.

Rule #1: /S/

If the sound just before the plural "s" is VOICELESS, the plural "s" will continue to be voiceless: It will stay a /s/ (also VOICELESS).

So plural words that end in the voiceless sounds /p/, /t/, /k/, /f/, /θ/ would stay an /s/!

Examples:

grapes /s/	weeks /s/	briefs /s/
bits /s/	backs /s/	baths /s/

Rule #2: /Z/

If the sound just before the plural "s" is VOICED, the plural "s" will continue to be voiced: We will pronounce the "s" as a voiced /z/.

So words that end in the voiced sounds /b/, /d/, /g/, /L/, /r/, /w/, /m/, /n/, /v/, /y/,/ð/ and all vowels (ALL ARE VOICED) turn into a /z/!

Examples:

cribs /z/	jars /z/	doves /z/
beds /z/	straws /z/	delays /z/
pigs /z/	clams /z/	teethes /z/
bells /z/	fans /z/	

Rule #3: /IZ/

Plural words that end in /s/, /z/, "sh," "ch," and "j" adds the sounds "iz".
The sounds that cause the plural "s" to be pronounced with /ɪz/ include:
/ ʃ / "sh",   /tʃ/ "ch",   /dʒ/ "j",   /s/,   /Z/.

Now, this might sound confusing, and you might be asking why? We add a vowel /I/ with the /z/because it's a way to separate the /z/ from another sound that is too similar. We might lose the meaning of the plural if we don't do this. So, we wouldn't say "mass> massss"; it would be "masses" or /mæsɪz/.

Examples:

wishes /ɪz/	witches /ɪz/	slices /ɪz/
flashes /ɪz/	bridges /ɪz/	classes /ɪz/
watches /ɪz/	judges /ɪz/	blazes /ɪz/

easy does it

eczema rash

feeling woozy

frizzy hair

frozen water

fuzzy bear

guzzle the water

hazel eyes

high gazebo

hot dessert

in a frenzy

in a tizzy

in the closet

in the plaza

jazzy band

laser focus

lazy days

lizard in the sand

losing his mind

mezzo-soprano

more dessert

music lessons

muzzled dog

nozzle on the faucet

nuzzle in

old dry raisins

old geezer

ozone layer

physical therapy

play the kazoo

possess things

present time

President of the USA

puzzle is complete

raising children

raspberry jam

razor blades

razzle dazzle

reason to live

refused to give in

set it ablaze

sharp scissors

sized up

sizzle on the grill

sleazy plan

snazzy jacket

spring season

thousand islands

Thursday is tomorrow

unzip the zipper

up the wazoo

visible minority

visit family

wedding proposal

what a doozy

wheezy voice

wicked wizard

End

always be kind

amuse me

because I had to

bees beehives

blues bands

buzz goes the bee

careful of spies

caught all of the cabs

chose to do it

Christmas elves

close the door

cries out loud

dabs on the spot

dries quickly

ease of use

easy does it

exercise your body

fifty grams

flies all around

flower vase

focus the lens

for a good cause

four days ago

French fries

fuse to the metal

get the tongs

good vibes

has he gone yet?

he goes all the time

hit all the bases

hold the reins

house the homeless

in the guise of

Is it hers?

Is that it?

jazz band

lives the life

lose your shirt

needs some help

news broadcaster

noise in the street

nose bleed

odds are in your favor

on all fours

ours and yours

pause the movie

phase it out

piles and piles of

please say yes

pose for the camera

propose to marry

raise awareness

reuse and recycle

rise and shine

nibs
noise
nose
odds
ours
pause
phase
piles
please
poise
pose
propose
raise
reins

reuse
rise
rose
rouse
skies
soles
spies
surprise
tales
taxes
taxis
tease
these
those

times
tongs
tries
use
vase
vibes
was
ways
whiz
whose
wise
wives
yours

Phrases:

Beginning

allowed zones
do it with zeal
he got zilch
he's a zealot
it has four zeds
school zone
striped zebra
the compound zinc
the letter zed
the zinnia smells good
tiny zygote
trip to the zoo
what's your zip code?

Zach did zigzags
zany friend
zap the bug
zapped my finger
zero interest in
zeroes in on
zest for life
zested the lemon
zests in the recipe
zesty seasoning
zig around
zigzag design
zip the zipper

zipped it up
zipper is stuck
zippy car
zips around quickly
zit on my face
zits are gone
zodiac sign
zombie apocalypse
zoned out
zoning bylaw
zoomed around
zucchini muffin

Middle

banzai tree
bazaar experience
benzyl alcohol
biohazard
blazon disregard
blizzard of the century
blue blazer

brazen scolding
breezy day
business plan
busy day
buzzer sounded
Cheesecake Factory
crazy friend

daisy bouquet
deserve a lot
designated driver
designer bag
dizzy ride
do it for the results
dozen eggs

Let's practice!

Beginning

Zach visited his favorite zebra at the zoo

There were zero zucchinis in Zoe's garden

I planted a zone of zinnia flowers in a zigzag formation

Middle

I raised a lazy lizard that is never busy

Daisy had cheesecake for dessert on Thursday

On Wednesday, my daughter played music all day

My cousin did puzzles and crafts with scissors

Ending

Phrases:

Underlined "s's" are pronounced as /z/, all other "s's" will remain pronounced as /s/

baked beans	babies' fingers	small nose
worker bees	potted flowers	soft pillows
say cheese	wear glasses	say please
fresh cookies	garden hose	win the prize
two dogs	car keys	going to sneeze
exercise outside	grab knees	three tacos

Sentences:

It is his

It was his

We won the prize

The team won two prizes

They own two dogs

It is polite to say please

Allergies made him sneeze

Don't lose your keys

He always forgets those pens of his

He is always with his friends

He is talking to the contractors and engineers

She is wise to make sales with her customers

211

He likes his cookies fresh

He ordered a plate of tacos

He's always losing his car keys

His glasses helped him see

I have a couple of proposals that have deadlines

It is because she was happy

Melt the cheese so we can dip chips in it

Please clean up those cheese crumbs off the stairs

She is holding her knees

She is pointing to her nose

That is a big stack of pillows

The baby's fingers were so tiny

The potted flowers were colorful

The worker bees make honeycombs

They decided to exercise outside

They served beans at the picnic

Those things are expected in this place

Use the hose to wash your car

Who knows if he was in his thirties or if he's lying

My eyes were in a daze

I looked at the pies two times

We are big fans of oldies music

Please put the girls' three bags in the closet

The computers in the offices were all replaced

She always practices after she finishes her exercises

She always places her tambourines in the same place

Reading:

As you improve your ability to add your voice to the /z/ sound, you will find your speed and naturalness improve when you move to the reading level. Again, it is really important to record yourself to adequately analyze your pronunciation and listen to the "buzz" sound of the /z/. Feel your vibration for /z/ as you read emails out loud, as you read your news articles on your phone or in the paper, as well as any time you are reading for pleasure. The more you practice adding your voice to the /z/ sound, the faster you will move on to using this sound in conversation.

Conversation:

Since you have mastered the voicing required for /z/ in reading and feel more confident in knowing when and when not to add your voice, begin to use your new sound as you speak with others. Using the sound in conversation is easier said than done! You first must overcome some of the emotional blocks that come with speaking differently with others. If you can push past this feeling of awkwardness at first, you will be able to focus on what is more important, and that is intentionally using your sounds with clarity and precision. Practice with strangers, practice with your children, practice with your friends. Set specific times in your day that you will focus on practicing your new pronunciation in conversation. I often recommend setting timers throughout the day as a reminder to focus on your new pronunciation for the next few minutes. You may also find that your ability to understand other native English speakers improves!

Chapter 18: Voicing & Final Consonants: Not to Be Skipped. Just Don't.

Description:

Voicing is the term that describes the physical act of adding vocalization or vibratory sound from your vocal folds. Put plainly; it means to turn on your voice. As we discussed in earlier chapters, we create our voices with our vocal folds. The vocal folds are located in our larynx. These vocal folds vibrate together to create our voice, and we produce no voice at all when they do not vibrate. In English, we have voiced sounds and unvoiced sounds. The voiced sounds include: /b/, /d/, /v/, /z/, /g/, /ʒ/, /dʒ/, /j/, /w/, /L/, /r/, as well as all vowels. The voiceless sounds include /h/, /p/, /t/, /s/, /ʃ/, /tʃ/, and /k/.

Common Differences:

The most common sound differences that non-native North American English speakers make concerning voicing are to drop the voicing altogether. As with all other difficult consonants and vowels, if a particular sound in English does not exist in your first language, you are more likely to have difficulty producing that sound. If you have not been surrounded by the native pronunciation of English regularly, it will be more difficult to pick up on those very subtle differences. For most of the clients I work with, it is a general theme that voicing the consonants at the ends of words proves to be the greatest area of difficulty, and we focus hard on feeling the differences in voicing. Others have difficulty voicing consonants in all word positions, whether it is the beginning, middle, or ends of words.

For this reason, I highly recommend an in-depth phonological assessment be completed by a trained professional (SLP) who is proficient in IPA (International Phonetic Alphabet). This is the best way to identify YOUR particular speech differences that exist as compared to the General North American English pronunciation. An assessment will help you to pinpoint precisely what you should be working on to avoid wasting time. In the meantime, however, it will be really helpful to work on voicing as there is likely an issue here that you may not have been aware of.

Something important to understand is that certain sounds have a "sister," if you will, a voiced and an unvoiced variant. By "sister sound," I mean that one sound is produced exactly the same as the other, by the tongue, lips, and jaw, except that only one of them is pronounced with the voice ON, and the other is pronounced with the voice OFF.

Below are the "sister" pairs of voiced vs. voiceless variants to be aware of. The first of the pairs is the voiced sound, the second is the voiceless.
/b/ is voiced >/p/ is voiceless
/d/ is voiced >/t/ is voiceless
/v/ is voiced >/f/ is voiceless
/z/ is voiced >/s/ is voiceless
/g/ is voiced >/k/ is voiceless
/dʒ/ "j" is voiced >/tʃ/ "ch is voiceless

Notice how the same parts of the tongue produce each pair of "sister sounds," and the lips are in the exact same position. The only difference is that one is louder, and the voice is on, while the other has no voice.

For simplicity, I will focus on the sounds that are TYPICALLY devoiced as there are common trends in speakers. For example, my clients who have issues with particular vowels are essentially never dealing with a voicing issue. However, if my client is dealing with a /z/ issue, it is almost always a devoicing issue that we must address.

Hear it!
The first thing you will want to learn is how to discriminate between a voiceless and voiced sound. You will likely need a combination of hearing and tactile cues, such as listening and feeling the vibration on your throat so that you can tell the difference between the sounds. Start by saying the voiceless "h." Hear how the sound is quiet. Compare that to the "aaaaa" sound. You will notice there is sound as well as a vibration in the throat. Listen to how a voiceless sound only emits air, not vibration or a humming voice sound. Now try the voiced version. Hear how the voiced vibration of the vocal folds is a louder, humming sound. Some clients find it helpful to think of it as if you're humming "while" saying the sound. For the clients that have a tough time comparing the difference between voiced versus voiceless sounds, I like to tell them to "yell" the sound from their throat to make it louder. Now be careful not to add a vowel after, so /d/ should be /d/ not "duuh", and /b/ should be /b/, not "buuh". E.g., "dog" would be correct with a voiced /g/, but "doguh" would be incorrect as an extra vowel was produced.

215

<u>Feel it!</u>

For the clients I have worked with, the strategy that often helps, especially when listening and differentiation are challenging, is to feel for the vibration physically. Place your hand on your throat. It doesn't truly matter where, but near where the "adam's apple" or bony protrusion on your throat is.

Say "aaaaaaa," and feel how the throat vibrates on your hand. Now say "hhhhhhhh" and feel how your throat does not vibrate.

Now, go through the "sister" sounds above and compare the voiced (vibration on your hand) sounds versus the voiceless sounds (no vibration felt on your hand).

<u>Do it!</u>

I cannot stress enough how important it is NOT to skip the steps above! Before moving on to more complex practice, you must be confident that you truly can hear and feel the difference between voiced and voiceless sounds. If you are one of the lucky few who found the above exercise extremely easy, let's move on!

<u>Isolation:</u>

Unless you have had a detailed assessment of your speech patterns, it may be difficult to know which sounds are causing you the most difficulty with voicing. I recommend working on all of the above sounds, especially at the ends of words, until you get to the sentence level. The sentence level will often uncover the real difficulties you are having.

Say the sound with your voice turned ON:

b, b, b, b, b

d, d, d, d, d

g, g, g, g, g

vvvvv, vvvvvv, vvvvv

zzzzz, zzzzz, zzzzz

jjjjj, jjjjj, jjjjj

<u>Syllables:</u>

Feel for the voicing on the consonant.

ba, bay, bee, bo, bu	ab, abe, eeb, ob, ub	aba, aybay, eebee, obo, ubu
da, day, dee, do, du	ad, ade, eed, od, ud	ada, ayday, eedee, odo, udu
ga, gay, gee, go, gu	ag, aig, eeg, og, ug	aga, aygay, eegee, ogo, ugu

216

va, vay, vee, vo, vu   av, ave, eev, ov, uv   ava, ayvay, eevee, ovo, uvu

za, zay, zee, zo, zu   az, aze, eez, oz, uz   aza, ayzay, eezee, ozo, uzu

ja, jay, jee, jo, ju   aj, aje, eej, oj, uj   aja, ayjay, eejee, ojo, uju

Words:

I will focus on final consonants, which is a significant issue for most non-native North American English speakers. Be aware, however, that you may also have problems with voicing at the beginning and middle of words as well. Try to compare voicing in words in these positions to help you determine if this issue exists in other word positions. Below are some minimal pair words to help you hear the voicing differences in words. This exercise will also help you understand just how important adding a little thing such as voicing truly is in order to be understood in English. The final consonant matters, and so does voicing!

B vs P

cab /cap	pub /pup	tab /tap
cub /cup	rib /rip	crab /crap
lib /lip	robe /rope	

D vs T

bad /bat	ride /write	aid /eight
God /got	add /at	feed /feet
had /hat	bed /bet	

G vs K

bag /back	dog /dock	jog /jock
pig /pick	dug /duck	log /lock
clog /clock	bug /buck	

V vs F

live /life	wave /waif	prove /proof
save /safe	leave /leaf	strive /strife
serve /surf	of "uhv" /off	

Z vs S

lose /loose	Ks /case	plays /place
dies /dice	eyes /ice	prize /price
lies /lice	ones /once	

"J" vs "ch"

ridge /rich   badge /batch   ledge /letch

age /H   purge /perch   Marge /March

surge /search   bodge /botch

<u>Sentences:</u>

B

The baby wore a ro<u>b</u>e and a bi<u>b</u> in his cri<u>b</u>

Bo<u>b</u> and A<u>b</u>e went to gra<u>b</u> Ro<u>b</u>

A bear cu<u>b</u> stole my co<u>b</u> of corn and a spare ri<u>b</u> from the BBQ

It was my jo<u>b</u> to melt the ice cu<u>b</u>e in the la<u>b</u> and scru<u>b</u> the floor

That blogger has a jo<u>b</u> on YouTu<u>b</u>e giving out gli<u>b</u> advice

D

He ma<u>d</u>e the brea<u>d</u> in a woo<u>d</u> stove

My foo<u>d</u> tastes weir<u>d</u> when it's col<u>d</u>

I'm afrai<u>d</u> the re<u>d</u> bir<u>d</u> is dea<u>d</u> in the col<u>d</u> mu<u>d</u>

The ki<u>d</u> sli<u>d</u> down the sli<u>d</u>e with her frien<u>d</u>

I ordere<u>d</u> a sala<u>d</u>, not a han<u>d</u> full of ol<u>d</u> lettuce

I rea<u>d</u> about a boy who was sa<u>d</u> because he missed his da<u>d</u>

G

Never put a wi<u>g</u> on a bi<u>g</u> pi<u>g</u>

I can't jo<u>g</u> while I hold my bi<u>g</u> mug

Ta<u>g</u> fed his bi<u>g</u> pi<u>g</u> an e<u>gg</u> from his ba<u>g</u>

My do<u>g</u> du<u>g</u> and found a bug and a slug

The fro<u>g</u> and his do<u>g</u> go for a jo<u>g</u> to see a bi<u>g</u> pig

Dou<u>g</u> told me never to hu<u>g</u> a fro<u>g</u> if he can't stand on a log

The e<u>gg</u> fell on my leg but luckily landed in the ba<u>g</u> and not on the rug

V

I ha<u>v</u>e an old sto<u>v</u>e

Did you mo<u>v</u>e my glo<u>v</u>e?

I ga<u>v</u>e the hi<u>v</u>e a kick to turn it over

The shark do<u>v</u>e into the underwater ca<u>v</u>e

You should never sha<u>v</u>e while you dri<u>v</u>e

Fi<u>v</u>e Ali<u>v</u>e is my favorite drink to ha<u>v</u>e on a hot day

Z (notice "s's" at the ends of words)

We are big fan<u>s</u> of oldie<u>s</u> music

Plea<u>se</u> put the girl<u>s</u>' three bag<u>s</u> in the closet

She alway<u>s</u> play<u>s</u> her tambourine<u>s</u> in the same place

My eye<u>s</u> were in a da<u>ze</u>, so I only saw the spie<u>s</u> two time<u>s</u>

She said she alway<u>s</u> practice<u>s</u> once she finishe<u>s</u> her salad<u>s</u>

I paid the price to win the pri<u>ze</u> after the play<u>s</u> were over

"J"

With a<u>ge</u> comes knowle<u>dge</u>

The Ju<u>dge</u> was known to harbor a gru<u>dge</u>

Who would ever throw fu<u>dge</u> in the garba<u>ge</u>?

A lar<u>ge</u> ran<u>ge</u> of new images surged on the internet

He received a ba<u>dge</u> on sta<u>ge</u> when he was at Colle<u>ge</u>

The villa<u>ge</u> view is gorgeous at the e<u>dge</u> of the bri<u>dge</u>

Did the badgers escape from the ca<u>ge</u> under the bri<u>dge</u>?

She arrived at her cotta<u>ge</u> with her lar<u>ge</u> lugga<u>ge</u> in hand

In my lugga<u>ge</u>, there is a packa<u>ge</u> with a posta<u>ge</u> stamp

He ate a sausa<u>ge</u> and drank a bevera<u>ge</u> in the stora<u>ge</u> closet

I would like a sausa<u>ge</u> and a bevera<u>ge</u>, but no cabba<u>ge</u>, thank you

The marria<u>ge</u> ceremony took place on a sta<u>ge</u> in a villa<u>ge</u> nearby

If you speak the langua<u>ge</u> of love, you won't dama<u>ge</u> your marria<u>ge</u>

The man lunged away from the animal in the ca<u>ge</u> to avoid any dama<u>ge</u>

Reading:

Once you feel you have mastered voicing the sounds with which you have the most difficulty, it is important to move up in complexity. Reading out loud is an excellent sub-step to conversation practice. During reading, you can hone in on your fluency, naturalness, and speed. Practice reading aloud and recording yourself regularly. Review your voicing to ensure you feel the vibration as you speak and hear your voice as you listen to your recordings.

Conversation:

As you work on reading practice, you should begin to push yourself out of your comfort zone to try using your new pronunciation skills with others. At first, do your best to add a few more voiced consonants at the ends of words as you speak. You will begin to increase your awareness of the voiced sounds as a result, and you will find yourself correcting your own pronunciation more and more often. Once you start to habituate your new pronunciation, you will find that you are correcting yourself less often. It does take a significant amount of effort and intention at the beginning of conversation practice. Naturalness comes with practice so keep at it!

Final Consonants

I wanted to dedicate an entire section on final consonants because they are so incredibly essential in North American English pronunciation. I come across so many clients with various first languages, each with their own specific struggles and differences, but there is often one similarity amongst them; The final sounds in their speech are significantly affected either by deleting the sound altogether or by not accurately adding the voicing element of speech.

This chapter will discuss the deletion of sounds at the ends of words and why this impacts intelligibility and clear English pronunciation.

Description:
Final consonants are the last consonant sounds you hear in a word. So, in the word "egg," the final consonant is /g/. Be aware, too, that I am referring to the spoken word, not the written word, as spelling does not dictate pronunciation in many cases. For example, for words with silent letters like "comb," the final sound that we say is what is important, not what is spelled. In this case, the last consonant sound is /m/.

Common Differences:
The most common issue I see my non-native English-speaking clients have with final consonants overall is deletion. The final sound is simply not pronounced or is produced so quickly that it is nearly imperceptible. The deletion of the final consonant in words in English will have a profound effect on intelligibility (others understanding you). Regardless of the sound, by merely focusing on the final consonants in words and ensuring you are producing that part of the word clearly, you can significantly improve your clarity and accuracy in English pronunciation. Let's take a look at some examples of final consonant deletions and how they can profoundly impact meaning:

Final Consonant Minimal Pairs:

beep	bee	keep	key	pipe	pie

sheep	she	weed	we	dime	die
peep	pea	toad	toe	dome	dough
toot	two	tied	tie	mine	my
meet	me	load	low	plane	play
bite	bye	road	row	moon	moo
late	lay	need	knee	rain	ray
boat	bow	feed	fee	noon	new
light	lie	seed	see	boil	boy
boot	boo	week	we	nose	no
shoot	shoe	make	may	couch	cow
fort	four	bark	bar	drive	dry
treat	tree	team	tea		
date	day	time	tie		

Hear it!

Go through the list of minimal pair words above. Now, it may seem strange to think that you have any issue with saying your final consonants, and when practicing at the word level themselves, most speakers can clearly pronounce the last sound. The problem often arises in more complex situations, such as sentence level and reading tasks. Despite what level you may delete your final consonants, or if even at all, do the exercise to be sure you hear the last consonant sound in the word list.

Feel it!

In this exercise, there is no specific direction for what to "feel" exactly. It is truly just the understanding that the final consonants must be present in English. I will touch on the many reductions and linking rules that exist in English at a later time. However, I always recommend first understanding the fundamentals of clear pronunciation BEFORE making deletions when linking, etc. So, do not skip this step!

Do it!

So we have already compared the final consonants versus deletion of final consonants in words. Let's get on to the more complex stuff! Practice in the phrase and sentence level. Ensure you fully produce the last consonant in each word.

Phrases:
Once/s/ in/n/ a blue moon/n/
Reading/ŋ/ a book/k/
At/t/ the game/m/
Totally delicious/s/ food/d/

221

The wate**r**/r/ dripped/t/

He's/z/ one/n/ of/v/ them/m/

Sentences:

Oa**k**/k/ is/z/ strong/ŋ/ and/d/ also gives/z/ shade/d/.

Cats/s/ and/d/ dogs/z/ each/tʃ/ hate/t/ the other/r/.

The pipe/p/ began/n/ to rust/t/ even/n/ though it/t/ was/z/ new.

Open/n/ the crate/t/ but/t/ don't/t/ break/k/ the glass/s/.

Add/d/ the sum/m/ of the product/t/ of/v/ these/z/ three.

Thieves/z/ who rob/b/ friends/z/ deserve/v/ jail/L/.

The ripe/p/ taste/t/ of/v/ cheese/z/ improves/z/ with/θ/ age/dʒ/.

Act/t/ on/n/ these/z/ orders/z/ with/θ/ great/t/ speed/d/.

The hog/g/ is/z/ under/r/ the high fence/s/.

Move/v/ the vat/t/ over/r/ the hot/t/ fire/r/.

Reading:

For many, sentence-level practice is where you begin to realize how often you actually drop the final consonant in words. You may also recognize a few final sounds that you do not pronounce as clearly as expected. We will continue to work on sound rules for more sounds in future chapters, but this exercise raises your awareness of the final consonants in English words. If you were one of the many who now realize just how often you are prone to dropping the final sounds in words, reading practice would prove to be an excellent exercise to improve this issue. As usual, I want you to find a book, magazine, blog, website, email, or whatever you would like to read aloud and focus on the final consonants of each word. Feel and hear how it sounds when you focus intentionally on producing the last sound. This technique alone will help facilitate more precise English pronunciation overall. One thing to be careful of is to avoid sounding robotic. Again, we will discuss linking in full detail during a later chapter, but I want you to know that pronouncing the final consonant does not mean you must pause. after. each. word. If you are using clear final consonants, it is even more important to try your best to blend your words together as if there are no spaces between your words at all.

Conversation:

Now that you have had good practice reading aloud and maybe even some recording to help identify the issues you're having with final consonant deletion, you are ready for conversation. Begin with short, simple conversations while intentionally focusing on the last sound of each word you say. You will feel that it is

222

significantly more effortful and taxing on your brain to do this in conversation. The result at the beginning of conversation practice is that it will force you to slow your speech rate down slightly. That's okay. It is part of the process. As you become more aware of your final consonant productions, you will begin to pronounce these sounds with more accuracy over time. Practice, focus on blending, and keep at it!

Chapter 19: Consonant Clusters & Blends, Oh my!

Description:
The term consonant blend refers to multiple consonants together. In consonant blends, we string consonants together one after the other. Pronouncing words with consonant blends is often a frustrating and complex issue for most people. A blend can occur as just two consonants together, like in "**pr**ess," or even three consonants together, as in "**str**ess." Therefore, a consonant blend is more challenging to produce if you have particular trouble with one of the consonants in the group and a massive struggle if you have difficulty with two or even all of the consonants strung together. A person who has difficulty with /r/, /L/, and /d/ would have a heck of a time with the word "wo**rld**," for instance. For this reason, we must identify our weaknesses in articulation and practice these sounds in their most complex forms. Consonant blends are just that; a really complex form of multiple consonants together.

Now, I don't want you to get scared of consonant blends. Once you figure out how to feel your difficult sounds on their own and feel confident in producing them, you will use the skills you have learned for consonant blends in exactly the same way.

Common Differences:
When you have difficulty with a sound, let's say /r/, you should expect that any /r/ blend will likely also be difficult. By now, you will have identified at least some of your most difficult sounds, and you will be able to determine if you have as much or more difficulty when the sound is squished together with another consonant. Luckily though, not all sounds exist in blends. /v/, for example, is never blended with /p/ in English as a cluster. There are only a few consonant blends to be aware of; R-blends, L-blends, S-blends, and 3 and 4 consonant blends.

2-Consonant Blends

R-Blends

PR Words:

princess	press	prawn
pretty	printer	prison
pray	price	principal
pretzel	prince	present

PR Sentences

Prancer pricked his hoof

The prawn was an excellent price

The pretty princess eats pretzels all day

I pray that the printer will print my papers

The principal went to prison for stealing a present

BR Words:

bread	brick	braces
bridge	breakfast	break
broom	bracelet	broccoli
brush	brother	breeze

BR Sentences

I ate brown bread for breakfast

I can smell broccoli in the breeze

She left the broken broom under the bridge

The bracelet and the hairbrush were brown

His brother fell onto a brick and broke his braces

TR Words:

train	trampoline	tree
trim	trophy	tray
troll	trash	tractor
triangle	trumpet	truck

TR Sentences

Someone put my trumpet on a dirty tray

The troll lived in the trash under the big tree

Trim the bushes and trees in a triangular shape

The train was faster than the tractor and the truck

It's true that I won a trophy for trampoline jumping

DR Words:

drum	dryer	dream
dragon	drawer	dry
draw	drive	drink
dress	drill	drip

DR Sentences

I drove to the store to get my dream dress

The dreary dresser needs a drastic change

I've dreamed of getting a drum set all my life

The dryer dried the drink I spilled on my shirt

I put my drawing of a drill in the bottom drawer

FR Words:

frog	frying pan	freeway
fries	fridge	freezer
fruit	frame	frost
Frisbee	friend	front

FR Sentences

The fridge and the freezer are frosty

I was looking at the front of the picture frame

Francis loves French fries for some reason, but not fruit

My friend took the rest of the meal from the frying pan

Fred loves the feeling of freedom when he's on the freeway

KR Words:

crab	creek	cricket
crown	cry	crack
cream	crib	crocodile
crayons	crow	crawl

KR Sentences

The baby cried in his crib

The king had a crooked crown

I cringe whenever I see a crocodile

The crowd went crazy over the band

The crow grabbed the cricket from the creek

Why are there never any cream-colored crayons in the box?

GR Words:

grasshopper	grater	grapes
grow	grab	grill
grandma	grass	green beans
grandpa	group	grave

GR Sentences

A group of grapes always taste great

You're a great group of grape growers

The grub laid on the newly grown grass

I use a grater to process my wheatgrass juice

Grandma and Grandpa always grow green beans

THR Words:

throw	thrift	threaten
through	thrive	thrush
three	throat	thrust
throb	thread	throttle
thrash	thrill	threshold

THR Sentences

Throw the ball through the trees

There were three throbbing bruises on her arm

Bacteria can thrive in your throat

The thread was thrust through the material

He was threatened to pass the threshold of the perimeter

L Blends

BL Words:

blade	blocks	blackberries
blue jeans	blanket	blouse
black sheep	blue ribbon	blackbird

BL Sentences:

The blanket blew away

The blackbird flew in the blue sky

He's the black sheep of the family

She will only wear that black blouse

The knife blade was sharp and black

Those are my favourite pair of blue jeans

Blair loves blackberries and black sweaters

I put the blocks on the blanket, but the blanket still blew away

I won the blue ribbon at the blueberry fair for my amazing blueberry pie

FL Words:

flag	floor	flashlight
flamingo	flute	flat
fly	flower	flow

FL Sentences:

Be careful of flash floods

The flag flew high but landed flat on the floor

The floor was flooded, so the fly had nowhere to go

She played the flute in the flower garden while the florist arranged flowers

I left my flashlight in Florida by the flat-footed flamingos

SL Words:

slide	sled	slug
sleeping	sleeve	slow
slippers	sloth	slap

SL Sentences:

Your sleeve is slightly too long

The boy was sleeping with his slippers on

228

She slid down the slippery slide using a sled

The slippers kept the woman from slipping

The sloth moved slowly as he passed the slimy slug

PL Words:

plane	pliers	pluto
plant	planet	plaster
plum	playing	please

PL Sentences:

Please keep playing nicely together

The plane plummeted to the ground

My plant is growing plenty of tomatoes

She planted the plum tree two years ago

I plan to use the biggest plug on the planet

I used the pliers to do some plumbing around the house

CL Words:

cloud	clap	class
clear	claw	climb

CL Sentences:

The clouds were coming

Clearly, the clip was broken

The crowd clapped for the clown

The bear claw was behind clear glass

He dragged clay in the class with his dirty shoes

The climbers climbed the cliff without their climbing gear

GL Words:

glare	glad	glen
glamorous	glass	globe
glow	glue	gloat

GL Sentences:

Glen glared at his boss

Glamorous people are glorified

The lanterns glow brightly at night

Gloria was so glad she passed her exams

The glassblower blew beautiful glass bowls

I used clear glue to glue the globe pieces together

S Blends

SP Words:

spaghetti	spider	spill
speech	speed	spinach
sports	spa	sponge

SP Sentences:

I cleaned the spill with a sponge

I want to learn how to speak Spanish

The spaghetti sauce sprayed everywhere

My speech about spinach was spectacular

I need to go to the spa after all the sports I did this week

SK Words:

ski	school	scare
skip	sky	scarf
skin	skeleton	skunk

SK Sentences:

A skeleton has no skin

I skipped the ski trip this year

I always wear my scarf when I walk to school in the winter

I got a scar on my leg after scoring that goal

That skunk scared me so much that I fell and scraped my knee

SN Words:

snail	snake	sneak
snow	snack	snip
sniff	snore	snorkel

SN Sentences:

I always sneeze when it snows

The snake moved so much faster than the snail

I sneaked up to my friend using a snorkel in the pool
I snipped some paper into the shape of a snowflake
I like to have a big snack after snowboarding all day

SM Words:

smile	small	smog
smell	smart	smoothie
smoke	smack	smear

SM Sentences:

That ball is so small and smooth
I always smile when I smell the scent of smoke in the air
I feel smart when I drink my green smoothies every morning
It's smart to keep your low-beams on in the smog when driving
I accidentally smeared some grease on my smock when cooking today

ST Words:

stop	storm	steak
steel	stem	star
start	stickers	stick

ST Sentences:

Steve was very stern
That's a nice steel statue of a stegosaurus
He threw a stereo and a stool into the station wagon
I stopped at the bus station to watch the storm clouds
She stepped on sticks and strawberries as she passed me in the field

3-Consonant Blends

As the number of consonants increases, the complexity of the pronunciation increases. You may find it helpful to elongate or stretch the one sound that causes you the most difficulty. For many, the /r/ or /L/ is particularly difficult. In these instances, try to elongate that sound in the blend to ensure you feel you are adjusting the sound as you did in your previous practice.

STR Words:

strong	street	streamers
strawberry	stretch	stroller
string	stretcher	stream
straw	striped	straight

STR Sentences:

I saw strawberries in the street

We walked with our strollers in a straight line

They opened up the striped stretcher in the street

He needed a strong straw for his strawberry milkshake

SPR Words:

spring	sprain	sprite
sprinkler	sprouts	sprung
spray	spruce	spring roll
spread	sprinkle	

SPR Sentences:

I had a Sprite and spring rolls for lunch

I sprained my leg over a spruce tree root

I spread my blanket out on a cool spring day

We take out the sprinkler and spray the grass in the spring

SPL Words:

splash	splatter	splurge
splat	splinter	splendid
split	spleen	splendorous

SPL Sentences:

Want to split the bill?

He splashed and splattered in the water

I want to splurge on a splendid new outfit

She laughed so hard she almost split her spleen

SKR Words:

scream	scrambled	scribble
scrub	screen	screw
scrape	scrap	scripture
screwdriver	scratch	scruples

SKR Sentences:

The <u>scr</u>een was <u>scr</u>ewed on tightly

I <u>scr</u>ubbed the <u>scr</u>ibbles off of the wall

I <u>scr</u>eamed when I <u>scr</u>aped my knee with a <u>scr</u>ewdriver

Always cover your <u>scr</u>atches and <u>scr</u>apes with a Band-Aid

Final Consonant Blends

There are also consonant blends that exist at the ends of words. Focus on the sounds that you previously identified as being difficult for you. These are the sounds you will want to work on as they appear in consonant blends. The /t/'s in these blends should generally be true normal aspirated /t/'s. More discussion on /t/ is included in the /t/ chapter.

/st/-Final

best	last	past
fast	lost	rest
just	must	trust

/sk/-Final

ask	disk	mask
bask	dusk	risk
desk	husk	task

/sp/-Final

crisp	grasp	cusp
gasp	lisp	wisp
clasp	wasp	

/pt/-Final

kept	swept	hoped
attempt	slept	clapped
except	ripped	wiped
slipped	accept	dropped

/nd/-Final

and	mend	stand
end	lend	band
find	tend	hand

/nt/-Final

different	plant	bent
important	point	sent
parent	rant	rent

/nk/-Final

think	bank	sank
rink	link	drink
tank	sink	thank

/mp/-Final

bump	stomp	lamp
jump	camp	stamp
ramp	lump	pump

/rd/-Final

third	afford	word
bird	hard	yard
leopard	card	record

/nz/-Final

phones	dines	wins
lines	fines	tins
runs	drones	fans

/ts/-Final

pets	rats	belts
secrets	puppets	lots
pots	carpets	planets

/ths/-Final

baths	myths	fifths
goths	oaths	fourths
moths	paths	wreaths

/ld/-Final

child	cold	old
wild	held	rolled
sold	filled	filed

/lp/-Final

help	scalp	yelp
gulp	kelp	pulp

/lt/-Final

adult	felt	salt
difficult	guilt	belt
result	wilt	fault

/lf/-Final

shelf	golf	elf
self	wolf	Ralph

*Not "calf" and "half" as these "L's" are silent.

/vd/-Final

loved	waved	proved
arrived	moved	starved
lived	served	

/nθ/-Final

absinth	month	tenth
hyacinth	ninth	umpteenth
millionth	seventh	midmonth

/ðd/-Final

betrothed	breathed	soothed
unscathed	loathed	tithed
sunbathed	clothed	
	bathed	

3 and 4 Final Consonant Blends

/cts/-Final

abducts	deducts	depicts
objects	insects	addicts
reacts	detects	aspects

3 and 4 Final Consonant Blends Mixed

accents	glimpsed	sixth
against	grasped	stamps
aspects	helped	tempts
attempts	next	texts
contexts	prompt	twelfth
crisps	risked	world
diamonds	sculpts	

Even native English speakers have significant difficulty with some of the more complex 3 and 4 consonant blends as well. For this reason, we do often simplify these multiple blends in running speech by dropping one of the sounds, typically the middle consonant of the three. Since it is often so laborious for us to articulate each and every consonant, it is far simpler to reduce these into a similar-sounding, less complex pronunciation.

Below are some common examples of when North American English speakers reduce longer, more complex consonant blends. Again, look at the middle consonant of 3-consonant blends and see how they have dropped altogether!

/skt/turns to /st/:
ris<u>k</u>ed turns to "rist"
as<u>k</u>ed turns to "ast"
bas<u>k</u>ed turns to "bast"
mas<u>k</u>ed turns to "mast"
tas<u>k</u>ed turns to "tast"

/kts/turns to /ks/:

aspects turns to "aspecs"

acts turns to "aks"

ducts turns to "duks"

facts turns to "faks"

tracts turns to "traks"

elects turns to "uhleks"

evicts turns to "uhviks"

ejects turns to "uhjeks"

affects turns to "uhfeks"

infects turns to "infeks"

objects turns to "uhbjeks"

impacts turns to "impaks"

insects turns to "inseks"

/ndz/ turns to /nz/:

diamonds turns to "diamonz"

minds turns to "minz"

finds turns to "finz"

kinds turns to "kinz"

bends turns to "benz"

bands turns to "banz"

hands turns to "hanz"

lands turns to "lanz"

stands turns to "stanz"

wounds turns to "wounz"

friends turns to "frienz"

/mpt/ turns to /mt/:

prompt turns to "promt"

tempt turns to "temt"

unkempt turns to "unkemt"

exempt turns to "exemt"

attempt turns to "attemt"

preempt turns to "preemt"

contempt turns to "contemt"

camped turns to "camt"

/lfθ/turns to /lθ/:

/d/ + "Th"

I felt it important to add a special combination of sounds in this chapter; when the /d/ sound is followed by a "th" sound as in "ma<u>de the</u>." This particular combination of sounds is really tricky for speakers since these movements of the tongue are difficult. The /d/ sound involves placing the tongue tip on the roof of the mouth just behind the front teeth on the alveolar ridge, which is that bump behind your top teeth. The tongue then must slide out and between the teeth to create the "th." Do not allow the /d/ to "pop" or release air before the "th." You must slide to the "th." Below are some examples to practice. Feel how you will need to slide the tongue from the alveolar ridge over to between the teeth without releasing or letting go.

Give it a try!

Phrases:

add these numbers	had them here	mud throwing
bald thin man	hid them	old thug
bird themed	kid threw the ball	paid the price
bold throw	landed there	read the book
dad things	lend the tools	rode there
did that	lied then stole	sad thing
did they	load the truck	told them
did they win?	mad thug	wandered there
end that game	made this book	
had the	wild theme park	

Sentences:

That was a really wil<u>d th</u>eme park

Don't forget to loa<u>d the</u> truck with the apples

She wanted a bir<u>d-th</u>emed party

The neighbor said he would len<u>d the</u> tools to use for the shed

I need help to ad<u>d these</u> numbers together

I forgot I ha<u>d these</u> boxes here

My daughter ma<u>de thi</u>s book for you

There will be no mu**d** **th**rowing during recess

I rea**d** **th**at book last year, it was great

My da**d** **th**inks his jokes are hilarious

You can't trust him. He's already lie**d**, **th**en stole from us

That's one very ma**d** **th**ug

The sa**d** **th**ing is that I can't even remember it

If you en**d** **th**at game of monopoly, we can go out for ice cream

Di**d** **th**ey win the baseball championship?

"Th" + /d/

Wait, didn't we just do this?!

Nope. "th" + /d/ is another variation of this difficult sound combination. Here, we have the "th" before the /d/ within the same word. Just as in the words above, this combination of sounds is tricky, so they are worth practicing and getting used to. To pronounce these sounds together, we will avoid putting a pause or a break between the sounds. We will slide from the "th" position with your tongue between your teeth, and then move inward to the /d/ position with your tongue on the alveolar ridge.

Words:

bathed	seethed	tithed
betrothed	sheathed	unbathed
breathed	sleuthed	unscathed
clothed	smoothed	wreathed
loathed	soothed	writhed
mouthed	sunbathed	
scathed	teethed	

Sentences:

Even after the fight, I left unsca**thed**

I brea**thed** in the wonderful fresh spring air

I mou**thed** out the words to my friend in the library, but he didn't understand

She smoo**thed** out the tablecloth to prepare for dinner

The calm music easily soo**thed** the baby

I sunba<u>thed</u> all day and got the worst sunburn of my life
He ti<u>thed</u> to the church to help the poor
The worm wriggled and wri<u>thed</u> in the mud
I have always loa<u>thed</u> watching horror movies

Hear it!

As you work through the consonant blends that include your difficult sounds, listen and pay extra attention. Sometimes, it may mean that you will have to elongate or make the goal sound stretched out a little bit. For example, if /r/ is your main issue, the word "bread" may mean that you will need to ensure your /r/ is a little longer so that you don't drop it altogether. So this word will feel like you are pronouncing "berrrred," but in actuality, you will be finally pronouncing the /r/ that you had previously been dropping. Making an adjustment like a slight elongation can help you in big ways!

Feel it!

As with your previous sound practice work, whichever sound you focus on is the sound you will feel for. Refer back to your particular sound issues and review what you are to be feeling for. If, for example, you are working on "L" in the blend "plant," you will be feeling to ensure your tongue tip actually touches the alveolar ridge on the roof of your mouth.

Go through all the blends that include your problem sound, both at the beginning and end of words, to ensure you are confident in pronouncing your new sound in the most challenging circumstances.

Do it!

As you progress through the lists above, be sure to stick to your complexity ladder rules. Start with isolation, then practice in syllables, words, sentences, reading, and finally practice in conversation. If you have already practiced your sound in non-blend words, you will have some confidence to know that you can hear and feel the new pronunciation versus your old version. Practice daily to work toward naturalness and fluent pronunciation of your target sounds.

PART THREE: Vowels, Vowels, & More Vowels

Chapter 20: All About Vowels: This Is The Serious Stuff!

<u>Description:</u>

In the following few chapters, I will go into great detail about specific vowels in English. I will be focusing on the particular vowels that are typically the most difficult for non-native North American English speakers to pronounce. I will also provide you with much-needed explanations about exactly how to pronounce each sound and what to do with your lips, tongue, jaw, and voice. I will also give you some precise comparisons between the English pronunciation and the typical sound substitution struggles that my clients deal with every day.

A vowel carries elements of the syllable in a word, so we refer to a vowel as a "syllabic sound." Vowels are pronounced without any constrictions in the vocal tract, meaning the sound of a vowel is really just shaped by the tongue's position. The tongue's position is what is going to change the acoustics of the sound. All vowels are voiced, so our vocal folds must be vibrating while pronouncing the sound.

Vowel List

Below are the vowels of the General American English Accent, with examples of each sound's pronunciation.

<u>IPA Symbol: Vowels</u>

/^/	"uh"	<u>u</u>p, g<u>u</u>m
/a/	"ah"	<u>o</u>n, t<u>o</u>p

/æ/	"aa"	at, cat
/ə/	"uh"	(the same as /ʌ/) today, animal
/i/	"ee"	eat, very
/ɪ/	"ih"	it, in
/ʊ/	"ouh"	look, good
/u/	"oo"	who, do
/ɛ/	"eh"	bet, said
/aɪ/	"ah ee"	my, lie
/eɪ/	"eh ee"	day, say
/aʊ/	"aa oo"	how, cow
/oʊ/	"ow oo"	so, low
/oɪ/	"ow ee"	toy, boy

The IPA Quadrilateral

Now, doesn't that title sound fancy! The IPA quadrilateral is an abstract way to help explain where our tongue needs to go to make specific sounds. It seems confusing, but I promise, with a little clarification, it will help you better understand how to pronounce those tricky vowels.

The IPA quadrilateral chart is a representation of the space in your mouth.

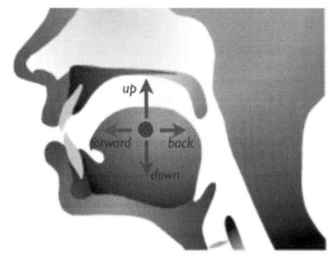

Image taken from: http://english.mimicmethod.com/english-vowels.html

If you see here, for example, that big round mass is your tongue. This representation is a side view of the head. The nose is to the left, and the back of the head is to the right. The top border of the oral cavity is the palate or the roof of the mouth. This image shows you how the tongue's mass can move in different directions in the mouth, which changes the sound of a vowel.

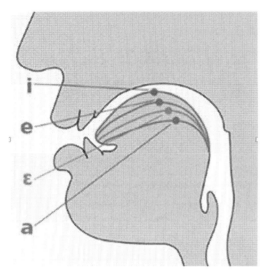

Image taken from: https://en.wikipedia.org/wiki/Vowel

Considering how high and low versus how forward or back our tongue must go for each sound, you will better understand this chart. In the picture above, you get an idea of how the slight variations in height can create an entirely different vowel sound. If you can grasp the feeling of where the tongue must go to make those sounds, you are far on your way to clearer English pronunciation.

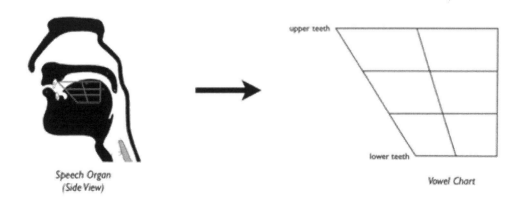

Speech Organ
(Side View)

Vowel Chart

Image taken from: http://english.mimicmethod.com/english-vowels.html

In the image above, the space in the mouth has been transferred into an abstract quadrilateral or wonky-looking rectangle. The quadrilateral represents the space in the mouth. It is not an actual square or even rectangle because the palate, or the roof of our mouth, is longer than the mandible or bottom of the oral cavity. The shape represents that space in the mouth. The tongue has more range of motion at the top of the mouth to move forward versus back than it does lower in the mouth as it is anchored in musculature.

Researchers have agreed on where each vowel can be plotted on this chart as it relates to tongue positions. It's important to note that each language has its own repertoire of vowels. Many vowels are shared between languages and some vowels are not.

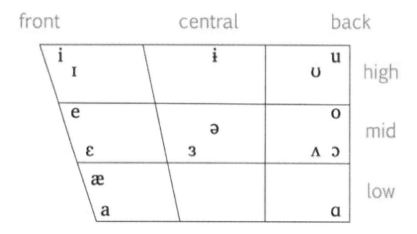

Image taken from: https://essentialsoflinguistics.pressbooks.com/chapter/3-3-need-to-add-tables-ipa-for-canadian-english/

Remember that this is an abstract model of the tongue and not an exact mapping of tongue position.

Many programs on the internet allow you to hear an example of each IPA vowel symbol and show you where they are plotted on the vowel chart with their IPA symbol. I highly recommend searching for an "interactive IPA Vowel chart" and listening to the various North American English vowels as well as the various vowels that are produced around the globe. It might just be me, but I think it's pretty cool!

Tongue Height:
Tongue height refers to the vertical movements up and down that the tongue makes to create a sound.

We produce some vowels with our jaw closed. When our jaw is closed, our tongue is placed high near the roof or palate of the mouth. Sounds such as /i/ "eee" and /u/ "ooo" are examples of high vowels. When the jaw is closed, we call this a "closed" vowel. When you say these sounds, feel how your jaw is closed, teeth are nearly together, and the middle of your tongue rises really close to the roof as compared to the sounds /a/ as in "hot" and /æ/ as in "cat" where the jaw is open. We call vowels with an open jaw position an "open vowel." When you say /a/ or "ahh," your jaw is open, and teeth are wide apart. Your tongue also moves downward along with your jaw, making this a "low" vowel.

Tongue Backness:
Another important thing to understand when practicing vowels is that the middle of our tongue not only moves up and down vertically, but also moves forward and back horizontally. Again, when we talked about /i/ "eee" and /u/ "ooo" our tongue was high for both of these sounds near the roof. Try to feel which sound you notice your tongue move forward for, and which sound you move your tongue back for. The movement is EXTREMELY minute, mere millimeters, but these slight changes up/down/forward/back are the subtle variances that change our vowel sounds. The /i/ or "eeee" sound is more forward, so it is a front vowel. The /u/ or "ooo" sound is more back, so it is called a back vowel.

Lip Roundness:
Finally, another element of vowels to understand is your lip position. The lips play an important role in vowel sounds, so you must be aware of how "spread" or smiling versus how "round" or puckered your lips are for each vowel. If you were to produce the schwa "uh" sound, which we transcribe in IPA with the /ə/ symbol, your lips would be neutral, with no rounding or spreading at all. Compare this with the /u/ or "oo" sound, which includes fully rounded and protruded lips (e.g. "uh" vs. "oo").

Monophthongs, Diphthongs, and Triphthongs

Now, by this point, you might be thinking: "Rebecca, you're making this up!" Nope. These are the terms used to explain how many vowels are strung together.

<u>Monophthongs:</u>

A monophthong is a single stable vowel. This vowel sound does not change from the beginning to the end. It stays the same, just as it does in the vowel "eeeee."

<u>Diphthongs:</u>

A diphthong is when a vowel transitions into another vowel. An example would be the /aɪ/ sound, as in "hi, my, die." If you notice, your mouth transitions from an open jaw position, where the tongue is placed low in the mouth "ah," then moves up to the palate as your jaw closes and your lips spread into a smile "ee." "ahhh eeee."

<u>Triphthongs:</u>

A triphthong is when a vowel transitions three times. An example of this would be "client." The vowel starts with an open jaw, low tongue position, "ah." We then change to a high tongue position with spread lips "eee." Then lastly, we move to a neutral forward tongue position with neutral lips /aɪɛ/ "eh." The vowels transition from an "ah" to "eee" to "eh." It would sound like "cl <u>ah</u> <u>ee</u> <u>e</u>nt."

This chapter was a quick overview of vowels. The IPA quadrilateral is a fantastic way to better understand exactly what we are doing when we pronounce different vowels. If you are a more visual learner, this may help you tremendously. If you are more of an auditory learner, search the internet for an interactive IPA vowel chart to help you hear the differences. Either method you use to learn will help you better understand how to accurately adjust your vowels to better represent those heard in the General North American English Accent.

Now don't worry. I'm not leaving you there with vowels. Next, we will delve deeper into each vowel. We will get lots of practice with each and learn how to hear and feel each vowel in speech so you can master them in conversation.

Chapter 21: /I/: I Warned You, This Might Blow Your Mind!

Description:
The /I/ is a sound I work on with nearly every client I see since it is a sound that does not often exist in other languages. This sound is often mispronounced because many non-native English teachers also make pronunciation substitutions with /I/ when speaking and teaching English to their students.

The /I/ is the sound that we say in words "it, is, in, and his." I hear my clients often complain that their English instructors told them to say the "eee" sound or /i/ when they see an "I" in English spelled words. Unfortunately, this is very far from accurate. In fact, English words spelled with "i" are nearly never pronounced as /i/ or "eee." This confusion results in clients saying "eat" for "it" or "ease" for "is."

To pronounce the /I/ sound, we must keep our lips only slightly spread, like the tiniest smile ever. Really, we should not be smiling wide at all. Our jaw should be relatively neutral and only slightly open, not closed with the teeth together.

As for tongue position, I usually like to have my clients say the "eee" sound first and feel what their tongue position feels like for them. Where is the tip of your tongue? The sides of your tongue, are they touching anything? Where is the middle of your tongue; is it high or neutral or low in the mouth? Typically clients can feel that for the /i/ or "eee" sound, the sides of the tongue are up against the upper inner teeth on each side. The tip of the tongue does not touch anything, and the middle of the tongue is very high near the roof of the mouth.

I then instruct my clients to compare this sound with the /I/ or "ih" sound. To create the /I/ "ih" sound, I have my clients hold the /i/ "ee" sound and then freeze their mouth and tongue. Now, slowly relax and lower the middle of your tongue slightly down. We're talking millimeters here! Just enough lowering makes the middle of your tongue go from a high arching and tense position to a more flat relaxed position. This is the /I/ "ih" sound. Once you can feel this tiny downward adjustment, I want you to compare /i/ to /I/. Over and over, go back and forth "eee," "ih', "eee," "ih." Feel how the middle of the tongue raises and arches up for "eee" /i/, and lowers ever-so-slightly and flattens for "ih" /I/.

<u>Common differences:</u>
As stated earlier, words spelled with an "i" are generally mispronounced, with the tongue placed too high in the mouth and sounding more like an /i/ or "eee" sound. The common pronunciation should be the /I/ "ih" sound, with the middle of the tongue pulled slightly down.

<u>Spelling:</u>
First, I want to go into some of the terms you often hear with vowels: "short I" vs. "long I," etc. I find these terms very misleading to non-native English speakers, as it implies that you must noticeably lengthen or shorten a vowel. Unfortunately, I have often come across clients who have taken this "rule" to heart and end up pronouncing all the "i's" they see the same, except they say some longer than others. This added vowel length results in unnatural English pronunciation, and I prefer to throw the long/short terminology out to avoid confusion. The difference in vowels is their articulatory placement in the mouth, which is the most important distinction. So let's focus on that and not get confused by how long a vowel must be because, truly, the length is usually imperceptible.

/I/ "ih" is generally spelled with either an "i" or a "y."

I (More than 93% of the time)	bit	kick	in	is
Y (around 3% of the time)	system	gym	hymn	polyp

Less common (less than 4% of the time) spellings include:

e	pretty
ei	forfeit, counterfeit
o	women
u	busy
ui	build, guilty, biscuit, guitar, circuit, liquid, penguin

The "i" _only_ sounds like /i/ or "eee" in three instances:

1. With a <u>silent</u> "e" at the end of the word in multisyllabic words: elite, police, tangerine
2. At the end of syllables followed by <u>another vowel:</u> stadium, piano, radius
3. At the end of <u>foreign</u> words: Hawaii, spaghetti, sushi, Helsinki

/I/ vs. /i/ minimal Pairs:
Let's look at why the slight lowering of your tongue can be the difference between being understood clearly versus a potentially embarrassing misunderstanding. Go

through the minimal pairs list comparing the /I/ vs. /i/ sounds below and think of the possibilities for potential confusion!

/I/	/i/						
bid	bead	hid	heed		pitch	peach
bin	bean	hill	he'll		risen	reason
bit	beat	hip	heap		shin	sheen
bitch	beach	his	he's		*shit	sheet
biz	bees	hit	heat		(I hope you see why
cyst	ceased	ill	eel		this matters!)
chick	cheek	is	ease		sick	seek
chip	cheap	it	eat		sill	seal
crick	creek	itch	each		sim	seem
did	deed	kid	keyed		sin	scene/seen
dip	deep	knit	neat		sit	seat
fill	feel	lick	leak		skid	skied
finned	fiend	lip	leap		skim	scheme
fist	feast	live	leave		slick	sleek
fit	feet	mill	meal		slip	sleep
fizz	fees	mitt	meet		slit	sleet
flit	fleet	pick	peek		still	steal
gin	gene	pill	peel		tick	teak
gip	jeep	pip	peep		till	teal
grid	greed	piss	piece		tin	teen
grin	green	pit	peat		Tim	team

Below are some phrases that also compare the /I/ and /i/.

<u>/I/ vs /i/ Phrases:</u>

big /I/ cheese /i/
green /i/ pill /I/
isn't /I/ she /i/?
it's /I/ easy /i/ /i/

little /I/ sheep /i/
middle /I/ East /i/
still /I/ eating /i/
these /i/ things /I/

very /i/ interesting /I/
fit /I/ my feet /i/
big /I/ city /I/ /i/
feeling /i/ / I/ ill /I/

<u>Hear it!</u>
Go through the minimal pairs list above and begin to train your ears to hear the slight, subtle difference between /i/ "ee" and /I/"ih." Focus on tensing the middle of your tongue up versus relaxing it lower to compare the vowels. Hear the difference and practice daily to improve your differentiation skills.

Feel it!

As you improve your ability to hear the differences in these vowels, you will want to also focus on how the tongue position change feels in your mouth. You will want to pay particular attention to the feeling of your tongue position if differentiation and hearing the difference between /i/ and /I/ is difficult for you. The middle of your tongue should be your focus. As /i/ or "ee" is likely an easy sound for you to pronounce, use this as your anchor sound. Go back and forth from /i/ to /I/ and feel the middle of your tongue slightly flatten and lower to /I/. Go through the minimal pair word and phrase lists to get a feel for the difference in pronunciation and what your tongue must do to make this sound.

Do it!

Okay, so now you can hear the difference between these vowels. You can feel the difference between the positions of your tongue for these two sounds. Let's get you on your way to using the /I/ in your life! Let's practice up the ladder of complexity from words to phrases, sentences, reading, and finally, conversation.

/I/ Words:

if	finger	rip
it	fish	river
is	him	scissors
in	his	sick
big	hit	spin
bridge	kiss	this
chicken	little	wish
cliff	pig	with
did	rib	zipper
ditch	ribbon	
driven	ring	

Phrases:

pink ribbon	kiss the pig	fish and chips
big hit	little ring finger	innocent victim
chicken wing	this wish	it is in his Instagram pics
he did it	jacket with a zipper	simple interests
in the ditch	big city	spring picnic
driven in the van	children's film	this is it
big middle finger	drink milk	trip to Italy
his issues	spilled milk	winter wind

it is what it is

it's a sin

critical thinking

this internship

As if!

listen to this

I insist on it

six sisters

in a minute

I insist

his wish

fish and chicken

a quick minute

filthy rich

sitting children

sip your drink

risky babysitter

sitting in it

his crib

interesting situation

innovative window

pick your shift

missing stick

winter mitten

exit the clinic

finish the fiction novel

big interview

miserable complaints

give me the sprinkles

twist the picture

rid of it

which one's pink?

profit from the rich

since that tricky situation

quick chick flick

thick lipstick

this system

go to the gym

sing a hymn

big polyp

pretty women

guilty of counterfeiting

liquid pill

busy penguin

build a circuit

dip a biscuit

Now try with no visual cues to identify the /I/ sound. Remember, look for those "i's" in words. The word "I," however, is an exception, so do not adjust this word. "I" is pronounced /aI/ or "ahheee."

Sentences:

It is his

It was his

I wish it didn't

I live in a big city

This is really tricky

It's a pity that Rick is sick

It was in his Instagram

It is in one of his instant pots

He is always with his friends

This is the ditch that the dishes fell into

Who knows if he was in his house

Is that what the little kid did to my things?

I have issues going indoors instead of outdoors

Will it be in the store with the price on it?

Did you rip your zipper during the spring picnic?

I feel ill about how much that bill for the liver was!

I am hoping this position is still available in a month

Don't you wish you could have fish and chips for dinner?

How did the pig dig his way out in that children's film?

This chicken soup is too thick

It is worse than this instant soup!

Chris fell from the cliff into the ditch when he lived in the big city

I have driven a million imports to Switzerland in the winter wind

The innocent victim survived only because the pink string was too thin

If I invite him to an informal dinner, will he have a drink with it?

In the beginning, it was difficult for Tim to quit drinking on his trip to Italy

Joe hurt his hip on the trip because he was drinking milk on that big hill

Tim will visit his little sister Kim in Virginia and do a little skit with his fiddle

The symbol on this ring has an interesting history. It will bring you good luck.

It was interesting how difficult it was to get into the cities in the Caribbean

/In/ Words

aging	drink	inland
begin	dying	input
being	eating	insist
berlin	filing	intact
bingo	finch	intend
blink	finger	intent
bring	finish	into
brink	fling	intro
cabin	flint	invest
caring	going	king
chin	grin	linen
cinema	hint	link
cling	icing	linked
clinic	inch	login
coping	indie	losing
cousin	indoor	loving
crying	infant	lying
ding	info	margin
dinner	inform	mince
doing	injury	mint

origin	since	think
pinch	sing	toxin
pink	singer	twin
prince	sink	tying
print	skin	win
rating	sling	wind
resin	spin	window
ring	spring	windy
rink	sting	wing
ruin	stink	wink
ruling	stint	winner
satin	string	winter
saving	swing	zinc
shin	thin	
shrink	thing	

Exceptions:

Although the words below have an "e" at the end, they are STILL pronounced as /I/ "IH" with the tongue lowered.

Engine

Hinge

Rinse

Binge

Sentences:

It's written in English

I will bring lots of drinks to the cabin

My skin felt cold in the frigid wind

I found a thin pink ring on the rink

Saving and investing is important

She will spin and sing with her twin sister

I can feel the spring air when I open my window

He grinned and winked at me. Did you see that?

You can win a mint if you begin that indie album

I intend to be the one eating the most at the cinema

I insist that you invite your loving wife to the party

Your cousin is coping well with her shrinking wardrobe

She will be going there and doing a lot of fun things, I think

I would have been the winner of the winter race, but I got an injury and didn't finish

My finger was caught in the filing cabinet, so I went to the walk-in clinic

The singer was informed that there was a crying infant in the audience

I'm going to binge-watch that movie about the king who killed the prince in his kingdom

Reading:

Go through an email and read it aloud. As you find all the /I/ words, you will be surprised just how often we use this sound in English. Read out loud as often as you can for practice. As you become familiar with the fact that the "i's" you see in English words are pronounced in this way, you will increase your differentiation and improve your English pronunciation. Record yourself reading aloud regularly. Choose a book or magazine, or blog. It doesn't matter! Just focus intentionally on producing the sounds clearly and accurately and review them after you have recorded yourself.

Conversation:

Begin to introduce this new sound into your daily conversations with people. At first, it will be very intentional, and you must focus with precision to find the /I/ sound as you speak. The increased intention will require you to slow down your pace and think as you speak. Of course, this process becomes faster and faster as you become familiar with some frequently used words, and you will increase that familiarity as you practice. Try it out; you will notice you will not be asked to repeat yourself as often once you get this sound under your belt!

Chapter 22: /æ/ as in "At, Hat & Apple"

Description:
The /æ/ symbol represents the sound pronounced in the English words "at, hat, and apple." The /æ/ or "aa" is produced with the jaw wide open and the tongue low and flat to the floor of the mouth. The lips are in a very tense open position, unlike the /a/, where the lips are more neutral and relaxed while open. It's kind of like a smile with the mouth open! The /æ/ sound can be felt as you widen the opening of the back of your throat.

Common Differences:
Typically, the /æ/ sound is substituted with the /a/ sound, so the word "hat" might be pronounced as "hot" and "map" might be pronounced as "mop." To fix this substitution, you must tense your lips in a more open smile and feel how the back of your throat should feel more open for the /æ/ than the /a/. The jaw opening is about the same for both of these sounds, so the opening will not change.

The lips are only neutrally open for /a/, compared to the purposeful spreading open mouth lip posture for /æ/.

Let's take a look at some minimal pairs for the vowels /æ/ vs /a/:

/æ/ vs /a/

cap	cop	lap	lop	sack	sock
fat	fought	map	mop	sat	sought
flap	flop	rack	rock	slap	slop
hat	hot	ran	Ron		
jack	jock	rat	rot		

Another issue many non-native English speakers have with the /æ/ sound is to produce an "eh" or /ε/ sound instead. The difference occurs when the jaw is not dropped low enough, and the lips are not spread into a wide smile. Overall the mouth is too neutral. Practice the comparisons below of /æ/ versus /ε/ to hear and feel the pronunciation difference. Remember, /æ/ requires an open jaw and spread open lip smile.

/E/ vs /æ/

any	Annie	head	had	pen	pan
bed	bad	hem	ham	pet	pat
beg	bag	Ken	can	pest	past
bet	bat	kept	capped	rent	rant
blessed	blast	kettle	cattle	said	sad
bread	Brad	left	laughed	send	sand
dead	dad	leg	lag	set	sat
den	Dan	letter	latter	slept	slapped
dense	dance	m	am	speckle	spackle
Ed	add	men	man	Steph	staff
effect	affect	mess	mass	tech	tack
ex	axe	met	mat	ten	tan
fester	faster	n	Ann	trek	track
flex	flax	net	gnat	wreck	rack
gem	jam	peck	pack		

Spelling:

A lot of the reason people have difficulty with the /æ/ sound is that the spelling in English is not consistent in representing the spoke pronunciation. Another reason why the /æ/ poses so much difficulty for speakers is because this sound requires a slightly greater mouth opening and lip spreading than may feel natural for speakers of other languages, as this sound is not often present in other languages. It does take some practice to feel comfortable with this open-mouth position sound.

In terms of spelling, the /æ/ is represented with an "a" most of the time, actually around 97% of the time. For the other one and a half percent, the /æ/ is represented as "al," as in "half" and "calf," where the "L" sound is silent. The other one and a half percent is represented as "au," like in the word "laugh," phonetically transcribed as /læf/. We also have the word "plaid," which is an exception word. Just because the /æ/ sound is usually represented with an "a" doesn't mean that the "a" only has one sound. Unfortunately, the "a" spelling can be pronounced in various ways. For the most part, however, this rule will help you identify the "a" in stressed syllables with no other vowels next to it. If other vowels sit beside the "a," like in "bear," or have a silent "e" at the ends of the words, like in "care," then other rules apply, so be careful. Try to look for the "a's" on their own.

Spelling:

"a" 97% of words

"al" as in half/calf 1.5% of words

"au" as in laugh 1.5% of words

"ai" as in "plaid" (exception word)

Here is a simple two-part rule that can help!

1. In a stressed syllable, the letter "a" is pronounced as /æ/. Examples: **a**pple, **fa**ster, **pla**ster.

2. In a one-syllable word, the letter "a" is pronounced as /æ/, unless the word ends with the letter "e." Examples: mat, hat, tap would all be /æ/, but mat<u>e</u>, hat<u>e</u>, tap<u>e</u> would not, they would be /ei/ "eh eee"

The "Wave" in /æ/

When using this sound, add an extra singing element or "wave" of your pitch from up to down. This is especially noticeable in one-syllable words. The result will be a slightly longer /æ/ sound.

Haaat (sing up and then down on the /æ/)

Maap (sing up and then down on the /æ/)

So to recap, we are looking for words with an "a" that have no vowels next to it (except "au"), NO "e" at the end of the word. Be aware of /w/ and /r/s too. When an /a/ is next to a /w/ or /r/, these also tend to change the "aa" vowel. An example would be "dawn" /a/, or "yard" /a/. Now, I know this does seem confusing… because it IS confusing! English isn't the easiest to figure out. However, if you look for those lonely little "a's" all on their own, your best bet is to assume it is an /æ/ sound. As you practice, you will better understand how to identify this sound and get faster and more efficient when doing so.

Go through the minimal pairs list and note how the /æ/ words will have a more tense open smile lip position, with the back of the throat more open than the "o" or /a/ words. Listen to your pronunciation and tune your ear to hear the difference.

Feel it!
Just as important as differentiation, is your ability to feel how you produce the /æ/ "aa" sound. Feel how wide and spread open your lips feel for /æ/ "aa" as if your smile is wider somehow. Feel what happens to the back of the tongue as you compare between /a/ "ah" and /æ/ "aa." These tiny subtle changes are what make all the difference for these vowels, so it is important that you can feel the differences in your tongue and lip positions.

A note about /æ/ with /n/ and /m/ after it:
The /æ/ sound changes slightly when a nasal sound comes after it, like in the word "man." The good news is that you don't need to do anything different from what was described above. So, why would it sound different if you're moving your mouth in the exact same way? Well, it is an anticipatory change. This means that you actually anticipate the /n/, which is a nasal sound before you finish the /æ/, so your tongue starts to make its way up to the palate in anticipation of the following /n/ nasal sound. So, the /æ/ in "at" will sound slightly different than the /æ/ in "an." I don't want you to get bogged down by this and spend even a second trying to change your /æ/ before the /m/ and /n/s. My goal is for you to be aware that the vowel might sound slightly different in this situation and that it is absolutely fine.

Do it!
Okay, let's practice the /æ/ sound in words first. Focus on opening the back of your mouth and smiling with your lips.

Words:

access	animal	average
action	answer	back
actor	appetite	bad
add	apple	bag
address	ashtray	bat
adverb	ask	cab
Africa	aspirin	can
after	attack	cap

cat

chapter

classes

contrast

crab

dad

enhance

exactly

factor

fad

family

fat

fax

gap

gas

had

happy

has

hat

impact

jab

lad

lap

mad

man

manager

map

master

mat

matter

Max

nab

nap

national

natural

package

pattern

ram

rat

rather

sad

sat

scrabble

slab

stack

tag

tap

tax

that

traffic

valley

Phrases:

a hat or a cap

after the cab

Appalachian valley

apple package

ask after

ask the actor

at a glance

at the Gap

average answer

average class

back at it

back at the apple orchard

back to back

bad actor

bad rap

bag on my back

that valley

black jacket

cat nap

expensive gas

fact of the matter

fast gas station

fat chance

fat rat

fat taxes

glad you're back

had a blast

had a happy day

happy lad

happy dad

he has a hat

last chance

last chapter

last fax

last man standing

mad hatter

mad man

massive tax

nab a snack

nap after lunch

national academy

national anthem

National Geographic

natural attraction

natural patterns

patterned package

plan of attack

practical habit

radical answer

rather mad

rather sad

sat back

sat there sadly

stack of tags

stack the slabs

tag Adam

take a nap

that crab

that's crass

that traffic

| that's exactly it | traffic jam | trap that rat |

<u>Sentences:</u>

Don't ask that

Have you traveled to Africa?

The animals are fast asleep

Fran did her math in the bathtub

After mass, I am going to cut the grass

Travis has a plaster cast on his hand

The graduate sang for the headmaster

The mine shaft was filled with laughter

They have a lot of brass in that jazz band

Andy has a big appetite for candy apples

Jack likes to play Candy Land and Scrabble

The actor took aspirin and sat by a fan

Cathy took the wrong path to the gas station

Jan, you shouldn't laugh when you eat taffy

My aunt Afra bought an antique ashtray in Africa

Sam had a bad attitude about his academic classes

Ask Pam if she can pass me half a glass of water

I think half of the office staff asks too many questions

Can't you come after your acting class at the national academy?

The more you practice, the faster and more natural you will feel

<u>Reading:</u>

Read daily to see and hear the /æ/ sound. Look for the "a's" as you read along, and feel as you open your mouth to make the accurate /æ/ sound. Compare with your old way until you can hear and feel the difference in pronunciation. The more you practice, the faster and more natural you will feel. You will eventually be ready to use your new sound in conversation.

<u>Conversation:</u>

The vowels are arguably the most difficult sounds to adjust in speech. Unfortunately, the vowels carry a great weight of meaning in English, so it is important to increase your accuracy to improve clarity and meaning. Begin to correct yourself as you speak. This will mean that you will sometimes find yourself repeating words multiple times until you get them. That's okay because this is a process, and it is what you need to go through to achieve the next level of mastery. Let yourself mispronounce words, catch them whenever you can, and adjust your tongue position as much as you can. This process does take time, and it does take focus and intentional speaking. If you find yourself speaking quickly to a friend, catch yourself, as you likely are not adjusting and focusing on your pronunciation. Again this does take a lot of intention at first. The speed and naturalness will come in time, so keep at it, and you will reap the rewards.

Chapter 23: /a/ as in "Hot" & "Pop"

Description:

The /a/ sound is similar to the /æ/ in jaw position. The jaw should be wide open, and your tongue will be very low in the mouth as a result. The tongue should be pulled downward and flat. The lips are relaxed like you are yawning. The lips should not be rounded.

Common Differences:

The most typical change that people make with the /a/ sound is substituting it with a sound that involves a more rounded lip position. People often pronounce the /a/ with rounded lips, similar to /o./ So the word "not" with the /a/ sound will sound more like "note" with the /o/ sound. A word like "raw" will sound like "row" with the /o/ sound. The /a,/ on the other hand, requires that we use a relaxed lip position. Take a look at these minimal pair words comparing /a/ and /o/.

/a/   vs. /o/

on	own	top	taupe	chalk	choke
not	note	sod	sewed	odd	ode
rob	robe	hop	hope	opera	Oprah
rod	road	off	oaf	pause	pose
rot	wrote	calm	comb	taught	tote
mop	mope	walk	woke		

Spelling:

The spelling for /a/ is a bit confusing. Over 80% of the time, we spell the /a/ "ah" sound with an "o." Words like "mop, hop, and rot" will all have the /a/ sound. Where it gets tricky is the other 20%. /a/ can be spelled with "au" as in the words "autumn" and "automatic." /a/ can be spelled with "al" as in words "calm, chalk, stalk, walk, and talk," with the /L/ being silent in these words. We do, at times, spell /a/ with an "a," such as in the word "want, father, and wander." This causes problems, as some of the spellings can overlap with the pronunciation of other sounds. Unfortunately, in these scenarios, the only thing left to do is memorize those "outsider" exception words. However, if you remember the basic generality, you will fix most of your /a/ issues; over 80% of them, to be exact! Words like "to" /tu/ and "so" /so/ are exceptions and will not be pronounced with the /a/ sound.

o   Most common spelling as in "on, off, not"

*Remember, if there is an "e" at the end of the word, the rule does not apply. E.g. "robe."

au   as in "auto"
al   as in "calm, chalk, stalk, walk, talk, all, always"
a   as in "want, father, wander"
aw   as in "crawl"

Less common spellings:
oa   as in "broad"
ou   as in "cough"
ow   as in "knowledge"

Hear it!
Read through the minimal pairs list above and listen to the difference in how they sound. When you round your lips for /o/ as compared to relaxing your lips for /a/, it impacts the sound. Watch for your jaw position as well. Hear how the sound changes if you open your jaw only slightly versus opening your jaw all the way down. Spend time comparing the differences between these pronunciations before moving on to word and sentence level practice.

Feel it!
If you have difficulty hearing and "differentiating" this /a/ vowel from /o/, I want you to feel the difference in your tongue, lips, and jaw. First, feel for your lip position. Feel your lips in an open rounded position, relaxing them and ensuring they are not rounded and tensed. Compare this relaxed lip to the rounded version, and you should feel the difference. Feel how open your mouth position is for /a/"ah" compared to your natural pronunciation of a word.

Do it!
Let's get down to it! Move up the ladder to more and more complex versions as you master each step. Don't move to phrases or sentences until you feel you have grasped a natural rapid rate for your words level practice.

Words:

along	golf	opt
applause	haunt	option
audio	hog	pause
audit	honor	pod
Bob	hop	pop
bomb	hot	pot
bond	job	Rob
box	jog	rock
broad	knot	rod
cause	launch	rot
cod	lock	sauce
cop	log	sauna
copy	long	shop
cost	loss	shot
cot	lost	sod
cross	lot	soft
dog	mob	solid
doll	model	song
dot	mom	spot
drop	naughty	stock
fault	nod	stop
fog	not	talk
fox	object	taught
fraud	odd	Tom
gaudy	off	top
gaunt	offer	upon
gauze	often	vault
gloss	on	walk
God	opera	wrong

Phrases:

a lot of dots	broad topics	frog on a log
a lot of gauze	car audio	haunt the mob
across the pond	caught a cod	high off your hog
along the top	cause a loss of blood	honor God
audience applause	common office problems	honorable cop
awesome cop	cost options	hop on top
Bob talks a lot	dog on a farm	hot in the office
body shop	dropped the mop	hot pot

hot sauce
hot sauna
job at the hospital
lock up the shop
locked vault
logical option
long job
long jog
long walk
loss of job
lost the offer
a lot of fog
a lot of options
modern topics
mom and pop
naughty octopus
non-stop
not a fraud

not very hot
not your fault
odd golf game
off your rocker
offer it often
on and off
on top
opera song
opt to talk
optional object
pause the talk
pop rocks
Rob and Bob
rotting awning
shot off
shot the fox
sleep on the cot
sloppy octopus

sod on the lawn
soft doll
soft object
solid options
solid rock
spot on
stock options
stock up on lip gloss
stocks and bonds
stop talking
talk to Bob
taught a lot
Tom shopped
top to bottom
walk and talk
write on the copy

Sentences:
I tried to dodge the mob
I want to solve this problem
John was offered the job
I wonder where I'll wander to next
He lost ten dollars from his pocket
All the closets in Cape Cod are small
I tried to dodge the mob at the sauna
Just hop on and off the top of this box
Bob finished his novel on rock concerts
This object should operate with a lock
My dad always talks about his jaw problems
I recall following the sound of the bird's call
I almost bought three copies of that movie
Don't you think Doctor Don is a little odd?
I do not recall having a shopping problem
Whoever shot the fox did it from this spot
The doctor operated on him at the hospital
The top of this model car has too much gloss
Some say if you jog a lot, it will harm your body

265

In Boston, whenever you stop, they honk a lot

The success of my trip depends on landing that job

I was caught off guard after turning the light switch on and off

Reading:

Now that you feel comfortable with differentiating the /a/ sound from the /o/, and you can feel exactly what you need to do to pronounce this sound accurately, you can move on to reading. Again, use whatever reading material you enjoy. Look at the words like a puzzle, searching for your new sound ahead as you read. Try your best to feel your pronunciation for /a/ "ah." Record yourself reading daily and review your pronunciation. If you read along as you listen to your speech, you can highlight the words you missed or mispronounced and try again afterward. Practice reading out loud regularly to get yourself familiar with the feeling of using this sound rapidly. The goal with reading is to increase your speed, fluency, and overall naturalness to prepare you for conversation.

Conversation:

Begin to use your new /a/ pronunciation in daily conversation with friends, family, colleagues, and acquaintances. The more variable the environments you use your new sound, and in more topics, the more you will be able to generalize your new skill into your daily life. Generalizing your skills takes time, and you will inevitably fall back into your old articulation patterns when you are engaged in fast-paced conversations or conversations with more emotion and energy. This is expected to happen, so be prepared to give yourself subtle reminders to focus on speaking with intentional articulation throughout the day. At first, you will need to be extremely focused when you speak. In time though, you will become accustomed to your new pronunciation. The more you use your new /a/ "ah" sound in conversation, the more comfortable and natural you will feel speaking with these new patterns.

Chapter 24: /ə/ as in "Uh" (A.K.A. the "Schwa")

Description:

Oh, the schwa! If you are like many of my clients, you have heard about this elusive sound but understand very little about it. The Internet is filled with videos about this sound, yet very few speakers actually understand how to use it. The schwa is the most commonly used vowel in English. It is the vowel sound at the beginning of the word "above," pronounced "uh buv." This sound is so tricky because the spelling of English words pretty much tells us next to nothing about when to use the schwa. There are at least 20 possible spellings of this vowel! Another reason the schwa is so difficult is because it is such a quick sound; it is often very difficult to hear.

The term schwa originates from the Hebrew term "emptiness," which really does seem fitting since the schwa often sounds like it lacks any actual vowel sound. The schwa symbol is /ə/. This sound is what you would produce if you were to say a very quick "uh," as in "**uh**-oh." The /ə/ sound is very short and only occurs in unstressed syllables (See chapter on syllables). When a word has multiple syllables, English rules require that you choose one of those syllables to be "stressed" or said louder, longer, and higher-pitched than the unstressed syllables. So in the word "a ni mal,"

the stressed syllable is the first syllable. "**A** ni mal." The other two vowels in the unstressed syllables turn to a schwa or /ə/, or a short "uh" sound: /æ nə məl/. "AA nuh muhl." The de-emphasis and neutralization of the vowels replaced by schwa help to take away attention from those syllables. So, the stressed syllable is better able to "be the star" of the word and stand out more to the listener.

The /ə/ sound is produced with a very neutral mouth position. What this means is, you essentially do nothing with your lips. Keep your lips slightly apart and your teeth neutral and slightly apart. The tongue is neutral as well. For the tongue to be "neutral" means, literally, just let it sit naturally in the center of your mouth; "uh." There you have it, the "schwa."

Common Differences:

The issue most speakers have with schwa is mainly just not knowing exactly when to use the sound. We can substitute the /ə/ for nearly all of the vowels in English. This

267

means that the use of schwa is tied to the stress structure of the word rather than the spelling.

<u>Spelling:</u>
The spelling of the schwa or /ə/ "uh" varies dramatically and is spread out in frequency amongst all vowels.

For example, we substitute the schwa for the letters:

"o"	26.79% of the time,	e.g., "<u>o</u>ccur" > "uh ker"
"a"	23.91% of the time,	e.g., "yog<u>a</u>" > "yow guh"
"i"	22.40% of the time,	e.g., "an<u>i</u>mal" > "an uh mul"
"e"	12.68% of the time,	e.g., "r<u>e</u>member" > "ruh mem ber"
"ou"	5.58% of the time,	e.g., "fam<u>ous</u>" > "fay muhs"
"u"	4.93% of the time,	e.g., "s<u>u</u>pport" > "suh port"

So you can see why spelling is not your best bet for finding those pesky schwa sounds. The best way to identify the schwa sound is to find the <u>unstressed</u> syllable.

<u>Do it!</u>
Let's take a look at some other schwa words to practice and move up the complexity ladder: isolation> syllable> word> phrase> sentence> reading> conversation.

<u>Isolation:</u>
Repeat the sound "uh," "uh," "uh," "uh," "uh"

<u>Syllables:</u>

puh	zuh	juh
buh	kuh	ruh
tuh	guh	luh
duh	shuh	wuh
suh	chuh	yuh

<u>Feel it!</u>
At times, you may have difficulty with hearing and discriminating the schwa. Discrimination will come with time, so in the meantime, you can use your ability to feel your tongue position to offset this difficulty. Remember, with the schwa, let your tongue rest in your mouth in a neutral position as in "uh" like "uh-oh." Feel how your tongue rests in the middle of your mouth naturally. Now compare that with how high the center of your tongue raises for the "eeee" or /i/ sound. /i/ vs.

/ə/. Repeat them over and over, and feel how the middle of your tongue goes up and down. "ee," "uh," "ee," "uh." The lower, more neutral tongue position is the schwa. Now feel the vowel schwa in the word list above as well.

I have found the most useful strategy for my clients is to deal with the most commonly used words first. We then move on to the most frequently used prefixes (don't worry, we'll discuss and practice next) and then move on to the harder rules to apply the schwa. If you do this, you will have a solid foundation of schwa far before you move on to the difficult stuff and will ultimately be more successful and avoid giving up on it as most people do. Let's not do that! So, I give you the Holy Grail "4 schwa words" to be aware of.

the	"thuh"
a	"uh"
of	"uhv"
to	"tuh"

Let's take a moment to look at these...and try not to panic!

The first thing to note here is that we use the schwa in natural flowing speech. It's not that you HAVE to reduce the vowels to schwa in these words every single time you say them. I am saying that most of the time, these words are reduced to schwa and rarely pronounced in the true vowel form. Listen to native English speakers for even one minute, and you will begin to hear the "uh" I am talking about.

The ("thuh") not ("thee"):
The word "the" will be reduced to schwa "thuh" as long as the next word does not start with a vowel. If the next word begins with a vowel, you can go back to the "thee" pronunciation.

Examples:
the book:	"thuh"
the day:	"thuh"
the cookie:	"thuh"
the owl:	"thee"
the author:	"thee"
the end:	"thee"

Let's Practice:
all the way out
at the end of the day
begs the question
but in the meantime
by the way
don't pass the buck
for the most part
get to the point
going off the grid
face the music
have to bite the bullet
he kicked the bucket
he paved the way
he's all over the place
he's on the run
he's the cock of the walk
he's under the weather
I call the shots
I'm on the fence
I'm on the job
in the face of fear
it's all the time
it's in the air
it's in the making
it's off the hook
it's on the ground
it's the law of the land
just toe the line
let's clear the air
let's just cut to the chase
on the spot
off the beaten track
on the contrary
on the go
on the other hand
one and the same
out of the blue
out of the way
over the counter meds
seize the day
she let the cat out of the bag
she made the cut

she's dressed to the <u>n</u>ines
shooting the <u>b</u>reeze
state of the <u>a</u>rt
that's beyond the <u>p</u>ale
that's out of the <u>q</u>uestion
that's over the <u>t</u>op
the <u>e</u>nd
the <u>o</u>nly one
under the <u>h</u>ood
we're on the <u>s</u>ame page
what a pain in the <u>n</u>eck
you're on the <u>b</u>all

The other situation in which "the" is pronounced as "thee" is when you might emphasize something. E.g. "that is theeeee best!"

Practice "thuh" with a neutral "uh" for the following phrases:
You're th<u>e</u> best
I'm going to th<u>e</u> store
That's th<u>e</u> one I wanted
I laughed so hard at th<u>e</u> movie last night

<u>A ("uh") not ("eh"):</u>
Similar to "the," the word "a" is often pronounced as "uh."

Examples:
a desk	"uh"
a fork	"uh"
a report	"uh"
a walk	"uh"

<u>Let's practice:</u>
<u>a</u> paper got jammed
do you have <u>a</u> clock here?
have <u>a</u> great evening
have <u>a</u> nice day
he had <u>a</u> plan
he's <u>a</u> lawyer
I grabbed <u>a</u> piece of paper
I had <u>a</u> report due today

I held <u>a</u> cup in my hand

I learned <u>a</u> lesson

I love <u>a</u> good story

I need <u>a</u> pen

I need <u>a</u> washroom break

I need to make <u>a</u> decision

she sat in <u>a</u> chair

that was <u>a</u> good decision

that's <u>a</u> great plan

there's <u>a</u> crumb on your shirt

we did <u>a</u> good job

we had <u>a</u> deal

we had <u>a</u> discussion

we're in <u>a</u> good place

what <u>a</u> beautiful place

what <u>a</u> day

what <u>a</u> game-changer

what <u>a</u> great game

won <u>a</u> prize

you had <u>a</u> great idea

To ("tuh") not too ("too"):

Similar to the word "the," "to" is often pronounced as "tuh" or /tə/. Again, if a vowel follows this word, then "to" should be pronounced as "tooo" or /tu/. Just as with "the," any time you are emphasizing the "to," you would no longer reduce it but pronounce it in its full form "tooo" or /tu/.

Examples:

To <u>the</u> store: "tuh"

To <u>my</u> house: "tuh"

To <u>your</u> client: "tuh"

To go shopping: "tuh"

To <u>our</u> place: "too"

To <u>a</u> class: "too"

To <u>open</u> it: "too"

Let's practice:

according to <u>le</u>gend	back to <u>back</u>	cater to <u>you</u>
appeal to <u>the</u> masses	bound to <u>hap</u>pen	come to <u>terms</u> with it

cut to the chase
day to day
desire to love
down to earth
drink to that
end to end
eye to eye
face to face
fall to the ground
get to go
go to my place
go to our place
have to understand
he's dressed to the nines
head to head
hold on to your hat
hot to trot
I look forward to it
I'll see to it
in order to get there
it boils down to this

it comes down to you
it will come to pass
it's up to date
kept up to speed
lead to win
lean into it
learn to speak mandarin
live up to your standard
look up to you
need to get around
next to me
not to mention
on to the next
people to see
places to explore
put down to paper
read to learn more
refer to the sign
resort to jokes
right to privacy
side to side

so to speak
speak to that point
stand up to him
stick to it
straight to the point
subject to reason
thanks to you
time to time
to and fro
to begin with
to no avail
turn to your partner
up to no good
used to do it
want to understand
way to go
what to do
where to go
willing to forgive
year to date
your right to vote

Schwa In Prefixes

First, let's talk prefixes. A prefix is that part of a word before the root of a word. A prefix can be added to many words to change its meaning. Examples of prefixes are a-/be-/re-/de-/to-/con- when added to the beginning of words. So, the prefix "re" can be seen in "remember, return, recite, redeem." (See other examples below).

When learning about the schwa, it is best to focus on some basic rules first to help you get a better grasp on what to do. One of the best ways to incorporate the schwa is to practice prefixes of words. Prefixes are those beginning parts of words (a, be, re, de, to, con, su) that you hear in many words. Prefixes are generally not stressed, which is why we can reduce them to the schwa. Practice reducing vowels in the prefixes of these words to "uh" or schwa instead of the actual vowel you see. The schwa is a neutral vowel, meaning the tongue is in a neutral or middle position in the mouth. It occurs in unstressed syllables and is pronounced as a quick "uh."

"A" prefixes:

above "uh"	Put the jar above the honey
amount "uh"	There's a large amount of work to do
attention "uh"	Give me your undivided attention
about "uh"	What's that book about?
another "uh"	I want another one
amaze "uh"	It will amaze you!
again "uh"	Let's try that again
around "uh"	Let's go around the block

"be" prefixes:

before "buh"	I'll go there before I go shopping
because "buh"	I'm hungry because I missed lunch
behind "buh"	The book is behind the box
between "buh"	I put the pen between the books
begin "buh"	Let's begin practicing
believe "buh"	I can't believe I never knew about the schwa!
behavior "buh"	I don't condone this behavior

"re" prefixes:

remember "ruh"	I can't remember where I put it
remain "ruh"	Please remain calm
report "ruh"	I finished the report today
review "ruh"	I'll review your rebuttal
reliable "ruh"	I am so very reliable
refine "ruh"	That is refined sugar
replenish "ruh"	We must replenish the food stores

"de" prefixes:

decide "duh"	She couldn't decide which color to choose
detergent "duh"	I'm out of detergent
determine "duh"	You've got to be determined
deprive "duh"	Don't deprive me of chocolate
delete "duh"	Oops, I deleted it!

274

deliver "duh"	I got the delivery today
debate "duh"	He won the debate
devour "duh"	My dog devoured the sandwich

"to" prefixes:

today "tuh"	I'll get groceries today
toward "tuh"	Go toward the last isle
together "tuh"	The two pieces go together as a set
tomorrow "tuh"	We can go there tomorrow
tonight "tuh"	I'll meet you there tonight

"con" prefixes:

control "cun"	I have no control over that
contain "cun"	It contains nuts
conduct "cun"	This metal conducts electricity
consent "cun"	I have his consent
confirm "cun"	Can you confirm this?
connect "cun"	It's great to connect with you again
consist "cun"	It consists of two ingredients
consult "cun"	I'll have to consult my doctor
concise "cun"	That report is concise
conceal "cun"	Don't conceal the evidence
confuse "cun"	I'm confused
confess "cun"	The suspect confessed
condone "cun"	I don't condone this behavior
confide "cun"	He confided in me

"su" prefixes:

submerge "suh"	The basement was submerged in water
submit "suh"	I'll submit the documents tomorrow
subscribe "suh"	Would you like to subscribe to our emails?
subtract "suh"	You can subtract the tax
suburbia "suh"	I live in suburbia
succeed "suh"	He's worked very hard and will succeed in his career
success "suh"	What a great success story
successor "suh"	You will be my successor when I'm retired
suggest "suh"	I would like to suggest another opinion
supply "suh"	There is an excess supply of this product

support "suh"	Thank you for your support
suppose "suh"	I suppose so
supposed "suh"	She was supposed to call today
suppress "suh"	He often suppresses his feelings
supreme "suh"	To be supreme is to be the best
surprise "suh"	What a welcomed surprise
surround "suh"	Surround yourself with supportive people
suspect "suh"	I suspect he didn't notice the sign
suspend "suh"	Johnny was suspended today
suspense "suh"	That episode left me in suspense
suspicion "suh"	I have a suspicion that he was the bad guy in the show after all
sustain "suh"	If you can sustain this position for a few seconds, you will gain strength

Let's look at the various examples of how schwa is represented in all the different vowels. Again, remember, it is not the vowel that dictates whether you make the "uh" sound or not. It is whether the vowel is in a stressed or unstressed syllable. The schwa can only occur in an unstressed syllable.

Schwa In Different Vowels

Schwa in "I" words

One typical issue people have with schwa is that they substitute the /i/ or "eee" sound for "i's" in unstressed syllables instead of using a schwa /ə/. So, the word "animal" would sound more like "aa nee mal." The schwa is the more common pronunciation used by native North American English speakers, so the pronunciation would sound more like "aa nuh muhl."

Examples:

The General North American Accent is pronounced using schwa /ə/ in the following words.

The stressed syllables have been capitalized here so you can better identify that the shwa occurs in the unstressed syllables. The underlined syllables contain the schwa.

CA pi tal:	"puh"	/pə/	Should sound like "ca puh tal"
A ni mal:	"nuh"	/nə/	should sound like "a nuh mal"

276

U ni form:	"nuh" /nə/	should sound like "u nuh form"
DI ffi cult:	"fuh" /fə/	should sound like "di ffuh cult"
PEN cil:	"suhl" /səl/	should sound like "pen suhl"
COU sin:	"zuhn" /zən/	should sound like "cou zuhn"
MEN tion:	"chuhn" /tʃən/	should sound like "men chuhn"
per MI ssion:	"shuhn" /ʃən/	should sound like "per mi shuhn"

We will need to pull our tongue down to a neutral flat position and say a quick "uh" sound instead to fix this issue. Feel your tongue pull down for the "uh" sound. You may need to open your jaw slightly to help to pull your tongue downward.

Schwa in "o" words

Another typical change people make to /ə/ for "o" words is substituting the /o/ or "oh" sound for "o's" in unstressed syllables. So, the word "octopus" would not sound like "oc tow pus," but rather, "oc tuh pus."

Examples:

com PU ter:	"cum" /kəm/	should sound like "cuhm pyou der"
con FIRM:	"cun" /kən/	should sound like "cuhn ferm"
com BINE:	"cum" /kəm/	should sound like "cuhm bine"
OC to pus:	"tuh" /tə/	should sound like "oc tuh pus"
GA llon:	"lun" /lən/	should sound like "gaa luhn"
PUR pose:	"puss"/pəs/	should sound like "pur puhs"
FA mous:	"mus" /məs/	should sound like "fay muhs"

Schwa in "a" words

Examples:

a BOVE:	"uh" /ə/	should sound like "uh bove"
a MOUNT:	"uh" /ə/	should sound like "uh mount"
FI na lly:	"nuh" /nə/	should sound like "fi nuh lly"
THOU sand:	"zuhnd" /zənd/	should sound like "thou zuhnd"
AT las:	"luhs" /ləs/	should sound like "at luhs"
SA lad:	"luhd" /ləd/	should sound like "sa luhd"

Schwa in "e" words

Examples:

re PEAT:	"ruh" /rə/	should sound like "ruh peet"
de VE lop:	"duh" /də/	should sound like "duh veh lup"
E ne my:	"nuh" /nə/	should sound like "eh nuh mee"
com pe TI tion:	"puh" /pə/	should sound like "com puh tih shun"

| I <u>tem</u>: | "duhm" /dəm/ | should sound like "eye <u>duhm</u>" |
| BUS <u>iness</u>: | "nuhs" /nəs/ | should sound like "biz <u>nuhss</u>" |

Schwa in "u" words
Examples:

<u>su</u> CCEED:	"suh" /sə/	should sound like "<u>suck</u> seed"
<u>su</u> PPORT:	"suh" /sə/	should sound like "<u>suh</u> port"
<u>tu</u> MUL tu ous:	"tuh" /tə/	should sound like "<u>tuh</u> mall chew us"
<u>su</u> PPLY:	"suh" /səp/	should sound like "<u>suh</u> ply"
FO <u>cus</u>:	"cuss" /kəs/	should sound like "fow <u>cuhs</u>"
VI <u>rus</u>:	"russ" /rəs/	should sound like "vi <u>ruhs</u>"
AU <u>gust</u>:	"gust" /gəst/	should sound like "Ah <u>guhst</u>"

Schwa in "y" words
Examples:

<u>sy</u> RINGE: "suh" /sə/	should sound like "<u>suhh</u> rihnj"
<u>py</u> JA mas: "puh" /pə/	should sound like "<u>puh</u> jaa muz"
VI <u>nyl</u>: "nuhl" /nəl/	should sound like "vy <u>nuhl</u>"
CA ta <u>lyst</u>: "lust" /ləst/	should sound like "caa duh <u>lust</u>"

Hear it!

Begin to listen to the schwa in other native English speakers. The next time you listen to two speakers, try to find the stressed words and syllables, then listen to the sounds and words in between; these are the unstressed syllables and words. Once you can identify the unstressed syllables and words, you will be able to hear that they're spoken very quickly and that they are pronounced with a schwa "uh" sound. Pay special attention to the 4 "holy grail" words: "to, the, a, of."

Let's look at some schwa sounds in words spelled with "I" in the unstressed syllable. Go through the word list, hear the short "uh" sounds, and compare them with your typical pronunciation. If you notice you are saying "eee," pull the middle of your tongue down, so it rests naturally in your mouth, and say "uh." Listen and compare until it is clear you can hear and differentiate between your sound and the schwa. The stressed syllables are CAPITALIZED, and the unstressed syllable with schwa is underlined.

A <u>ni</u> mal	AR <u>bi</u> trate	DET <u>ri</u> ment
AC <u>ci</u> dent	AR <u>ti</u> fact	MO <u>ni</u> tor
AP <u>ti</u> tude	CA <u>pi</u> tal	MUL <u>ti</u> tude

278

OP <u>ti</u> mist   PRO <u>mi</u> nent   U <u>ni</u> corn
PO <u>li</u> tics   SEN <u>si</u> tive   U <u>ni</u> form
PRE <u>di</u> cate   SO <u>li</u> tude   VE <u>ni</u> son
PRE <u>si</u> dent   SUB <u>sti</u> tute

Schwa In Suffixes

Words:
A suffix is the tail or ending added to a root word. "ity" is an example of a suffix, and it can be added to many words like "rarity, community, and equity." Many words that end in similar suffixes or "tails" like "ity" and "ical" include the schwa. The "ity" suffix would be pronounced as "uh dee." The schwa will replace the unstressed syllable vowel.

SO...
The suffix or ending of a word with –ity is pronounced /ədi/ or "uh dee" (we also turn the /t/ to a /d/ called the "flap /t/.")

The suffix or end of a word with –ical is pronounced /ɪkəl/ or "uh kuhl"

Let's practice. Add the pronunciation "uh dee" and "uh kuhl" in these words below.

"Ity":

ability	humanity	quality
activity	humidity	reality
authority	intensity	reliability
capability	majority	sanity
cavity	necessity	security
clarity	personality	severity
dignity	popularity	stupidity
electricity	possibility	university
festivity	publicity	vicinity

"ical":

chemical	critical	electrical
comical	economical	geographical

grammatical	medical	practical
historical	musical	technical
identical	nautical	typical
logical	physical	vertical
mechanical	political	

Try the schwa with more "i" words. The thing to note here, especially in words with multiple "i's," is that the UNSTRESSED syllable will include the schwa. So, the word "**DI**fficult," includes stress in the "di" part of the word, so it would sound like /dɪ fə klt/, with only the second vowel turning to schwa. Below the stressed syllables will be in upper case letters and bold, and the schwa will be underlined.

"I":

ACcident (ak "suh" dent)	**CRI**minal	o**RI**ginal
a**ME**rican	**DI**fficult	par**TI**cipate
Animal	fa**CI**litate	**PE**ssimist
ARticle	**GRA**titude	**PO**litics
CANdidate	**HE**licopter	**PRE**sident
CApital	**HE**sitate	**PRIN**cipal
CARnival	**HUR**ricane	**SEN**sitive
cer**TI**ficate	**IN**stitute	sig**NI**ficant
CItizen	in**TE**lligent	**SI**milar
com**PA**rison	**LA**titude	**U**nicorn
COMpliment	**MA**nicure	**U**niform
	Officer	**U**niverse

Final unstressed "a" words:

VIa	**MA**ma	**MO**cha
ERa	**SO**fa	**LLA**ma
DIva	**ME**ga	**AOR**ta
TUba	**NO**va	**TE**sla
SOya	**CO**la	**SAL**sa
PIta	**GA**la	**CO**mma
Aqua	**VI**sa	**NIN**ja
COma	**IDE**a	**AP**nea
TUna	**DA**ta	**SCU**ba
YOga	**A**rea	**SAU**na
AUra	Ko**A**la	**ZE**bra
LAva	**PAR**ka	**PAN**da

MANi<u>a</u>	Alph<u>a</u>	aNEmi<u>a</u>
oMEg<u>a</u>	Oper<u>a</u>	baNAn<u>a</u>
aROm<u>a</u>	maRI<u>a</u>	maRIn<u>a</u>
CObr<u>a</u>	aREn<u>a</u>	ASthm<u>a</u>
PASt<u>a</u>	DRAm<u>a</u>	TRAUm<u>a</u>
PIzz<u>a</u>	CHIn<u>a</u>	CInem<u>a</u>
PLAz<u>a</u>	EXtr<u>a</u>	aGEnd<u>a</u>
ULtr<u>a</u>	MEdi<u>a</u>	CAmera
VIll<u>a</u>	paJAm<u>a</u>	
DELt<u>a</u>	PHObi<u>a</u>	

Mixed Vowels: More Practice:

The Underlined unstressed syllables include the schwa sound. All stressed syllables are in bold and upper case letters. Many of these words have more than one schwa within the word, but for simplicity, I have only underlined the vowel in each category pronounced as a schwa.

A

<u>A</u>	/ə/
<u>a</u>MAZE	/ə/
<u>a</u>BOUT	/ə/
PLEA<u>sant</u>	/zənt/
<u>a</u>GAIN	/ə/
<u>ba</u>LLOON	/bə/

E

PRO<u>blem</u>	/bləm/
CE<u>le</u>brate	/lə/
E<u>ne</u>my	/nə/
THE	/ðə/

I

DU<u>pli</u>cate	/plə/
PRE<u>si</u>dent	/zə/
aMER<u>i</u>ca	/ə/
FA<u>mi</u>ly	/mə/

O

ON<u>ion</u>	/jən/

oCCUR	/ə/
to**DAY**	/tə/
FAmous	/məs/
to**WARD**	/tə/
GAllon	/lən/
PArrot	/rət/
BOttom	/dəm/
FREEdom	/dəm/

U
FOcus	/kəs/
su**PPORT**	/sə/
su**CCESS**	/sə/
CIRcumstance	/kəm/
ALbum	/bəm/

Y
SyRINGE	/sə/
a**NA**lysis	/lə/
penns**yl**VAnia	/səl/

Practice:

TIP #1: First, find the stressed syllable and identify each schwa amongst the UNSTRESSED syllable vowels.

TIP #2: The words "to, the, of, a" ("tuh, thuh, uhv, uh") are all produced with a schwa unless followed by a vowel.

WORDS: Find the "schwa" (answer key below):

above	adopt	confirm
amount	alone	combine
attention	apply	capital
about	ahead	animal
another	allow	uniform
amaze	occur	difficult
again	today	accident
away	toward	monitor
amuse	together	optimist
awake	tomorrow	politics
alarm	computer	president

prominent	humidity	clarity
sensitive	intensity	dignity
solitude	majority	geographical
substitute	necessity	chemical
unicorn	personality	historical
uniform	publicity	comical
activity	quality	critical
authority	reliability	physical
capability	sanity	technical
popularity	security	identical
possibility	severity	logical
electricity	stupidity	mechanical
humanity	vicinity	medical

WORDS: Answer Key:

aBOVE	**CA**pi**t**al	ma**JO**ri**t**y
aMOUNT	**A**ni**m**al	ne**CE**ss**i**ty
aTTENtion	**DI**ffi**c**ult	perso**NA**li**t**y
aBOUT	**AC**ci**d**ent	pu**BLI**ci**t**y
aNOther	**MO**ni**t**or	**QUA**li**t**y
aMAZE	**OP**ti**m**ist	re**A**li**t**y
aGAIN	**PO**li**t**ics	re**l**ia**BI**li**t**y
aWAY	**PRE**si**d**ent	**SAN**i**t**y
aMUSE	**PRO**mi**n**ent	se**CU**ri**t**y
aWAKE	**SEN**si**t**ive	se**VE**ri**t**y
aLARM	**SO**li**t**ude	stu**PI**di**t**y
aDOPT	**SUB**sti**t**ute	vi**CI**ni**t**y
aLONE	**U**ni**c**orn	**CLA**ri**t**y
aPPLY	**U**ni**f**orm	**DIG**ni**t**y
aHEAD	uni**VER**si**t**y	geo**GRA**phi**c**al
aLLOW	ac**TI**vi**t**y	**CHE**mi**c**al
oCCUR	**au**THO**ri**ty	his**TO**ri**c**al
t**o**DAY	capa**BI**li**t**y	**CO**mi**c**al
t**o**WARD	popu**LA**ri**t**y	**CRI**ti**c**al
t**o**GEther	possi**BI**li**t**y	**PHY**si**c**al
t**o**MOrrow	elec**TRI**ci**t**y	**TECH**ni**c**al
c**o**mPUter	hu**MA**ni**t**y	i**DEN**ti**c**al
c**o**nFIRM	hu**MI**di**t**y	**LO**gi**c**al
c**o**mBINE	in**TEN**si**t**y	me**CHA**ni**c**al

Med<u>i</u>c<u>a</u>l

<u>Phrases: Find the schwas (answer key below):</u>

security uniform	confirm today	about another
sensitive personality	computer monitor	another alarm
logical animal	president in politics	apply ahead
difficult activity	university activity	tomorrow's alarm
logical optimist	adopted animal	bananas for breakfast

<u>PHRASES: Answer key:</u>

se**CU**r<u>i</u>ty **U**n<u>i</u>form	con**FIRM** t<u>o</u>**DAY**	<u>a</u>**BOUT** <u>a</u>**NO**ther
SENs<u>i</u>tive pers<u>o</u>**NA**l<u>i</u>ty	com**PU**ter **MO**n<u>i</u>tor	<u>a</u>**NO**ther <u>a</u>**LARM**
LOg<u>i</u>cal **A**n<u>i</u>m<u>a</u>l	**PRES**<u>i</u>dent in **PO**l<u>i</u>tics	<u>a</u>**PPLY** <u>a</u>**HEAD**
DIff<u>i</u>c<u>u</u>lt ac**TI**v<u>i</u>ty	un<u>i</u>**VER**s<u>i</u>ty ac**TI**v<u>i</u>ty	t<u>o</u>**MO**rrow's <u>a</u>**LARM**
LOg<u>i</u>cal **OP**t<u>i</u>mist	<u>a</u>**DO**pted **A**n<u>i</u>m<u>a</u>l	b<u>a</u>**NA**n<u>a</u>s for **BREAK**f<u>a</u>st

<u>Sentences:</u>

Use the words above in sentences. Make an extra effort to emphasize and highlight the stressed syllable by saying them louder, higher pitch, and longer. The unstressed syllable is where you will place your "uh" schwa sound.

Remember that even words with just one syllable can be unstressed in a sentence, so these words will often carry the schwa sound (to, a, the, of). Think of it as just another way of making that unstressed word be emphasized even less by making the vowel neutral and quick.

<u>Examples: (answer key below)</u>
Here are some examples of schwa in a sentence:

What are you doing tonight?
I have to focus on my work today
I ate a carrot and a banana for breakfast
I read an atlas with the most amazing maps
She was amazed about his success
I didn't know how to respond to that question
My manager went around the department
I love to nap on the sofa when I'm alone
The circus performance blew us away
He suggested a better supply system for our company to succeed

I believe it's the second time it happened today

Do the review today

I'm going to go to the store

I have to go to the washroom

He has to review the report because it's due tomorrow

SENTENCES: Answer key

What are you doing to**NIGHT**?

I have t<u>o</u> **FO**c<u>us</u> on my work t<u>o</u>**DAY**

I ate <u>a</u> **CA**rr<u>ot</u> and <u>a</u> ba**NA**n<u>a</u> at **BREAK**f<u>a</u>st

I read an **AT**l<u>as</u> with th<u>e</u> most <u>a</u>**MA**zing maps!

She was <u>a</u>**MAZED** <u>a</u>**BOUT** his s<u>u</u>**CCESS**

I didn't know how t<u>o</u> re**SPOND** t<u>o</u> that **QUE**st<u>io</u>n

My **MA**n<u>a</u>ger went <u>a</u>**ROUND** th<u>e</u> de**PART**ment

I love t<u>o</u> nap on the **SO**f<u>a</u> when I'm <u>a</u>**LONE**

The **CIR**c<u>us</u> per**FOR**mance blew us <u>a</u>**WAY**

He s<u>u</u>**GGES**ted <u>a</u> better s<u>u</u>**PPLY SYS**t<u>e</u>m for our **COM**pany t<u>o</u> suc**CEED**

I be**LIEVE** it's th<u>e</u> **SE**c<u>o</u>nd time it **HA**pp<u>e</u>ned t<u>o</u>**DAY**

Do th<u>e</u> re**VIEW** t<u>o</u>**DAY**

I'm going t<u>o</u> go t<u>o</u> th<u>e</u> **STORE**

I have t<u>o</u> go t<u>o</u> th<u>e</u> **WASH**room

He has t<u>o</u> re**VIEW** th<u>e</u> re**PORT** be**CAUSE** it's due t<u>o</u>**MO**rrow

/ʌ/ "Uh" in Stressed Syllables

I wanted to make a short note about the "uh" sound in stressed syllables. You can hear this sound in words like "mug, bug, sun, and gum." The /ʌ/ sound is exactly the same as the "uh" in the schwa; only it is slightly longer, louder, and higher-pitched since it occurs in stressed syllables. Your meaning will be impacted if you tend to produce an /a/ "ah" sound instead of /uh/. So, "nut" will sound more like "not." The fix is to keep your jaw in a neutral position and not open it as widely as you might with /a/ "ah." Keep your tongue resting in the middle of your mouth.

Spelling:

U   "up" (>90% of spelling) – If words have an "e" at the end, this rule does not apply.

o_e   "one, none, done, come, some, love, glove, dove"

<u>Less Common Spelling:</u> (words to memorize)

o   " wonder, son, brother, mother"

oe   "doesn't "

ou   "young, double, trouble"

au   "because"

a   "was, what"

<u>Auditory Discrimination:</u>

/^/ "uh"	nut	rub	bun	but
/o/ "ow"	note	robe	bone	boat
/a/ "ah"	not	Rob	bonne	bought

<u>Minimal Pairs:</u>

/a/ vs /^/

body	buddy	fond	fund	paunch	punch
bon	bun	golf	gulf	pock	puck
Bonnie	bunny	gone	gun	pomp	pump
bog	bug	got	gut	poppy	puppy
boss	bus	haunt	hunt	pot	putt
bought	butt	hog	hug	Rob	rub
call	cull	honk	hunk	Ron	run
cause	cuz	hot	hut	scoff	scuff
clock	cluck	jog	jug	shot	shut
cob	cub	knob	nub	slosh	slush
calm	come	lock	luck	sob	sub
cop	cup	log	lug	soccer	sucker
cot	cut	loll	lull	sock	suck
cough	cuff	long	lung	stock	stuck
dock	duck	lost	lust	talk	tuck
dog	dug	mock	muck	Tommy	tummy
doll	dull	mod	mud	stomp	stump
Don	done	non	nun	wander	wonder
fawn	fun	not	nut	wrong	wrung

<u>Practice words:</u>

Be<u>cause</u> "buh KUZ"	bump	does
bug	club	doesn't

286

duck	none/nun	thumb
dumb	of	ugly
flood	one/won	uncle
fudge	plunge	under
fun	pug	up
gum	rub	us
hung	shut	was
much	son/sun	wasn't
mug	such	young

Practice Phrases:

all done	hungry tummy	shirt cuff
bear cub	in the gulf	shut up
because it stung	in the muck	soft bun
big blunder	is it any wonder	son of mine
big bug	jug of water	stuck in the office
big cup	just because	such dumb luck
bump in the road	lick a sucker	take a plunge
catholic nun	love and lust	tasty nut
clubhouse logo	lug a barrel	thumbs up
clucking duck	mini putt	tiny nub
collapsed lung	much too much	tree stump
cut my knee	my buddy	trust fund
cute bunny	need a hug	tuck in your shirt
dirty mud	no fun	ugly duckling
dirty scuff	none of it	Uncle Bud
does it matter?	not a dull moment	underwater excursion
doesn't seem so	of mine	up and down
duck hunt	on a bus	was it there
dug a hole	one more	wasn't afraid
dumb luck	pizza hut	wet slush
fudge sundae	pump the brakes	what a lull
fun games	punch the bag	what a suck
gum tree	rub it in	with us
gut feeling	rub the lamp	young duck
hockey puck	scary bug	young puppy
hung it up	scary mummy	

Practice sentences:

I prefer this cuff much more than that one
I had so much fun at the club last night
My son laid in the sun all day long
I wonder how much chewing gum I had today
I took care of my uncle's puppy
The volcano has begun to erupt
I hung too much in my closet
He doesn't sound dumb at all when he reads a script
It's up to us to discuss the important topics
Gus is always in such a rush
There's a bump under my thumb
None of it is up to you
I'm so lucky I unlocked that door
Don was done with his work
There's a beautiful duck on the dock
Bonny is great at baking buns
The bug fell in the bog
I told my boss my car had broken down and I needed to take the bus
I bought a new car, but I don't know how to drive a stick shift
I bought a clock that clucks like a chicken each hour
The bear cub stole my cob of corn
The cop dropped his cup of coffee on the floor
I covered my cough with the cuff of my shirt
My dog dug the biggest hole in my yard
Playing with dolls is never dull for my daughter
I went golfing in the Gulf of Mexico
I got that sinking feeling in my gut
Never hug a hog if you want to stay clean
Let's go to the hot dog hut
I always jog with a jug of water
When I run long distances, my lungs have trouble
Her mommy dressed as a mummy for Halloween
That is not a nut
I put the puck in my pocket
Our new puppy ate a poppy
Rob rubbed his eyes
I scoffed at the scuff on my shoe
She sobbed when she dropped her submarine sandwich
He gets a sucker after each soccer game

The stock market seems to be stuck
I stomped on the tree stump
I wonder where he'll wander to next
He wrung the rag wrong, so it's still sopping wet

Reading:

The schwa sound can take a little more time to get used to than other sounds, given the complexity and variability involved. It is best to get yourself familiar with this sound when listening and spend more time practicing while reading aloud. Reading and recording yourself speaking will give you a stronger understanding of when to use the schwa and help you pay greater attention to the stress in your pronunciation of English words. Read out loud often. Find the unstressed syllables and practice your pronunciation of schwa daily. My clients often find it helpful to listen to transcripts of speakers on the Internet and listen to the stress patterns as they read along with a video. You can find transcripts of nearly everything. TedTalk videos are an excellent source for listening to great speakers as there is a corresponding transcript of their speech below each video. Either way you decide to practice, use reading aloud as a tool to gain familiarity with the schwa sound.

Conversation:

Slowly insert the schwa into your everyday conversations. Again, this sound is not something to change in every single word at all times. Rather, it is a form of naturalness that increases as you use the schwa more and more. You can start with words like "the" and "a," as they will come up often. As you increase your familiarity with more and more schwa words, you will find using this sound regularly to be less and less difficult. Practice with strangers. Practice with yourself by recording your speech on your phone or computer. Conversation is the most challenging phase, as you will need to overcome the unfamiliar feelings you will experience as you speak differently. Keep at it. If your goal is to be understood by others and to speak with a closer approximation to the general North American English accent, this sound will take you far in reaching your goals.

Chapter 25: /ʊ/ as in "Look & Put"

<u>Description:</u>
The horseshoe-looking symbol /ʊ/ represents the sound produced for words like "look, good, put, and foot." Linguists refer to this sound as the "upsilon." This sound causes issues for many speakers since the spelling can really throw you off! Most non-native English speakers are astounded by the pronunciation of this sound. They are shocked to learn that they have been explicitly taught to pronounce it as the "oo" or /u/ sound by their non-native English-speaking teachers, or they were convinced of the /u/ pronunciation because of its spelling. It is entirely understandable too! This sound is frequently used for a few particular words and can cause confusion if not pronounced as expected. With this sound, meaning can be affected by a slight change in your lip and tongue position.

The /ʊ/ sound is produced very similarly to the "uh" sound, like the schwa. I often show my clients to just say the schwa or "uh" sound while slightly rounding and protruding their lips, and voila!

The upsilon /ʊ/ sound is produced with the tongue in a neutral position, meaning you will relax your tongue and let it sit and rest in your mouth. So, if you just say "uh," your tongue is in a perfect position. Notice, too, that you must slightly lower your jaw so that your teeth are just slightly apart. A crucial element of this sound, however, is the lip position. The lips are slightly rounded but NOT fully rounded like in the "ooo" sound. Think about it as if you are just about to make your lips into a pucker, but you stop before you've completed. Your lips should feel almost protruded, as if you are trying to push them out and away from your face but not rounded into a small circle like a /w/ or "ooo" sound.

<u>Common Differences:</u>
The most typical mispronunciation of the /ʊ/ sound is to produce the "oo" or /u/ instead. The result is words like "look" /lʊk/ sounding more like "Luke" /luk/. To increase the accuracy of this sound, we must lower the middle of our tongue to a more neutral position, similar to how your tongue position is for "uh," and then add a slight lip pursing instead of fully rounding your lips.

<u>Spelling:</u>

One of the many reasons this sound is challenging for non-native English speakers is inconsistent spelling. There are various ways to spell the /ʊ/ sound, with an o, u, ou, or even oo. The double "oo" spelling adds extra difficulty as there really is no way to differentiate whether we pronounce it as /u/ "oo" vs. /ʊ/, so the speaker must memorize the words. Luckily, there are really only a handful of words spelled with the "oo" and pronounced as /ʊ/, so this will make your work a little easier.

Let's look at the various ways we can spell the /ʊ/ sound: This is an exhaustive list, so try your best to memorize these. Memorizing the upsilon sound will prevent you from getting confused with the other vowel pronunciations.

"o":

bosom	wolves
wolf	woman

"oo" pronounced as /ʊ/:

book	hood	stood
brook	hook	took
cook	look	wood
crook	rook	wool
foot	shook	
good	soot	

*the words "hoof" and "roof" can be pronounced as /u/ or /ʊ/ as both are accepted pronunciations in English

"u" pronounced as /ʊ/:

bull	butcher	pull
bullet	cushion	push
bush	full	put
butch	pudding	sugar

"ou" pronounced as /ʊ/:

could
would
should

Hear it!

Now that you are more familiar with the words associated with this sound, try to hear the difference in pronunciation when you change your tongue and lip positions. Let's start with some minimal pairs to get familiar with the difference in sound. As you pull your tongue up for the /u/ or "oo" sound, you should notice your lips rounded tightly. When you compare the /ʊ/ sound, you should feel how the middle of your tongue pulls down to the neutral middle position, and your lips are more relaxed in a protruded position.

Minimal Pairs /ʊ/ vs /u/:

look	/Luke	would	/wooed	could	/cooed
pull	/pool	stood	/stewed	cookie	/kooky
full	/fool	soot	/suit	hood	/who'd
should	/shooed	took	/toque		

Feel it!

As you improve your differentiation skills, you should also focus on how the middle of the tongue feels as it shifts lower for the /ʊ/ sound. The tongue position should be nearly the same as if you were to say "uh" as in "uh-oh," then slightly purse and round your lips outward to create the /ʊ/ sound. Look in the mirror to see how the lips change position between the two sounds. Your lips should look like they're flat and only slightly rounded, not like a /w/ or "oo" at all. Get accustomed to how different this sound feels in the mouth because being able to feel that difference will get you far in your ability to distinguish if you have correctly adjusted your tongue position or not. For many, the ability to hear the difference comes a little later. The sounds continue to seem similar to the ears until intentional listening exercises improve this issue. Your brain may not be able to differentiate the difference quite yet, so focus on the feeling of lips and tongue positions. If you focus on the tongue position and "feeling" of the lip protrusion, you will give your ears time to adjust and improve your differentiation skills over time.

Do it!

Since you have spent the time hearing the difference between /u/ and /ʊ/, and you feel comfortable with your tongue and lips position when you produce the /ʊ/ consistently, you are ready to move forward and practice.

Isolation:

Repeat the sound in isolation: /ʊ/, /ʊ/, /ʊ/, /ʊ/, /ʊ/

Syllables:

Try the sound in different syllables to get the hang of the production in different sound environments.

Pʊ	Dʊ	Kʊ
Bʊ	Sʊ	Gʊ
Tʊ	Zʊ	ʃʊ

Words:

book	foot	shook
bosom	full	should
brook	good	soot
bull	hood	stood
bullet	hoof	sugar
bush	hook	took
butch	look	wolf
butcher	neighborhood	wolves
cook	pudding	woman
cookie	pull	wood
could	push	wool
crook	put	would
cushion	rook	

Phrases:

good looking	wouldn't he have finished?	don't trust the crook
wooden hook	you stood on my foot	look for it
pull the wool	what a woman	it's in the nook
push and pull	sofa cushions	finish the book
sugar cookie	she took the wood away	big bully
he shook his foot	good job	the Brooklyn bridge
fully cooked	book a visit tomorrow	he shook the bottle
took a look	look away	chocolate pudding
good book	push the button	I'm putting it here
it couldn't be so	pull the trigger	bushels of berries
she shouldn't do that	put it away	berry bushes

Sentences:
Look at the butcher
Brooke was a rookie at cooking
Pull the wool from the cushion
You shouldn't look at the sun

That's my favorite cookbook

I put your hoodie on the hook

You should read the good book

Those sugar cookies look good

Put the sugar in the sugar cookies

He's a crook, but he's good-looking

I would like to know if I should do it

He took a look at my chocolate pudding

The man put the book on his wooden desk

Put the wooden hook on the hood of my car

He shook the bottle near the Brooklyn Bridge

I'm putting the bushel of bush-berries here

Would you eat a bushel of fully cooked apples?

I would love to read my friend's script if I could

He shook his hoof before he stomped on my foot

The bull stood near the brook to look at the water

Butch used to live in a good neighborhood in Brooklyn

I stood as I pushed and pulled the bush out of the ground

I shouldn't have looked at his rook when we played chess

She took the book away from the dirty wood stove

I looked at the full bag of wood, and then I shook it for bugs

How much wood would a woodchuck chuck if a woodchuck could chuck wood

Reading:

Now that you feel more comfortable identifying the tricky /ʊ/ words, it is now time to increase the complexity of your reading skills. Read a novel, a magazine, go through a website or blog, or even read your emails aloud. Search for your new /ʊ/ words and use clear pronunciation focusing on your lips and tongue position. At first, these words will feel like they're hard to find, but soon, you will realize there are a handful of words, like "look, put, and good," which are extremely common words you use frequently. Start practicing with the focus of using your new sound quicker to feel more natural and fluent.

Conversation:

As you improve your confidence with the upsilon sound /ʊ/, you will find that adjusting your pronunciation for this sound will become easier. Remember, the very change that you make in this sound will impact the meaning of your words. If your goal is to speak English clearly and confidently, taking yourself out of your comfort zone and adjusting the pronunciation for this sound will help you on the path to being understood more often. Practice this sound with anyone you can, and push yourself to search for this sound as you speak intentionally.

Chapter 26: /i/ as in "Eat" & "He"

Description:

The /i/ or "ee" sound is produced with the lips spread into a smile. The jaw is in a closed position, and the middle of the tongue is raised high and close to the roof of the mouth. As with all vowels, we turn our voices on for this sound.

Common Differences:

Many mispronunciations of the sound /i/ include a lower tongue position or less lip spreading than is required for General North American pronunciation. Many substitutions for this sound include either the /I/ "ih" as in words "it, is, and him" or a more forward tongue position substitution such as /ɛ/ as in "pet, let, and end." No matter your difference when producing the /i/ "ee" sound, the issue lies in the lip spreading and the height of your tongue.

Spelling:

There are many different spellings of the /i/ "ee" sound. Generally, though, it is not what you'd expect. Typically my clients will have learned either by assumption, due to spelling, or by direct instruction from their non-native English-speaking teachers that words spelled with an "i" are pronounced /i/ or "ee." This assumption, of course, is incorrect. The /i/ or "ee" sound is generally spelled with an "e." Below are a few spelling variations that make the same sound, /i/ or "ee."

Most common Spellings: (98% of the time)

e: we, me, these, meme (44%)

y: baby, many (40%)

ea: meat, team

ee: meet, feed

i: sushi

Less common Spellings: These are best dealt with by memorizing the few exception words

ae: algae

ay: quay

ei: seize, protein

ie: brief, piece

eo/oe: people, phoenix

i_e in multisyllabic words: regime

iu/ia/io – after another vowel at the end of syllables: radio, audio
The ends of foreign words: spaghetti, sushi, Helsinki

Exceptions!
Let's take a look at a few exceptions to the rules because, as you already know, English is full of exceptions to keep us on our toes!

The "i" only says /i/ in three instances:

With a silent "e" at the end in multisyllabic words
police   prestige   tangerine

At the end of syllables followed by another vowel
stadium   piano   radio

At the ends of foreign words
spaghetti   sushi   Helsinki

Hear it!
Begin to train your ears to hear the difference between the /i/ "ee" sound versus the /ɛ/ "eh" sound. Go through the minimal pairs list that contrasts these vowels. The /i/ words require you to pull the middle of your tongue up to the roof and smile. The/ɛ/ words require you to push your tongue forward with a more neutral lip position.

/i/ vs /ɛ/ Minimal Pairs:

teen	ten	seal	sell	deed	dead
heal	hell	wheel	well	bead	bed
teal	tell	bean	Ben	read	red
deal	dell	keen	Ken	seed	said
feel	fell	wean	when		

Feel it!
For many, the ability to hear and differentiate between similar vowels is extremely difficult. I instruct my clients to focus on the "feeling" of their tongue position to better master the accuracy, as frequently, a client's differentiation is inconsistent. By feeling your tongue's position, you can overcome your differentiation problem. First, you must ensure you are spreading your lips into a smiling position for /i/"ee." The /i/ "ee" sound is also slightly higher in tongue positioning, so ensure your jaw is

more closed, as compared to a more neutral position for /ɛ/. Lastly, you must feel what the middle of your tongue is doing for the /i/ "ee" sound. Practice feeling how the middle of your tongue raises high, nearly touching the roof or palate of your mouth. When you compare this with /ɛ/ "eh," the middle of the tongue will drop lower to a neutral height position and go forward. Feel the difference by repeating one after the other. "ee," "eh," "ee," "eh." Go through the minimal pair list of words above once more to feel how your tongue is raised for /i/ "ee."

Do it!
Once you feel that you have a good grasp of the difference in how the /i/ "ee" sounds and you can feel your tongue position for /i/ "ee," move up the ladder of complexity. The goal is to move towards the conversation level.

Isolation:
Repeat: /i/, /i/, /i/, /i/, /i/

Syllables:

pee	jee	eez
bee	ree	eek
tee	lee	eeg
dee	wee	eesh
see	yee	each
zee	eep	eej
key	eeb	ear
gee	eat	eel
she	eed	eew
chee	ees	eey

Words:

beam	deal	grease
bean	delete	greet
bee	ear	he
bleed	eat	heal
breeze	email	heat
brief	eve	here
clean	fee	jeans
clear	feed	jeep
coffee	feel	keep
complete	free	key

leaf

leap

leave

me

meet

meme

monkey

morphine

near

need

niece

pea

Pete

piece

please

priest

queen

read

receipt

reek

see

seed

seek

seem

she

sheet

sleep

speech

Steve

stream

teach

team

teenager

teeth

theme

these

thief

treatment

veal

we

zeal

zero

Phrases:

feed the ee!

we read

eat a bean

he was healed

heat the jeep

feel the need

see a bee

mean city

keep the beet

we eat veal

a genie's dream

clear view

these three nieces

a piece of meat

leave the keys

need some peace

please see me

we cheer

a weird fear

Pete's Pizza

clear veneer

meet a creature

mean teacher

keep the peace

let's meet

easy street

don't be mean

speak with me

green seeds

leave my team

legal people

clear hearing

chief speaker

clear the field

need to keep it

new career

heal the wound

water leak

eat the pizza

beaded cloth

take a seat

east coast

great idea

hear the noise

don't fear

easy does it

each year

knead the dough

tweak the paper

squeaky easel

leaky eaves

please don't tease

eat a feast

green leaf

Sentences:

I have a clear view through the mirror

These three nieces are the only nieces I have

Throw a piece of meat on the BBQ

Leave the keys for me to drive the car later

I really need some peace and quiet, please

Please see me after your meeting with the client

We always cheer for our team

I have a weird fear of meeting my hero

Pete's Pizza is the cheesiest pizza on the street

Read these brief deals

Don't feed a seal meat

Eve, do you see a seed?

A thief might steal these jeeps

The vet will heal the pet's heel

We will feed the three monkeys

We need to see the team succeed

Steve and Pete will never eat a beet

Steve, can you please keep Pete on the team?

/i/ in "Y" Words

For many, the /i/ "ee" sound difficulty arises in primarily one situation; words that end in "y" as in "happy" and "many." The issue that speakers have with the "y" is that they produce more of a lower tongue position as in /I/ "ih," so "happy" /hæpi/ would sound like "happih" /hæpI/ and "many" /mɛni/ would sound like "menih" /mɛnI/. Practice the words and sentences below to feel your /i/ "ee" pronunciation at the ends of these words.

Examples:

alley	curry	entry
angry	daddy	every
badly	daily	fairy
belly	dairy	family
berry	diary	fancy
Bobby	dirty	fatty
busy	dusty	fifty
candy	early	forty
carry	empty	fully
crazy	enemy	funny

glory	mercy	silly
handy	money	sixty
happy	moody	sorry
hairy	mummy	story
heavy	newly	study
hobby	noisy	sunny
honey	only	teddy
hungry	party	Terry
hurry	penny	truly
irony	rally	unity
ivory	ready	very
lobby	risky	weary
lucky	rocky	worry
marry	shiny	

Sentences:

She's pretty

We are fancy-free

That cost a pretty penny

I came early to the noisy party

I am craving some really fatty foods

I'm ready to carry the heavy weights

You need to speak carefully to the family

I'm sorry the juice machine is empty

I'm really only hungry for honey cookies

I'm very happy you came early to the party

I am happy when I am busy doing my work efficiently

Reading:

Now that you have mastered the sentence level, let's move it up a notch! Find more complex reading material to practice your new sounds. You will notice it is slightly tricky as there are many spelling variations for the /i/ "ee" sound. As you practice, you will become more familiar with the typical spelling options for this sound. Practice, practice, practice! If you find your reading is starting to sound a bit robotic and choppy, I do have a recommendation. Read the sentence in your head first, then look up and say the sentence as if you are speaking to someone. Practicing like this will help you increase your naturalness and fluency.

Conversation:

Your final goal is to introduce this sound into your daily conversational speech. I often encourage my clients to think of their speech like a running narration or ticker tape; you can think of reading the words as they come past your lips in speech. This exercise can help you identify the /i/ "ee" sound a little easier if you are a visual learner. The goal is to heighten your awareness of this sound in all situations, all environments, and with many different conversation partners to generalize your skills. The only way to feel natural is to go through the often awkward phase of trying out a new sound for the first time with others. Push through this discomfort, and you will find that you can improve your clarity and meaning with far fewer requests for you to repeat yourself to others.

Chapter 27: /ɛ/ as in "Head & Bet"

Description:
The /ɛ/ sound is produced with the jaw slightly open, the middle of the tongue is in a neutral position in terms of height but pulled forward towards the front teeth. The /ɛ/ sound exists in the words "bed, head, and red."

As with all vowels, this is a voiced sound, so the vocal folds should be vibrating.

Common Differences:
The typical substitutions made for /ɛ/ are numerous. The reason for such variability has to do with the fact that this is a neutral height vowel, which is often difficult to know where to place your tongue. I usually have clients who substitute this sound with five or more different vowels, which shows that the speaker is unsure exactly how to create this sound. They are also likely having issues hearing and differentiating this sound in the first place.

Among the many sound substitutions, speakers can place the tongue too far back in a more neutral position to "uh," so the word "pet" /pɛt/ will sound like "putt" /p^t/. Speakers may place their tongue too low, resulting in an /a/ "ah" sound, so the word "men" /mɛn/ might sound like "mahn" /man/.

Spelling:
We can spell the /ɛ/ sound in a few different ways in English.
The most typical spelling for /ɛ/ is "e."
"e": let, leg, sell, end, debt, well
"ea": bread, head, dead
"ie": friend
"ai": said
"a": any

Take some time to compare the /ɛ/ sound with other vowels to see which vowel you struggle with the most. Focus on paying attention to your tongue position for the /ɛ/. For /ɛ/, pull your tongue forward from the neutral "uh" position.

Auditory Discrimination:
/ɛ/ "eh"   let   wet   bet   sell

/eI/ "eh ee"	late	wait	bait	sail
/I/ "ih"	lit	wit	bit	sill

/ɛ/ vs. /æ/ Minimal Pairs:

*Remember, for /ɛ/ "eh," keep your mouth and jaw in a neutral position, but for /æ/ "aa," open your jaw wide.

/ɛ/ vs /æ/

any	Annie	guess	gas	pen	pan
bed	bad	head	had	peck	pack
beg	bag	hem	ham	pest	past
Ben	ban	Ken	can	pet	Pat
bet	bat	Kent	can't	rent	rant
blessed/blast		left	laughed	S	ass
bread	Brad	leg	lag	said	sad
kept	capped	lend	land	send	sand
dead	dad	letter	ladder	set	sat
den	Dan	M	am	shell	shall
Ed	add	med	mad	slept	slapped
excess	access	men	man	Steph	staff
expend/expand		mess	mass	ten	tan
fester	faster	messed/mast		trek	track
flex	flax	met	mat	vet	vat
gem	jam	N	Ann	wreck	rack

Hear it!

Practice the minimal pairs lists above and listen to the slight differences of each vowel sound. As you keep your jaw in a neutral position and pull your tongue forward, the /ɛ/ will be easier to distinguish.

Feel it!

When comparing this vowel to others, you can use a mirror to view how open or closed your jaw position is. Remember, for /ɛ/ "eh," the teeth are only slightly parted, and the lips are nearly in a neutral position. Feel how the sound changes as you pull the middle of your tongue forward ever so slightly. Pronounce the word lists as you naturally would, then compare the new tongue and jaw position for the new sound /ɛ/ "eh." Feel the difference and make a note of that feeling; you may need to rely on the feeling of the sound for a while until you are better able to hear the difference.

Once you feel comfortable with the difference in sound and how the pronunciation feels different in your mouth and jaw, you're ready to move on to some more difficult practice. Let's do this!

Isolation:
Repeat: /ɛ/, /ɛ/, /ɛ/, /ɛ/, /ɛ/

Syllables:

peh	reh	ek
beh	leh	eg
teh	weh	esh
deh	yeh	ech
seh		ej
zeh	ep	er
keh	eb	el
geh	et	ew
sheh	ed	ey
cheh	es	
jeh	ez	

Words:

ahead	event	leg
bed	every	let
beg	fed	letter
Ben	fell	level
best	felt	med
bet	gel	men
check	gem	met
death	get	net
den	head	never
effort	help	next
egg	Jeff	peg
elm	jet	pet
else	Ken	press
end	led	red
entire	ledge	ready
estate	left	rep

305

reverend	ten	well
said	test	went
sector	them	west
sense	then	wet
set	twelve	when
spent	vet	yes
Ted	web	yet
tell	wed	zen

Phrases:

Ben is the best	in any event	well spent
Ben will fix the net	it's the end	went west
bend your elbow	Jeff on a jet	when is the end
best friends	let him pet the cat	worth the effort
big bed	or else	Ken led them
check it out ahead	plenty of empty nests	on a ledge
check the den	remember your pen	left and right
death is scary	said it yet	my leg aches
elect the president	say yes to the dress	let it go
elegant dress	sense of urgency	empty letter
Elm trees	set aside	edge of the level
entire estate	she will wed Ed	med school
everyone went	spent the end of it	men at work
felt it when he fell	spent the yen	met his friend
get better every day	tell them	get it in the net
get the gem	Ted will tell	never ever
get the red hen	ten tests	next order
he fed the dog	the egg is cracked	Peggy's pet
head upstairs	the gel was let out	press the button
heavy bet	the vet got wet	ready, set, go
help Ed	the vet helped my dog	I read the ledger
I beg of you	the web broke	rendered useless
I bet he said yes	then they went	I said it again
I want to fly in a big	twelve or eleven	end of the sector
red jet	well said	

Sentences:
Ed was elected president
Jeff never has any food left

The weather gets better every day
Everyone ate the fresh yellow eggs
She said I was too heavy for the ride
I met my best friend Fred seven years ago
Everyone says Ben is the best at everything
Bend your elbow to get the net out of the water
Ed, Ned, and Fred are best friends
I processed the check ahead of time
Check that every speck is cleaned off the deck
The women danced in elegant dresses around the Elm trees
The entire estate will be left to the heir
We must ensure that we elect the best president possible
Everyone went to the play, and it was worth the effort
Tell them that the letter was empty
I went west last summer, and I'll go again with my friends
There are plenty of empty webs on the trees
The men left their equipment at work
Peg needs help to remember her pen
I can't catch my breath whenever I see that elegant dress
Jen's lesson went well, but I expected it to end at eleven
I'll make a heavy bet that the hotel has a guest in every bed
There are plenty of empty nests on that ledge of the window
Jenny's best friend, who lives at the end of Elm Street, never eats eggs for breakfast

Reading:

Expand your practice to more complex reading tasks, such as reading books, emails, and websites out loud. As you are able to identify the "eh" sound with the various spelling options, you will become more familiar and comfortable with your new pronunciation. Work towards reading faster and with a more natural rhythm. As you become faster at pronouncing these sounds, you will become better prepared to begin to use this sound in conversation. You don't need to be perfect at this sound before you try in conversation. You just need to get a firm grasp on how to pronounce this sound and in what situations. Your speed and naturalness will be proportional to the amount of practice that you do. It takes time, so keep practicing daily!

Conversation:

The goal is to speak English clearly and confidently, but sometimes, it can feel daunting even to try your new pronunciation skills with others. If you never step out of your comfort zone and practice in daily conversation, this new pronunciation skill will remain challenging and laborious for you. It is not until you begin to use it with greater frequency that you will see all of the benefits of your hard work. It takes time, and you will NOT be perfect at the start. The best thing you can do is try; put yourself out there, and catch the words with /ɛ/ "eh" as best as you can as you speak with others. Keep at it!

Chapter 28: /u/ as in "Do" & "Too"

Description:
In the International Phonetic Alphabet, the "oo" sound is represented by a /u/. This sound is produced with tightly rounded lips. The middle of the tongue is high up in the mouth and far back.

Common Differences:
The two most common substitutions for the /u/ sound are to place the tongue too low instead of up near the roof, resulting in the /ow/ sound. So words like "tune"/u/ would sound like "tone" /ow/, and the word "soup" /u/ would sound more like "soap" /ow/. The fix here is to raise the tongue to a higher position so it approximates or comes close to the roof of the mouth.

Another typical substitution for the /u/ sound is to use the /ʊ/ sound. What this means is that not only is the tongue too low in the mouth, but the lip rounding is inadequate or not quite rounded enough. So words like "Luke" /u/ "oo" will sound like "look" /ʊ/, and "pool" /u/ "oo" will sound like "pull" /ʊ/. The fix in this situation is two-fold. The speaker must raise the middle of the tongue towards the roof of the mouth and round their lips more.

Here is a small list of comparisons between the three vowels just described.

Practice the difference in the words below to increase your auditory discrimination skills for /u/ "oo."

/u/ "oo"	Luke	pool	fool	shooed
/ʊ/ "eu"	look	pull	full	should
/o/ "ow"	cloak	pole	fold	shoulder

Spelling:
The most common way to spell the /u/ sound is with the double "oo." As you already know, this spelling confuses speakers trying to differentiate the /ʊ/ since they share spelling features. The best course of action for this problem is to memorize the smaller list of /ʊ/ words spelled with "oo."

Below are the various ways to spell the /u/ "oo" sound:
o: as in do, to

ou: as in you

oo: as in food, school, choose

u: as in flu

ew: as in new, view, chew

u_e: as in rude, flute

ui: fruit, juice, suit

Isn't that frustrating? There are so many ways to spell this sound in English, and so many of these spellings overlap with other vowels. The spelling problem is what makes this sound so difficult. Of all the vowels, the schwa and "o" are the most difficult to grasp in terms of spelling. The advice I have here is to group the spelling words that cause you the greatest difficulty with your pronunciation. Focus on one spelling group at a time until you feel you have a good grasp of when to use the /u/ "oo" sound.

A Note About /u/ vs. /ju/ or "You"

Often there can be confusion about the "oo" /u/ vs. the "you" /ju/ sounds. There are a few words that have a tiny "y" sound before the /u/. The "y" sound is transcribed as a /j/ in IPA, which might sound a little confusing, so stay with me here.

In the words below, you will still pronounce the /u/ "oo" sound as described earlier, but there is a tiny "y" sound first. The result is a "you" sound. Below are some words to be aware of that have the "you" and NOT the "oo." So for the word "beautiful," it would not be pronounced "boo duh fuhl" but rather "b**you** duh fuhl."

beautiful	hue	preview
communicate	human	rebuke
commute	January	refuse
computer	menu	refute
confuse	mule	review
continue	music	spew
cube	mute	union
curfew	nephew	unit
few	pew	united

<u>u</u>nicorn	<u>u</u>sed	v<u>iew</u>
<u>u</u>niversity	<u>u</u>seful	<u>you</u>
<u>u</u>se	val<u>ue</u>	<u>you</u>th

"EW" Spelled Final Words

Many words that end in "ew" are pronounced without the "y" sound. This often requires memorization because English spelling does not inform you of the pronunciation at all in this case. For these words, just pronounce the /u/ "oo."

/u/ as in "oo":

new	flew	slew
dew	blew	threw
grew	brew	screw
drew	chew	renew
crew	stew	cashew

/ju/ as in "you":

few

curfew

spew

nephew

pew

*Sew- is an exception word pronounced as "so."

<u>Hear it!</u>
Listen to the differences in the minimal pairs list above. Pay specific attention to the rounding of your lips, ensuring they are in a tight rounded position, like a little tiny /w/ circle. Feel where you place the center of your tongue. For the /u/ words, raise your tongue close to the roof of your mouth.

<u>Feel it!</u>
Begin to visualize what your tongue is doing. Feel how the sounds change as you raise and lower the center of your tongue. Look in the mirror and make a note of your lips, ensuring they are in a tightly rounded position. Notice how this articulation position feels to you as compared to your typical pronunciation and

mouth position. Get accustomed to feeling the difference, and as you practice the words and sentences below, keep your focus on this difference.

Do it!
Let's practice and move up the ladder of complexity.

Isolation:
Repeat: "oo": /u/, /u/, /u/, /u/, /u/

Syllables:

poo	joo	ooz
boo	roo	ook
too	loo	oog
doo	woo	oosh
soo	yoo	ooch
zoo	oop	ooj
koo	oob	oor
goo	oot	ool
shoo	ood	oow
choo	oos	ooy

Words:

approve	Google	resume
balloon	goose	room
bloom	hoop	rude
blue	June	school
boot	kangaroo	scoop
booze	loop	scooter
broom	loose	shoot
choose	lose	soup
conclude	Luke	stew
crew	mood	stoop
do	moon	student
doom	move	sue
droop	news	super
dues	noon	swoop
flu	pool	through
flute	prove	to
food	remove	too

312

tooth

tube

Tuesday

tulip

tuna

two

who

you

you'll

youth

zoo

/u/ Phrases:

approve your review

bamboo shoes

beef stew

birthday balloon

blooming flowers

blue moon

check out YouTube

chewing gum

chicken coop

choose Google

cool pool

crude attitude

cruel duel

cut the coupon

dirty boots

do your homework

flower bloom

fruit juice

fruit loop cereal

full moon

good afternoon

good food

good mood

good move

growing roots

hula hoop

in June

it's a fluke

loop de loop

loose goose

lose the group

lose your keys

Luke's in the pool

new flute

new goose

new room

new shoes

new students

old news

prove to you

remove the tube

resume being rude

rude dude

schoolroom

scoop the soup

see you soon

soupspoon

spoon of sugar

student room

sugar substitute

super cool

super value

thank you

through the roof

through the tube

to the zoo

truth and lies

tune your music

two new rooms

two new suits

who are you?

zoom lens

Sentences:

I'll prove it to you

Did you get a new flute?

See you very soon

Have a great afternoon

I think I'll choose the goose

He got a brand new blue suit

That song was through the roof!

The flowers are blooming in June

Luke, your right boot is chewed up

Remove the students from the room

Thank you and see you again soon!

The truth will be viewed through lies

I'll prove to you that Luke's still in the pool

That's a super value for tickets to the zoo

The soup spoon was replaced with a scoop

There's never boring news in the newsroom

The kangaroo looked at the blue moon

She looks crude with that ruby in her tooth

Lou's new blue shoes were covered in glue

I refuse to listen to music played on a flute

You can produce the new tune in my studio

The scoop and broom are useful at the zoo

Do you think it was rude to go into the pool?

Why do they use gloomy colors in this room?

The students watched YouTube with their tutor

I don't need proof that you're telling me the truth

Who was that rude guy who made the crude comments?

Reading:

As you begin to feel more comfortable with the mouth position for this sound and increase your differentiation skills, expand your skills to reading aloud. Spend 20 minutes each day dedicated to finding the /u/ "oo" sound in books, magazines, emails, or while searching on the internet. Any time you see a /u/ "oo" word, say it out loud.

Conversation:

Begin to use your new /u/ "oo" sound in daily conversation. When you say "thank you," focus on the lips and tongue position. When you use the word "do," feel your lips purse into a round position. Set reminders for yourself throughout the day to focus on this sound in conversation. A few alarms set for yourself throughout your day will do a great deal to help you focus on your pronunciation intentionally when you speak.

Chapter 29: Diphthongs /aI/ & /eI/: As If Two Vowels Weren't Enough!

The term diphthong refers to a vowel that has two parts. For example, in the word "my," the "y" vowel pronunciation changes from an /a/ to an /i/ sound, "m ah ee." Most speakers, even native English speakers, are not aware of this transition, yet it is extremely important when it comes to speaking English intelligibly. In this chapter, we will go through the various diphthongs in English and explain them in detail. After you practice, you will undoubtedly have an exceptional understanding of what you have been doing differently with your pronunciation. Not only that but, you will understand what to do to adjust the difference.

/aI/ as in "Hi, My, Pie"

Description:
The diphthong /aI/ begins with an open-mouth posture. Your jaw should be open wide with your tongue low in the mouth, then transition to a smile and pull your tongue up to the roof like an "ee" sound; "ah ee."

Common Differences:
The most typical issue is to drop the final element of the diphthong or the tail of the diphthong. Often, not only is the tail missing but the /a/ sound is produced with too little jaw opening so that it will sound more like "uh" /^/. The word "my" will sound more like "ma" or "muh" rather than "mah ee." To fix this issue, I recommend opening your mouth wider to ensure your tongue is very low in the mouth. Opening your jaw allows your tongue to move lower, thus changing the quality of the vowel acoustics. The next step is to add the tail /i/ or "ee." Move from an open mouth "ah" to the smile "ee" and quickly transition from one to the other. The transition must be blended, meaning there is NO SPACE between the two vowel sounds. The /aI/ should not sound like "ah" pause "ee."

Spelling:
Most common English spellings for the /aɪ/ includes:

igh: as in "bright"

i_e: as in "time, nice, fine"

y: as in "my, fly, dynamic, python, spy, coyote, rhyme"

Other spellings for /aɪ/:

ie: as in "pie, lie, tried, tie"

ei: as in "kaleidoscope, poltergeist, Rottweiler"

i: as in "find, sign

uy: as in "buy"

I + other vowels: as in "trial, riot"

Hear it!

Go through the word list below and hear how the two vowels glide into one another. Be intentional about transitioning your mouth from open "ah" to spread lip positions "ee." Hear how the vowel changes, and attune your ear to the difference compared to your typical pronunciation. You may notice that the vowel takes longer to pronounce as a result of this extra movement. That is expected since this vowel has two parts and therefore must be slightly longer as a result. So, take your time to ensure you add the "tail of the sound."

Feel it!

Focus your mind on your jaw, specifically. I want you to feel how open your jaw is and how it transitions to a near-closed position. Feel how your tongue moves as you move your jaw up. You should feel that your tongue starts very low in the mouth for "ah" and moves upwards towards the palate or the roof of your mouth for "ee." Feel how your lips begin in an open, relaxed position and move to a spread smile. Go through the word list and feel each of these components of the sound. Being able to not only hear but also feel the difference will help you acquire this sound.

Do it!

Let's practice up the ladder of complexity before moving to the conversation level to ensure you have a good grasp of this diphthong.

Isolation:

Repeat: "ah ee" /aɪ/, /aɪ/, /aɪ/, /aɪ/, /aɪ/

p/aɪ/ "pie"	j/aɪ/	/aɪ/z
b/aɪ/ "bye"	r/aɪ/	/aɪ/k
t/aɪ/ "tie"	l/aɪ/	/aɪ/g
d/aɪ/ "die"	w/aɪ/	/aɪ/sh
s/aɪ/	y/aɪ/	/aɪ/ch
z/aɪ/	/aɪ/p	/aɪ/j
k/aɪ/	/aɪ/b	/aɪ/r
g/aɪ/	/aɪ/t	/aɪ/l
sh/aɪ/	/aɪ/d	/aɪ/w
ch/aɪ/	/aɪ/s	/aɪ/y

Words:

acquire	desire	frying
alibi	despise	giant
analyze	diagram	guy
apply	dial	height
arrive	diary	higher
aspire	die	horizon
bicycle	diet	hybrid
biology	dire	hype
blind	dry	hyperactive
buy	dryer	ice
buyer	dying	idea
buying	dynamic	ideal
child	dynamite	identical
client	empire	idle
climate	entire	iron
climb	expire	item
combine	eye	kind
coyote	fight	liar
crisis	file	library
cry	find	life
cyber	fine	light
cycle	fire	line
denial	flyer	lion
deny	flying	lying
denying	fry	mild

mind	quite	sky
minus	rely	smile
modernize	reply	society
modify	require	style
my	ride	surprise
nice	rifle	tie
night	right	tire
nylon	riot	title
organize	rise	try
paralyze	rye	type
pioneer	satisfy	violet
polite	science	wild
prior	sigh	wire
private	sight	wise
prize	sign	
quiet	signify	

Phrases:

a dire cyber attack	denied the pie	giant tire
a dire tale	desire to fly	hi and bye
a fad diet	despise crying	high wire
acquire a rifle	die trying	higher kite
acquired alibi	dry ice	hired and fired
analyze the trial	dying desire	hyper child
apply the wire	dynamic rights	ice pile
arrive on time	entire box of wires	identical child
aspire to be wise	exiled empire	irate pirate
bicycle guy	expired rice	iron item
bicycle tire	eye to eye	kind child
blind eye	fight the crime	liar on trial
bright light	fight the fine	light the dynamite
buy a kite	final trial	light the fire
buying a tire	find the fire	lime pie
by design	find the light	lying lion
by the by	fire crisis	modified design
child in line	fish fry	my alibi
client diary	five minus nine	my crazy life
cry my eyes out	fly by	my hair dryer
cyber crisis	flying higher	my local library

nice guy	quiet child	scientific diagram
nice night	quiet ride	scientific mind
nylon pylons	quite surprised	submit the file
organize the night	rely on my reply	tie-dye
polite denial	require a reply	try to climb
polite guy	rifle riot	wide horizon
prior fires	right on time	wild climate
private diary	satisfied client	wild fire
prize of the night	satisfying ride	wild idea

Homophones With /aɪ/

Homophones are words that have different spellings and meanings but are pronounced the same. Here is a list of /aɪ/ homophone words:

aisle	/I'll	high	/hi	sighs	/size
bite	/byte	eye	/I	sight	/site
buy	/by	knight	/night	time	/thyme
site	/cite/sight	mined	/mind	whine	/wine
die	/dye	right	/write	Y	/why
fined	/find	sighed	/side		

Sentences:

The liar was on trial

I aspire to be a scientist

Friday night was a wild party

I require a higher quality dryer

The lion was trying to be quiet

Why is the price so high for that light?

I hate lime pie, but I don't mind apple pie

I might as well take care of the crying child

Why did the guy try to light the fire tonight?

The man had to fight all night in the bright light

My wife was wise to be polite about winning the prize

I have no idea which item it was either (also pronounced "ee ther")

He had to acquire an alibi after starting a dire cyber attack

319

I aspire to be wise about my health instead of starting a fad diet

The bicycle guy arrived on time despite a broken bicycle tire

I cried my eyes out when they went blind after staring at the bright light

Don't deny the pie to the child in line

I have a dying desire to play with dried ice

The giant tire went flying by on the highway

I never thought that if I were to buy a kite, it would fly into a high wire

The liar on trial wanted to fight the crime he committed to avoid the fine

The biggest prize of the night was quite a surprise

A satisfied client requires a reply right on time

Submit your modified design and don't rely on my reply

If I don't stop that rifle riot, I'll die trying

I'll never find the flashlight in this box of wires

There's a nice, polite guy at my local library

Only a scientific mind could accurately analyze this trial

The kind child offered me his Key Lime Pie

He had a weak alibi for lighting the prior wild fires

If you light that dynamite, you'll cause a fire crisis in this dry weather

I had the nicest night of my life

It was a wild idea to wear a tie-dye suit to the wedding

Do you have five minutes to say hi and bye to your friends at the fish fry?

He was hired and fired on the same day

I found the private diary that she left behind

Reading:

Once you have read through the sentences above, read other passages and practice daily. You will hear the sound more clearly and begin to feel the mouth movements. When this becomes quick and natural for you, move to more complex reading samples to get yourself accustomed to using this sound in unpredictable texts.

Conversation:

Begin to listen for this sound when other people speak. Once you have a good grasp of when to use the sound, begin to use this adjustment with your own pronunciation. Don't be afraid to correct yourself and repeat a word after having mispronounced it. The "dysfluent" phase is when you find yourself repeating words and self-correcting as your speak. This is an important phase to work through. Repeating yourself will happen less and less as you get used to using this sound in a faster way. You will find that you will need to correct yourself less and less and slowly begin to catch the sound as you speak. With more practice, you will be able to process the sound before you say the word, and this is the phase where your naturalness will evolve.

/eɪ/ as in "Hey, Day & Way"

Description:
The /eɪ/ diphthong is produced with the /ɛ/ "eh" followed by the /i/ "ee" sound. The /ɛ/"eh" is pronounced with the teeth slightly apart. The tongue is neutral in the middle of the mouth, only pulled forward slightly toward the front teeth ("eh.") The diphthong sound will then transition to "ee" by spreading your lips into a tight smile. The tongue moves upward toward the roof or palate of the mouth. "eh-ee" is the sound it creates, as each sound is seamlessly blended into the next with no pauses or stops.

Common Differences:
The typical change non-native English speakers make with the /eɪ/ sound is to drop the tail /i/ sound. This is exactly like in the sound /aɪ/. The result of dropping the tail "ee" sound is that words like "take" might sound more like "tech." The word "age" or "eh eeej" will sound more like "edge." The fix here is to ensure you are producing both vowel sounds and add extra emphasis on the final tail of the diphthong. Of course, adding an extra vowel sound to a word will feel very strange. Adding a sound will also elongate the sound, so it will take a bit longer to say. The extra sound addition will take some time to get used to, but it is an important step in ensuring your English pronunciation is clear.

Spelling:
As with many vowels in English, there are quite a few variations in spelling for the /eɪ/ diphthong.

Most common spelling:
a_e: as in "race, same, name"
ay: as in "ray, play, say"
ai: as in "rain, train, wait, brain"

Less common spelling: ("e" is usually the first of two vowels)
ei: as in "weight, eight, neighbor"
ey: as in "hey, they, obey"

ea: as in "break, great, steak"

a: as in "lazy, crazy"

Hear it:

Go through the words below to compare the sounds of the diphthong /eɪ/ "eh ee" versus the /ɛ/ "eh." Compare the /ɛ/ sound on its own without the tail sound first. Extend the "ee" sound after the "eh" sound to hear the transition from one vowel to another. If you are unsure, record yourself and hear the longer elongated "ee" tail sound to compare.

/eɪ/ vs /ɛ/ Minimal Pairs:

late	let		waste	west		main	men
chase	chess		aid	Ed		fail	fell
wait	wet		ace	S		sail	sell
fade	fed		wage	wedge		raid	red
take	tech		taste	test		whale	well
age	edge		gate	get		Yale	yell

Feel it!

Spend time focusing on how your mouth moves for this diphthong. First, think about how your lips move. Look in a mirror as you see your lips open in a relaxed position from "eh" and transition to the wide-spread smile of the /i/ "ee" sound. Think about how your tongue moves from a neutral position to a high position in the mouth. For some, the middle or sides of the tongue can be felt, making contact with the palate. For others, the tongue merely grazes the roof. Feel for yourself what it feels like, and focus on the feeling as you practice the word lists, sentences, and reading tasks below. Start with the minimal pairs list above to help yourself feel the difference between the two words. As you can tell, if you drop that tail of the diphthong, you will change the meaning, which will result in others misunderstanding what you want to say. Add that tail, and all of a sudden, your meaning becomes clear.

Do it!

Once you have mastered the minimal pairs list above, you will better grasp the sound and the feeling of the diphthong /eɪ/. Now it is time to move on to bigger and better things! Let's get it to the conversation level! But remember, don't skip any steps here. Take your time to master each level before you push on to more complex speech tasks.

Isolation:

Repeat: "eh ee" /eI/, /eI/, /eI/, /eI, /eI/

Syllables:

s/eI/ "say"	j/eI/	/eI/z
d/eI/ "day"	r/eI/	/eI/k
p/eI/	l/eI/	/eI/g
b/eI/	w/eI/	/eI/sh
t/eI/	y/eI/	/eI/ch
z/eI/	/eI/s "ace"	/eI/j
k/eI/	/eI/t "ate"	/eI/r
g/eI/	/eI/p	/eI/l
sh/eI/	/eI/b	/eI/w
ch/eI/	/eI/d	/eI/y

Words:

able	convey	lake
ace	cradle	late
ache	danger	lay
afraid	David	layer
age	day	laying
aid	decorate	lazy
aim	delay	made
angel	dictate	mail
April	drain	main
ate	educate	may
baby	eight	name
bacon	explain	nature
base	fail	neighbor
basis	faint	obey
behavior	fate	paint
betrayal	game	paper
brain	gate	patient
break	gave	place
cable	gray	play
came	great	portrayal
cave	hey	pray
change	information	race
complain	Kate	rage

323

raid	say	they
rain	skate	train
raise	stain	vein
range	stay	wage
rate	steak	wait
ray	straight	waste
remain	strange	wave
safe	stray	way
sail	table	weight
same	take	
save	taste	

Homophones with /eI/

Again, homophones are words with different meanings and spellings but are underlined pronounced exactly the same. Take a look at the list below and notice the differences in spelling; this will help you familiarize yourself with the different spelling options for "eh ee." All of these are pronounced the same.

break vs. brake	sail vs. sale	Wales vs. whales
great vs. grate	steak vs. stake	weigh vs. way
male vs. mail	tale vs. tail	weight vs. wait
plane vs. plain	wave vs. waive	
rain vs. reign	waste vs. waist	

<u>French Words:</u>
You might notice that many words derived from French that have "é," "ê," or "et" are also pronounced as the diphthong /eI/. Here are a few French /eI/ words:

ballet	crepe	protégé
beret	décor	elite
buffet	déjà vu	résumé
café	entrée	lingerie
cliché	fiancé	
crème brûlée	gourmet	

Phrases:

a new neighbor
ace of spades
aches and pains
afraid to obey
afraid to say it
aim for a range
aiming to convey
Angel's face
April fools game
ate a plate of food
baby cradle
baby crate
baby gate
bacon shavings
bake a cake
break a chain
Cain and Abel
came to the game
change your name
chase the base
choose your fate
complain in vain
crazy behavior
crazy brain
crazy rage
Dave caved
David paints
day and age
day to day
decorate the cake
delay my pay
dictate the race
drain the main sink

eighty-eight
escape from jail
explain and educate
explain the play
fail to negotiate
Friday in May
gave away my plate
gray snake
great cradle
great danger
great day
great information
grey stain
grey table
hate mail
hate the pain
hey, are you okay?
lame game
late pay
lay on the hay
lazy Sunday
made my day
main sail
make paper
minimum wage
name of the game
naval train
paid for my place
paint the paper
paperweight
patient safety
play the game
pray and have faith

quaint place
rainy Monday
raise my pay
remain safe
safe from the rain
sail away
same game
save my place
save the date
say my name
skate today
stay away
stay in one place
stay on the paper
steak and potatoes
straight away
strange day
take a day off
take away
take me to the great lakes
taste the bacon
tasty flavor
the fate of nature
the grey baseball
the same game
the same name
they say it
train station
wait at the table
wait for the day
waste away
way to play
weigh on the scale

Sentences:

The waiter gave us a good table
Great haste makes great waste
We came late to play the game

I own ei̲ghty-ei̲ght pa̲perwei̲ghts

Th̲ey pl̲ayed that ga̲me until ei̲ght

It r̲ained and h̲ailed in A̲pril and M̲ay

K̲ay ga̲ve me a pl̲ace to st̲ay for the d̲ay

She has the sa̲me na̲me as the d̲aisy flower

It isn't s̲afe for St̲acey to stand on the t̲able

He had to st̲ay aw̲ay after he esc̲aped from j̲ail

M̲ainly I want to lose we̲ight for my wedding d̲ay

My n̲eighbor from M̲aine moved aw̲ay yesterd̲ay

D̲ave ca̲me in by the side ga̲te to esc̲ape the r̲ain

Th̲ey will wa̲ke up to the smell of b̲acon and a freshly b̲aked ca̲ke

Reading:

As you get more comfortable with the spelling associated with the diphthong /eɪ/, you will find it easier to identify this sound in more complex reading. I suggest reading daily to improve your awareness of this sound while reading out loud. It is beneficial to read out loud while recording yourself. I highly recommend doing this! I can't emphasize this enough. It's as simple as grabbing your phone to record your voice as you read. Listen and read along with the recording to find the /eɪ/ sounds. Read along to videos that have scripts attached. I recommend slowing the playing speed to help you to focus on this new sound. Repeat the speaker using the clear "eh ee" diphthong.

Conversation:

Now that you have mastered the reading level, bring your skills into the real world of speaking. Be sure to focus on how the sound feels. Since conversation is so extremely rapid, you will need to slow down to give yourself a chance to adjust to the change. So, be careful and take your time. Pause often. Slow down. It's okay! You will need to focus your attention on your pronunciation and feel and hear the tail sound of these diphthongs. Try these sounds out in conversation with strangers. That might sound crazy and scary to you. The nice thing about strangers is that they have no preconceived notion about what you typically sound like, so it is an excellent exercise to do without having to feel too self-conscious. Look to see if you notice any reaction from your listener. Likely there will be none at all, and that is the goal! That means you sound natural. Keep at the practice and work on it daily to habituate your movements.

Chapter 30: Diphthongs /oʊ/ /aʊ/ & /oɪ/

/oʊ/ as in "No, Snow & Go"

Description:
The /oʊ/ "oh ww" sound is made by transitioning from a neutral tongue position and slightly rounded lip position to a very tightly rounded lip position. The tongue also transitions from that neutral position "uh" up towards the roof "www." This transition of lip and tongue movements is extremely quick, but it is important to produce both vowel portions of this diphthong. It will sound like "oh ww."

Common Differences:
As with most diphthongs, the greatest issue most speakers have with this sound is that they drop the tail end of the vowel. The result of dropping the "ww" or tail portion of the diphthong is that it produces just the "uh" sound. So words like "robe" will sound more like "rub," and "dome" will sound more like "dumb." As you can imagine, this can lead to some pretty interesting and potentially embarrassing miscommunications! The fix here is to ensure you are fully pronouncing the "ww" tail portion of this diphthong in its entirety.

Spelling:
There are a few options for spelling for the sound /oʊ/. Here are a few examples of the spelling for /oʊ/:

Common spellings: (>96% of the spelling)
o_e: as in "robe, hope, stove"
oa: as in "coach, road, oak, toad, whoah"
ow: as in "snow, throw, arrow"
o: as in "no, so, zero"

Less common spellings:
au: as in "chauffeur, bureau"
ew: as in "sew"
ou: as in "shoulder"

Hear it!
Take some time to listen to the difference in sound between the "uh" and the "oh ww" diphthong. Remember, the diphthong /oʊ/ will be slightly longer to produce

and involves lip rounding at the end. Listen to the "w" sound at the tail-end of the vowel to ensure you pronounce this sound fully. Here are some words to show you the difference in pronunciation between the diphthong /oʊ/ "uh www" and the /^/ "uh."

<u>Auditory Discrimination</u>
/oʊ/ vs. /^/ Minimal Pairs:

note	/nut	home	/hum	coat	/cut
robe	/rub	hone	/hun	soak	/suck
bone	/bun	motor	/mutter	roast	/rust
boat	/butt	colt	/cult	boast	/bust
(embarrassing!)		folk	/f*ck (yup!)	though	/the
phone	/fun	yolk	/yuck	dough	/duh
stone	/stun	ghost	/gust	dome	/dumb

Another typical change people make with the /oʊ/ sound is pronouncing the /oʊ/ with only slightly rounded lips, similar to an /a/ "ah," rather than using a fully rounded tight lip position. So the word "note" with the /oʊ/ sound will sound more like a British pronunciation of "not." A word like "low" will sound more like "law" with the /a/ "ah" sound. Take a look at these minimal pair words comparing /oʊ/ "oh ww" and /a/ "ah."

/oʊ/ vs. /a/

bone	bonne	goat	got	node	nod
choke	chalk	goes	gauze	note	not
coal	call	hoe	haw	oaf	off
coast	cost	hole	haul	oaks	ox
coat	caught	hope	hop	ode	odd
coax	cocks	Joan	John	Oprah	opera
(embarrassing!)		Joe	jaw	or/ore	are
code	cawed	joke	jock	owe	awe
cold	called	known	non	own	on
comb	calm	load	laud	phone	fawn
cope	cop	loan	lawn	pole	Paul
flow	flaw	lord	lard	poor	par
for	far	low	law	Pope	pop
form	farm	mode	mod	port	part
goad	God	mole	mall	pose	pause
goal	gall	mope	mop	road	rod

robe	Rob	slow	slaw	toll	tall
row	raw	stoke	stalk	tote	taught
sew/so	saw	taupe	top	woke	walk
sewed	sod	toad	Todd	wrote	rot
shown	Sean	toast	tossed		

Feel it!

Spend some time reviewing the list above and looking in a mirror at your lip position. The greatest impact you will have with this sound is to increase your lip rounding at the end of the diphthong. Watch and feel as you round your lips into a tiny circle for the "www" sound. Feel how the vowel is slightly longer due to adding the lip rounding at the end. Compare the diphthong to your old pronunciation. Take note of how different the words feel on your lips and tongue. This feeling is what you are going to now focus on in your practice of this sound.

Do it!

Now that you can hear the difference of the diphthong compared to your previous pronunciation, and you can truly feel the difference that rounding your lips makes, you are ready to move on to more complex practice. Move through each stage until you are confident you can both hear and feel the diphthong /oʊ/ "oh ww."

Isolation:
Repeat:"oh ww" /oʊ/, /oʊ/, /oʊ/, /oʊ/, /oʊ/

Syllables:

s/oʊ/	ch /oʊ/	/oʊ/s
t/oʊ/	j/oʊ/	/oʊ/z
d/oʊ/	r/oʊ/	/oʊ/k
p/oʊ/	l/oʊ/	/oʊ/g
b/oʊ/	w/oʊ/	/oʊ/sh
z/oʊ/	y/oʊ/ /oʊ/p	/oʊ/ch
k/oʊ/	/oʊ/b	/oʊ/j
g/oʊ/	/oʊ/t	/oʊ/r
sh/oʊ/	/oʊ/d	/oʊ/l

Beginning Words:

oaf	oat	obey
oak	oath	oboe
oasis	obese	ocean

odor

ogre

oily

okay

old

older

omega

omen

omission

omit

only

onus

opal

opaque

open

opium

oppress

Oprah

opus

oral

orange

orbit

orca

order

organ

oval

ovary

ovation

over

overpay

overt

overnight

overlook

overactive

overtly

owe

own

ozone

Beginning Phrases:

standing ovation

over and out

don't overpay

overt versus covert

I owe you

he owns that orca

order it over again

orange oboe

organ donor

old omen

what an oaf!

that's a huge oak tree

you live in an oasis!

I love oatmeal

omega 3 fatty acids are good for you

I think that's an omen

that was a lie by omission

it's only 3 hours away

the onus is on you

the curtain is opaque

open the door

there's an opium crisis

Oprah's a great interviewer

my oral presentation is tomorrow

this is the last <u>o</u>range
I wish I played the <u>o</u>rgan as well as you
she got a standing <u>o</u>vation
I'm s<u>o</u> <u>o</u>ver it
do I <u>ow</u>e you any change?
I <u>ow</u>n this one

<u>Middle Words:</u>

approach	gold	poetry
boast	grown	pole
boat	hoe	poor
bold	hold	port
bone	hole	road
bonus	home	roast
born	hope	robe
both	host	roll
close	hotel	rose
coach	Joe	shoulder
coal	joke	slow
coast	joy	so
coat	known	soak
code	load	soap
Coke	loan	social
cold	lonely	solar
cone	lord	sold
cope	low	soldier
core	moan	sort
don't	moat	soul
door	mold	soy
dote	moment	stone
dough	most	stove
foe	motel	taupe
fold	motor	toad
ford	no	toast
four	node	toe
ghost	nose	told
goal	note	toll
goat	notice	tone
goes	phone	Tony

331

total   whoah

vote   zone

Middle Phrases:

that's the best appr<u>oa</u>ch

it's not good to b<u>oa</u>st

what a fast b<u>oa</u>t

that man was b<u>o</u>ld to say that

thr<u>ow</u> him a b<u>o</u>ne

that's a b<u>o</u>nus!

b<u>o</u>th of my kids are in school

cl<u>o</u>se the door

I'm a soccer c<u>oa</u>ch

c<u>oa</u>st to c<u>oa</u>st

put on your c<u>oa</u>t

it's c<u>o</u>ld

d<u>o</u>n't f<u>o</u>ld the d<u>ou</u>gh

you look as white as a gh<u>o</u>st

they scored the final g<u>oa</u>l

I want to go h<u>o</u>me

it's l<u>o</u>nely in this h<u>o</u>tel

that's the m<u>o</u>st m<u>o</u>ld I've ever seen

m<u>o</u>st m<u>o</u>tors d<u>o</u>n't run that long

I n<u>o</u>ticed my ph<u>o</u>ne isn't working

I parked on the sh<u>ou</u>lder of the r<u>oa</u>d

s<u>oa</u>k the s<u>oa</u>p in water

you could r<u>oa</u>st it or put it on the st<u>o</u>ve

I t<u>o</u>ld a t<u>o</u>tal of two people

End Words:

ago	bio	cargo
albino	bistro	casino
also	bongo	cello
although	bozo	chemo
amigo	bravado	combo
amino	bro	condo
audio	bronco	crypto
auto	cameo	demo
bingo	camo	disco

ditto	lotto	snow
domino	low	so
echo	macho	solo
ego	mango	speedo
euro	mayo	stereo
expo	memo	stucco
fro	metro	studio
gazebo	Mexico	taco
ghetto	mono	tango
go	nacho	tempo
halo	no	though
hello	patio	throw
hero	photo	toe
hippo	piano	tomato
hobo	polo	torpedo
hydro	potato	torso
indigo	pro	trio
inferno	promo	turbo
info	pronto	tuxedo
intro	psycho	typo
jumbo	radio	vertigo
keto	ratio	veto
kimono	retro	video
know	rhino	zero
limo	rodeo	
logo	show	

End Phrases:
that was long ago
I also came along to the show
she dressed in camo for the hunt
want to hear my demo song?
I heard an echo in the cave
let your ego go
I want to go home
he's my hero
the hippo was named bongo
I don't know the info on this topic
we took a limo there

your new logo is great

the mango fell low to the ground

I never put mayo on my nachos

listen to the radio show

I see so much snow

the solo artist is in the studio

I went to Mexico to eat a taco and a nacho

never throw a tomato

I stubbed my toe

didn't you get the memo?

who has veto power?

I see zero signs of rain in the sky

I love to play Marco-Polo in the pool

Homophones:

Some words that are spelled differently with different meanings yet have the same pronunciation are called homophones. Here are a few homophones that exist with the diphthong /oʊ/:

lone	loan		poll	pole		so/sew	sow
no	know		role	roll		sole	soul

Mixed Phrases:

coast to coast

cold Coke

don't smoke over here

golden ornament

homeowner

low profile

mostly over

no home phone

old stone road

old toast

open road

show on the road

slow-motion in the ocean

tow motor

no notice

Mixed Sentences:

<u>O</u>h n<u>o</u>!

I'll have an espress<u>o</u> to g<u>o</u>

<u>O</u>pen the <u>o</u>ld c<u>o</u>ld C<u>o</u>ke bottle

That gh<u>o</u>st can't sh<u>ow</u> his b<u>o</u>nes

J<u>oa</u>n, please use s<u>oa</u>p to wash your cl<u>o</u>thes

J<u>oe</u> n<u>o</u>ticed the g<u>o</u>ld was too heavy to h<u>o</u>ld

I want to g<u>o</u> r<u>o</u>llerblading from c<u>oa</u>st to c<u>oa</u>st

The h<u>o</u>me<u>ow</u>ner couldn't <u>o</u>pen the <u>o</u>ld st<u>o</u>ve

If you r<u>o</u>ll this d<u>ou</u>gh too much, it w<u>o</u>n't gr<u>ow</u>

I invested all the money I <u>ow</u>n in <u>o</u>ld p<u>o</u>stage stamps

Do you kn<u>ow</u> the j<u>o</u>ke about the g<u>o</u>lden <u>o</u>rnament?

I h<u>o</u>pe it doesn't sn<u>ow</u> while we're on the <u>o</u>pen r<u>oa</u>d

I d<u>o</u>n't kn<u>ow</u> if B<u>eau</u> came to the <u>o</u>ld st<u>o</u>ne r<u>oa</u>d h<u>o</u>me

D<u>o</u>n't <u>o</u>pen the wind<u>ow</u> in the c<u>o</u>ld when it's 20 bel<u>ow</u>!

We v<u>o</u>ted that you cannot sm<u>o</u>ke <u>o</u>ver here anym<u>o</u>re

The sl<u>ow</u>-m<u>o</u>tion vide<u>o</u> is alm<u>o</u>st <u>o</u>ver

It's hard to ph<u>o</u>ne h<u>o</u>me from a b<u>oa</u>t if you have n<u>o</u> ph<u>o</u>ne

I will keep a l<u>ow</u> pr<u>o</u>file and w<u>o</u>n't give out the c<u>o</u>de even under <u>oa</u>th

Reading:

By now, you have a really good grasp of the different spelling variations for the /oʊ/ "oh ww" sound. Expand your skills to more complex reading, like books, magazines, articles, websites, and emails. You can use any reading task you come across in your day, but be sure to say the words aloud. Better yet, record yourself reading aloud so you can study and focus on your pronunciation.

Conversation:

Finally, you are ready to try this sound in conversation with your co-workers, friends, new acquaintances, and family. Your aim is to expand the final rounded lip element of the diphthong to enhance clarity and accuracy in your speech. A conversation is far faster and much more complex than reading aloud. You have to process what you are going to say, you have to listen to your conversation partner, and you now will have to pay attention to your pronunciation along the way. You WILL make mistakes, and you WILL mess up! Be open to the fact that this is a process. You are overcoming an old habitual motor pattern that you may have practiced for years or even decades! This motor-muscle memory is not something that will go away in a day or a week of practice. You're in this for long-term changes.

Work at it. Focus on your articulation, and slowly your speed will increase. You will notice fewer and fewer misunderstandings with others as you better grasp your articulation issues and adjust them.

/aʊ/ as in "How, Cow & Now"

Description:
The /aʊ/ "ah ww" sound as in "ouch" is another common diphthong in English. As you may recall, diphthongs transition from one vowel to another. The first element of the diphthong is the /æ/ "aa" sound. We pronounce the /æ/ "aa" with the jaw open in its lowest position. The tongue is also very low in the mouth and pulled forward, like in words "at" and "apple." The position transitions to the /u/ "oo" sound, with the jaw closed, the tongue rising upwards toward the palate, and the lips moving to a tightly rounded position. The result is the "aa ww" sound.

Common Differences:
The most typical change non-native North American English speakers make with this sound is to drop the tail of the diphthong "ww," or they do not open the jaw wide enough for the /æ/ "aa" portion of the sound. Either change will impact the clarity and accuracy of this sound. The fix is to either ensure you are opening your jaw and pulling your tongue down at the beginning of the sound or to focus more attention on adding the rounded lip position for /u/ at the tail end of the diphthong. A precise speech transcription by a speech-language pathologist will help you identify exactly what changes you might be making with this sound.

Spelling:
ou: as in "about, found"
ow: as in "cow, flower"

You should be aware that not all "ou" and "ow" words are pronounced as /aʊ/, as seen in the words below. Unfortunately, English does no favors by telling us anything through spelling, so memorizing these few outlier words will help you differentiate the pronunciation.

ou: /ʊ/: Should, would, could
ou: /a/ "ah": bought, sought

336

ow: /oʊ/ "oh ww": show, mow, know, sow, low

Hear it!

Go through the minimal pairs list below and compare the pronunciation. Each pair includes the diphthong with the "tail" "ww" with rounded lips at the end versus the word with no diphthong tail. Listen to the difference in pronunciation, and hear the lengthening and tail of the sound. If you hear no difference from your typical pronunciation by adding the "ww" sound, it may be that you are not opening your mouth wide enough to produce a clear /æ/ "aa." Try each version to decipher what you are doing. If you feel discomfort in your pronunciation of the /aʊ/ from your typical pronunciation, you likely have found your difference!

/aʊ/ vs. /a/ Minimal Pairs:

bound /bond	proud /prod	browse /bras
cloud /clod	scout /Scott	cow /caw
foul /fall	shout /shot	cows /cause
found /fond	trout /trot	down /dawn
mouse /moss	wound (verb) /wand	drown /drawn
mouth /moth	hour /are	owl /all
noun /non	brow /bra	row (quarrel) /raw
pound /pond	brown /brawn	

Feel it!

The key to knowing if you are pronouncing this sound is to hear the difference and feel how your mouth moves differently. Focus on your jaw opening. Feel how you are opening your jaw to an open position for "aa." Then feel how your lips transition from wide-open to a tiny tight rounded "ww." Go through the word lists and minimal pair lists again to focus on "feeling" your mouth position rather than focusing on how it sounds, because, as we already know, our ears can trick us.

Do it!

Let's work up to conversation and start with isolation.

Isolation:

Repeat the sound "aa ww": /aʊ/, /aʊ/, /aʊ/, /aʊ/, /aʊ/

Syllables:

k/aʊ/	ch /aʊ/	b/aʊ/
w/aʊ/	p/aʊ/	t/aʊ/

d/aʊ/ y/aʊ/ /aʊ/g
s/aʊ/ /aʊ/p /aʊ/sh
z/aʊ/ /aʊ/b /aʊ/ch
g/aʊ/ /aʊ/t /aʊ/j
sh/aʊ/ /aʊ/d /aʊ/r
j/aʊ/ /aʊ/s /aʊ/l
r/aʊ/ /aʊ/z /oʊ/w
l/aʊ/ /aʊ/k

Words:

our council mouth
out counsel noun
outcome count pound
output county power
owl coward profound
brow crowd proud
cow crown round
eyebrow discount row (quarrel)
how doubt scout
now down shout
about drown shower
account encounter sound
allow flounder sour
amount flour/flower south
announce foul surround
around found thousand
background frown towel
blouse gown tower
bound ground town
boundary hour trout
brown house vowel
browse loud wound (verb wind)
cloud mount wow
clown mountain
compound mouse

Phrases:

a thousand sounds   best towel in town   county sheriff
allow a small amount   bound by doubt   crowded brown couch
announcement about cows   boy scout   crown counsel
around the mountain   count down   discount gown
beautiful flower   counting clouds   doubting clown

338

down and out
down town
encountered a clown
foul aroma
found a flounder
found a hound
found a mountain range
found out
fresh trout
frilly gown
frown upside down
ground flowers
high tower
house mouse
how about now
I found the vowel
it is loud downtown
jeweled crown
large amount
large discount
last hour

loud crowd
loud house
mount the horse
mouth to mouth
no doubt
not a coward
nouns and vowels
oh wow!
on the ground
out of town
outhouse
pound on the door
power struggle
powerful mouse
powerful sound
profound ideas
pronounce the noun
pronounce your vowels
proud mama
proud scout
round table

scary encounter
shout out loud
shower caddy
shower towel
sound of a noun
sound the alarm
sour candy
sour taste in the mouth
south Carolina
surrounded by friends
surrounded by towers
Thousand Islands
thousands of pounds
throw in the towel
too loud
verbs and nouns
white flour
wound it around
wow, what a shower

Sentences:

I found a mouse

Now I know how she found it

Always pronounce that last vowel

I heard a loud, powerful sound downstairs

There's a large amount of clowns crowded downtown

I don't know how to pronounce those nouns and vowels

I'm feeling a bit down and out

I'm counting all the horses I see around the mountain

In an emergency, you might have to give mouth to mouth

The proud scout shouted with a powerful voice

That left a sour taste in my mouth

I'll eat a thousand pounds of flour cookies

I found out about the announcement too late

Our power went out about an hour ago

The announcement is in about an hour

The flowers are so beautiful down south

She found the cow behind a mound of dirt

How do you pronounce the word account?
I looked at the clouds for hours and hours
The sound was coming from around the corner
She put her gown down on the round brown table
The clouds turned brown around the dusty mountain town
The hound was making a strange sound from his rounded mouth
I had to shout out loud to find out
Is your spouse wearing a brown blouse?

Reading:

Now that you understand how to pronounce this sound naturally and have a greater grasp of this sound's spelling, you can move on to more complex reading items. Look for this sound in books and record yourself reading with your full mouth movements for the diphthong. Don't drop the tail. After you're done, review the video to check your mouth movements and listen to the sounds. Read along with your video recording to see if you caught every single /aʊ/ in the reading. Remember, you'll want to do this regularly to increase your familiarity with this sound and build it into a habit. I recommend daily practice reading aloud and recording yourself to get used to the new movements to feel natural until you no longer feel you have to do so intentionally.

Conversation:

Even if you're at the reading level, you will want to begin using this sound as much as you possibly can in daily conversation. It will require significantly more focus at the onset of your practice and mean that you will need to be intentional with every word you say. At first, you will miss so many diphthongs, but any that you do notice, do not let yourself pass without correcting yourself. I highly recommend just saying it over again with the new pronunciation. You will improve your processing speed, and the need to repeat yourself will be less and less as you practice. Keep at it, and don't expect perfection. Nobody speaks perfectly, not even native English speakers, so give yourself a break and let yourself mess up a little bit. This is a process. It takes time. Conversation practice will take you out of your comfort zone, so embrace the silly feeling you might encounter and just work through it. It's all about getting used to it!

/oɪ/ as in "Boy, Toy & Soy"

Description:

The /oI/ or "oh ee" diphthong is similar to other diphthongs, as, of course, there are two vowels that transition from one to the other. The first element of the diphthong is the "oh" sound. This sound is made with a slightly open jaw position, which means the tongue is somewhat lower than the neutral position. The lips are round in a tight circle, then transition to a smile. You will slowly transition the tongue from the lower position and pull it up so that you will feel the sides of your tongue pressing up on each side of the roof of the mouth or the upper molars for /i/ or "ee." The jaw, lips, and tongue transition simultaneously, making this, along with all diphthongs, slightly more difficult for speakers to produce than just your typical everyday vowel.

Common Differences:

The most typical change that speakers make to this sound is to drop the tail end of the diphthong, the /i/ or "ee." The result of dropping the /i/makes words like "toy" sound like "toe." The simplest fix to this issue is to focus on feeling the /i/ "ee" sound by adding a smile and pulling your tongue up at the end of the diphthong. At first, this will feel strange since you are adding an extra sound that you have never added before. It takes time to get used to.

Another common change made to this diphthong is reducing the amount of lip rounding for the "oh" part of the sound. The fix in this situation is to ensure your lip rounding is complete by using a mirror to focus on a tight rounding position and add the tail /i/ smile afterward.

Spelling:

The /oI/ sound is spelled in two different ways:
"oy": as in "boy, toy, soy, joy"
"oi": as in "coin, coil, foil"

Hear it!

Take some time to go through the minimal pairs list below. Decide for yourself which substitution you believe you are making, and listen to the difference in pronunciation as you add the /i/ "ee" sound in the diphthong.

/oI/ vs /oʊ/ Minimal Pairs:

boil	/bowl	coin	/cone	foil	/foal
boy	/bow	coil	/coal	join	/Joan

joy	/Joe	toil	/toll	soil	/soul
noise	/nose	toy	/toe		
oil	/'ol	toying	/towing		

/oI/ vs /a/ Minimal Pairs:

boil	/ball	foil	/fall	toil	/tall
coin	/con	joy	/jaw	soil	/Saul
coil	/call	oil	/all	doily	/dolly

Feel it!

Once you are confident you can hear the difference in your typical pronunciation versus the "oh ee" diphthong, go through the minimal pairs once more. Don't focus so much on the sound this time, but pay attention to your lips and tongue. Notice how your lips transition from a tight circle to a spread-out smile. Feel how your tongue moves from a low position in the mouth to a high position in the mouth for each word. Grab a mirror and see how different your mouth looks when you focus on these lip changes. As you feel this difference better, you can rely on yourself to know when you pronounce this diphthong (even without a mirror).

Do it!

Go through the practice below, starting from isolation, syllables, words, phrases, and sentences. These steps will help you create a high level of awareness in your speech. Self-awareness is essential before we move on to the conversation level.

Isolation:

Repeat: "oh ee" /oI/, /oI/,/oI/,/oI/,/oI/

Syllables:

s/oI/	j/oI/	/oI/z
b/oI/	r/oI/	/oI/k
t/oI/	l/oI/	/oI/g
p/oI/	w/oI/	/oI/sh
d/oI/	y/oI/	/oI/ch
z/oI/	/oI/p	/oI/j
k/oI/	/oI/b	/oI/r
g/oI/	/oI/t	/oI/l
sh/oI/	/oI/d	/oI/w
ch /oI/	/oI/s	

annoy

annoyance

annoying

avoid

boil

boy

choice

coil

coin

coy

destroy

destroying

employ

employer

enjoy

exploit

foil

join

joy

loyal

noise

oil

oyster

point

poison

royal

soil

soy

spoil

toil

toy

toying

voice

void

voyage

Phrases:

a new voyage

annoying choice

avoid poison

avoid the moisture

be loyal

boil the water

boiling point

broiled oysters

check the soil

coy boy

destroy your enemies

destroyed coin

don't annoy

don't be coy

enjoy toiling the soil

exploited employee

join the group

labor and toil

loyal employee

oily oysters

olive oil

pay the coin

point to the spot

pointy toy

poison control

royal decree

spoiled the boy with toys

tasty oysters

the boy's appointment

use the tinfoil

voice your opinion

void cheque

want a new toy

what a loud noise

Sentences:

I avoid oily oysters

How did Roy avoid Floyd?

I bought the toy in Detroit

You have to destroy the poison

The gardeners toiled on the royal soil

The boy was annoying and a little paranoid

That was an annoying choice to buy pointy toys

I was destroyed by Joy's choice to broil the oysters

The loyal employee was exploited by his employer

If you avoid moisture, you avoid destroying the collector coins

Any noise annoys an oyster, but a noisy noise annoys an oyster the most

Reading:

After thoroughly practicing the /oI/ "oh ee" diphthong in sentences and complex tongue twisters, you can now move on to other reading texts. Remember, it is a

343

really useful strategy to read aloud and record yourself and review yourself speaking as you read along with the text. This type of practice will help you increase your articulation skills and your ability to differentiate and become more aware of this sound.

Conversation:

Once you feel you have a good grasp of the /oɪ/"oh ee" sound in English words, it is time to use what you know! Practice with literally anyone you speak; the store clerk, the mail carrier, friends, family, colleagues, clients. This is a tough step! My clients find it helpful, though, to remind themselves that this is a method to increase your clarity, ensure your meaning is understood, and feel confident that you are expressing yourself accurately in your current surroundings. Your comfort level will increase with time, and you will feel yourself self-correcting your articulation more and more. With practice, you will find that your diphthong pronunciation gets quicker and more natural. Keep it up!

PART FOUR: But What About...

Chapter 31: English Exceptions: When The Rules Don't Apply

So, by this point, you have learned quite a lot! You have a significantly greater understanding of the sounds in English and have had a chance to improve your awareness, differentiation, and pronunciation of English sounds. "But, what about all those exceptions in English?" you may be asking.

In this chapter, I will delve deeper into the different types of exceptions to English pronunciation and their rules.

Now, I know, you're probably thinking, "The last thing I need is more rules to memorize!" I'm with you. The goal here is to shed some light on some of the patterns in these English exceptions so you can better deal with them rather than always memorizing vocabulary. Unfortunately, there is no escaping at least a little bit of vocabulary memorization when it comes to English since there are instances where the rules just don't apply.

Common Words That Don't Sound Like They Are Spelled

I wanted to start with this list because, unlike some of the other lists in this chapter, you will surely use these words regularly in conversation.

one   rhymes with "sun"
do   rhymes with "boo"
who   rhymes with "boo"
shoe   rhymes with "boo"

two	rhymes with "boo"	
is	rhymes with "fizz," the /s/ is pronounced as a /z/	
his	rhymes with "fizz," the /s/ is pronounced as a /z/	
was	rhymes with "fuzz," the /s/ is pronounced as a /z/	
of	rhymes with "love," the "o" is pronounced as "uh," and the "f" is pronounced like a /v/	

Homophones

Homophones are two words that are spelled differently and have different meanings but <u>sound the same</u>. The root of the word homo means "the same," and phone means "sound." Examples of homophones are "to, too, and two." Although this seems frustrating, do consider that basically, every language has some homophones; it's just part of the package. As our focus here is on pronunciation, I will not go deep into the meaning differences of each of these sets of homophones, but be aware that there may be different spellings for words you use that are pronounced the same.

<u>Homophone Words: A pretty exhaustive list!</u>

ad, add	bazaar, bizarre	brews, bruise
ail, ale	be, bee	bridal, bridle
air, heir	bean, been	broach, brooch
aisle, I'll, isle	beat, beet	bur, burr
allowed, aloud	beau, bow	but, butt
altar, alter	berry, bury	buy, by, bye
arc, ark	billed, build	canvas, canvass
ate, eight	bite, byte	cast, caste
aural, oral	blew, blue	cede, seed
aye, eye, I	boar, bore	ceiling, sealing
bail, bale	board, bored	cell, sell
bald, bawled	boarder, border	censor, sensor
ball, bawl	bold, bowled	cent, scent, sent
band, banned	boos, booze	cereal, serial
bare, bear	bough, bow	cheap, cheep
baron, barren	brake, break	check, cheque
base, bass	bread, bred	chord, cord

cite, sight, site

coarse, course

colonel, kernel

complement, compliment

core, corps

council, counsel

creak, creek

crews, cruise

cue, queue, Q

currant, current

dam, damn

days, daze

dear, deer

descent, dissent

dew, due

die, dye

doe, dough

draft, draught

dual, duel

earn, urn

ewe, you

fair, fare

feat, feet

few, phew

find, fined

fir, fur

flair, flare

flea, flee

flew, flu, flue

flour, flower

for, fore, four

foreword, forward

forth, fourth

foul, fowl

friar, fryer

gait, gate

genes, jeans

gorilla, guerilla

grate, great

greys, graze

groan, grown

guessed, guest

hail, hale

hair, hare

hall, haul

hangar, hanger

hay, hey

heal, heel, he'll

hear, here

heard, herd

he'd, heed

heroin, heroine

hi, high

higher, hire

him, hymn

ho, hoe

hoard, horde

hoarse, horse

holey, holy, wholly

hour, our

idle, idol

in, inn

it's, its

key, quay

knave, nave

knead, need

knew, new

knight, night

knob, nob

knot, not

know, no

knows, nose

lain, lane

laps, lapse

leach, leech

lead, led

leak, leek

lean, lien

lessen, lesson

license, license

licker, liquor

lie, lye

links, lynx

lo, low

loan, lone

locks, lox

loot, lute

made, maid

mail, male

main, mane

maize, maze

mall, maul

mare, mayor

marshal, martial

meat, meet

medal, meddle

might, mite

mind, mined

miner, minor

missed, mist

mode, mowed

moor, more

moose, mousse

morning, mourning

muscle, mussel

naval, navel

none, nun

ode, owed

oh, owe

one, won

packed, pact

pail, pale

pain, pane

pair, pare, pear

palate, pallet

pause, paws

pea, pee, P

peace, piece

peak, peek, pique

pedal, peddle

peer, pier

pi, pie

plain, plane

pole, poll

praise, prays, preys

principal, principle

profit, prophet

quarts, quartz

rain, reign, rein

raise, rays,

rap, wrap

read, red

read, reed

real, reel

reek, wreak

rest, wrest

right, rite, write

ring, wring

road, rode

roe, row

role, roll

root, route

rose, rows

rote, wrote

rye, wry

sale, sail

saver, savor

scene, seen

sea, see

seam, seem

sear, seer

seas, sees, seize

sew, so, sow

shear, sheer

shoe, shoo

side, sighed

sink, synch

slay, sleigh

soar, sore

sole, soul

some, sum

son, sun

spade, spayed

stair, stare

stake, steak

stationary, stationery

steal, steel

straight, strait

sweet, suite

tacks, tax

tale, tail

taught, taut

tea, tee, T

team, teem

tear, tier

teas, tease

there, their, they're

threw, through

throes, throws

throne, thrown

thyme, time

tic, tick

tide, tied

to, too, two

toad, towed

told, tolled

vain, vane, vein

vial, vile

wail, whale

waist, waste

wait, weight

waive, wave

war, wore

ware, wear, where

warn, worn

wax, whacks

way, weigh, whey

we, wee

weak, week

weather, whether

we'd, weed

we'll, wheel

were, whirr

weald, wheeled

which, witch

whine, wine

whirled, world

who's, whose

woe, whoa

wood, would

yoke, yolk

yore, your, you're

you'll, yule

Homonyms

Homonyms are words that have the <u>same spelling</u> and <u>sound the same</u> but have different meanings. Many of the words with multiple syllables change meaning when you stress one syllable over another. For example, we stress, or place greater emphasis on most nouns and adjectives in the first syllable, so the word "subject," stressed in the first syllable "**SUB**ject" would be the noun, where if you were to stress the second syllable as in most English verbs, the word would sound like "sub**JECT**." Stressing the syllable is done by making the syllable louder, longer, and higher pitched. If you are unaware of some of the double meanings, refer to the dictionary for both descriptions.

<u>Homonym Words:</u>

accent	down	manifest
address	drain	match
back	duck	may
ball	fall	mean
bank	file	median
bar	fine	mind
bark	firm	mint
bat	float	model
battery	fly	mouse
brace	foot	nail
buck	gas	notice
building	grave	novel
can	harbor	object
character	hoe	odd
chest	implant	one
club	import	palm
console	increase	park
content	insert	patient
contract	insult	perfect
crane	invite	permit
date	jam	pin
default	just	pitch
degree	kind	play
dessert	land	pop
discharge	leaves	pound
discount	left	present
dismiss	lie	proceeds
display	lighter	progress

project	roll	spring
protest	rose	story
quarter	round	subject
rebel	ruler	survey
recall	saw	suspect
record	scale	tie
refund	seal	top
reservation	second	train
right	sheer	type
ring	show	update
rock	sink	wave

Silent Letters

Here are the most common words categorized by the silent sound.

<u>Silent B:</u>

bomb	dumb	subtle
climb	jamb	succumb
comb	lamb	tomb
crumb	limb	womb
debt	numb	thumb
doubt	plumb	

<u>Silent C:</u>

abscess	fascinate	obscene
ascent	fluorescent	resuscitate
conscience	incandescent	scenario
conscious	isosceles	scene
crescent	luminescent	scent
descend	miscellaneous	science
disciple	muscle	scissors

<u>Silent D:</u>

handkerchief	handsome	Wednesday

Silent G:

align	design	gnome
assign	feign	high
benign	foreign	light
Champaign	gnash	reign
cologne	gnat	resign
consign	gnaw	

Silent H:

honor	heir	vehement
hour	homage	
honest	vehicle	

H is silent after G and R in:

ghastly	ghost	rhyme
gherkin	rhinoceros	rhythm
ghetto	rhubarb	

H is also usually silent after W:

what	where	white
wheel	while	why
when	whisper	

BUT "H" IS pronounced in:
WHO!

Silent K:

knack	knickers	knot
knave	knick-knack	know
knead	knife	knowledge
knee	knight	knowledgeable
kneel	knit	knuckle
knelt	knob	
knew	knock	

Silent L:

alms	calf	colonel
balm	calm	could
balk	chalk	embalm

folk	psalm	Stockholm
half	qualm	talk
Lincoln	salmon	walk
Norfolk	should	would
palm	stalk	yolk

Silent M:

mnemonics

Silent N:

autumn	condemn	solemn
column	hymn	damn

Silent P:

corps	psyche	psychotic
coup	psychedelic	psychosis
cupboard	psychiatrist	pterodactyl
pneumonia	psychiatry	ptosis
pneumonic	psychic	raspberry
psalm	psycho	receipt
pseudonym	psychologist	
psoriasis	psychology	

Silent T:

Silent T Words Ending With -STLE

apostle	hustle	thistle
bustle	nestle	whistle
castle	rustle	wrestle
gristle		

Silent T Words Ending With -STEN

christen	chasten	moisten
glisten	fasten	
listen	hasten	

Silent T Words With -FT

often
soften

French Words With a Silent T at the End

ballet	depot	rapport
buffet	chalet	ricochet
fillet	gourmet	

Other Words With Silent T: No rules for these crazy rogues!

Chestnut (only the first t is silent)

mortgage

Christmas

Silent U:

baguette	fatigue	guilty
biscuit	guess	guise
build	guest	guitar
built	guide	intrigue
catalogue	guild	league
circuit	guile	prologue
colleague	guillotine	rogue
disguise	guilt	silhouette

Silent W:

awry	wreck	write
playwright	wren	writhe
sword	wrench	wrong
wrangle	wrestle	wrote
wrap	wretch	wrought
wrapper	wriggle	wrung
wrath	wring	wry
wreak	wrinkle	
wreath	wrist	

Other silent letters:

aisle	The "s" is silent	pronounced "eye uhl"
asthma	the "th" is silent	pronounced "az-ma"
colonel	"olo" is substituted	pronounced "ker-nel"
conscience	"scie" is substituted	pronounced "con-chinse"
indict	the "c" is silent	pronounced "in-dite"
island	the "s" is silent	pronounced "eye-land"
jeopardy	the "o" is silent	pronounced as "e" "je-per-dy"
liaison	the 2nd "i" is silent	pronounced "lee-ay-zon"

pharaoh	the "a" is silent	pronounced "fair-roe"
queue	the 2nd "ue" is silent	pronounced "cue"
receipt	the "p" is silent;	pronounced "ruh-seet"
zucchini	"cch" said as /k/	pronounced "zoo-key-knee"

Two Accepted Pronunciations:

We're Flexible!

In English, there are a few words that most people accept as being pronounced in two ways. Each is pronounced slightly differently by various speakers, and each pronunciation is widely accepted.

Basil	/eɪ/ "eh ee" vs /æ/ "aa"
Apricot	/eɪ/ "eh ee" vs /æ/ "aa"
Roof	/u/ "oo" vs /ʊ/ rhymes with "book"
Aunt	/a/ "ah" vs /æ/ "aa"
Process	/a/ "ah" vs /oʊ/ "oh ww"
Direct	/aɪ/ "ah ee" vs /ə/ "uh"
Economic	/i/ "ee" vs /ɛ/ "eh"
Either	/aɪ/ "ah ee" vs /i/ "ee"
Envelope	/a/ "ah" vs. /ɛ/ "eh"
With	/ð/ voiced vs /θ/ voiceless

When "Ch" is Pronounced as "K"

Below is a list of words spelled with a "ch" but pronounced as a plosive stop sound /k/.

anchor	chaos	choir
archaeology	character	chorus
architect	charisma	choreograph
archive	Christmas	Christian

echo   ache

chemical   zucchini

When "Th" is Pronounced as "T"

Below is a list of words spelled with a "th" but pronounced as the plosive stop sound /t/.

Thomas   Thai   Theresa

Thompson   Thyme   Esther

Thames   Thailand

Spelling Inconsistencies for "Ough"

Words containing "ough" are confusing since there are multiple ways to pronounce it, and the spelling will not help indicate this. These are words you will need to memorize. Here are some examples.

Pronounced as "ot" as in "pot"   thought, bought, fought, brought, ought
Pronounced as "uff" as in "stuff"   enough, rough, tough, slough
Pronounced as "oo" as in "moo"   through
Pronounced as "oh" as in "go"   though, although, dough, thorough
Pronounced as "off"   cough
Pronounced as "ow" as in "cow"   bough, doughty

Dropped Syllables

You may have already noticed that some words in English are just plain not pronounced as they are spelled. It almost seems as if English speakers are making up their own rules and dropping parts willy-nilly. What is happening is that an entire unstressed syllable is dropped altogether.

Take "business," for example. This word looks as if it should be three syllables: bus-i-ness. The middle unstressed syllable is dropped and becomes "bizz-nuss." In some cases, a sound is dropped, but not always the syllable (as in "iron" pronounced as "eye-urn").

Why do English speakers do this? Well, generally, English speakers reduce vowel sounds to say words more efficiently. Dropping syllables also helps us to direct more attention to the stressed syllables. Some words are reduced depending on the speaker, dialect, and context or situation. English speakers reduce the unstressed syllables so much that entire syllables are at times dropped. Some words are so commonly spoken that they are always spoken with the dropped syllable as a general rule. These changes have become the norm over time.

Generally, the syllables that are dropped are the unstressed syllables. The term to describe this dropped syllable phenomenon is called "elision." Here is a list of common words to be aware of in terms of syllables.

Asian	The word is just plain different☺	"ay zhun"
Australia	The "i" is dropped	"aws trail yuh"
billion	"ion" pronounced as "yun"	"bill yun"
business	The "i" is dropped	"biz nuss"
Christian	The word is just plain different☺	"krish chin"
comfortable	The word is just plain different☺	"cumf ter bull"
controversial	The word is just plain different☺	"con truh ver shuhl"
diamond	The "a" is dropped	"die mund"
diaper	The "a" is dropped	"die per"
drawer	The word is just plain different☺	"jrow er"
environment	The "o" is dropped	"en vie ern ment"
evening	The "e" is dropped	"eev ning"
eventually	The "u" is dropped	"uh ven chuh lee"
favourite	The "ou" is dropped	"fave ruht"
flood	The "oo" is pronounced "uh"	"fluhd"
gardening	The "e" is dropped	"gard ning"
genius	The word is just plain different☺	"jean yus"
iron	The "o" is dropped	"eye ern"
jewel	The "e" is dropped	"jew ul"

man<u>sion</u>	The word is just plain different☺	"man chin"
marr<u>ia</u>ge	The "i" is dropped	"mare udge"
mill<u>ion</u>	"ion" pronounced as "yun"	"mill yun"
mis<u>c</u>ellan<u>eou</u>s	The word is just plain different☺	"miss uh lay nee us"
mo<u>du</u>le	The word is just plain different☺	"mah jewl"
naus<u>ea</u>	The "e" is dropped	"naw zhuh"
<u>o</u>c<u>ea</u>n	The word is just plain different☺	"oh shin"
offi<u>cia</u>l	The word is just plain different☺	"uh fish uhl"
on<u>io</u>n	"ion" pronounced as "yun"	"uhn yun"
opin<u>io</u>n	"ion" pronounced as "yun"	"uh pin yun"
<u>p</u>n<u>eu</u>monia	The word is just plain different☺	"nuh moan yuh"
powerf<u>ul</u>ly	The "u" is dropped	"power flee"
rest<u>au</u>rant	The "au" is dropped	"rest ront"
sopho<u>m</u>ore	The "o" is dropped	"sof more"
tuition	The word is just plain different☺	"too wish un"
usu<u>a</u>lly	The word is just plain different☺	"uzh uh lee"
vege<u>t</u>able	The "e" is dropped	"vej tuh bull"
We<u>dn</u>esday	The /d/ is silent and "e is dropped	"wenz day"

Try practicing some of these strangely pronounced words in sentences.

Sentences:
We bought the vegetables in the evening for our restaurant business.
I love to wear diamonds and jewels to business meetings.
I never iron diapers.
We're going out Wednesday evening.
I never feel comfortable eating vegetables at restaurants.

OR/OL words:	The "o" is dropped for all
lab<u>o</u>ratory	Pronounced "lab ruh tow ree"
the<u>o</u>ry	Pronounced "thee ree"
fav<u>ou</u>rite	Pronounced "fave rut"
Cath<u>o</u>lic	Pronounced "cath lick"
choc<u>o</u>late	Pronounced "chock lit"
mem<u>o</u>rable	Pronounced "mem ruh bull"

Sentences:
The sophomore is learning science theory.
This is my favourite laboratory.

357

The Catholic priest learned religious theory during his education.

That's my favourite kind of chocolate.

ER words:	The "e" is dropped for all
average	Pronounced "av ridge"
beverage	Pronounced "bev ridge"
camera	Pronounced "caam ruh"
desperate	Pronounced "des priht"
different	Pronounced "diff rint"
every	Pronounced "ev ree"
generally	Pronounced "jen ruh lee"
interesting	Pronounced "in trus ting"
miserable	Pronounced "miz ruh bull"
opera	Pronounced "ahp ruh"
several	Pronounced "sev rull"
temperature	Pronounced "tem pruh cher"
veterinarian	Pronounced "vet ruh nair ee un"
aspirin	Pronounced "ass prin"

Sentences:

Every camera is different.

I checked my temperature and took aspirin for the pain.

The veterinarian walked my miserable dog to me after he got his shots.

There are several beverages that I enjoy.

What is the average number of interesting facts you have memorized?

ALLY words:	The "a" is dropped for all
alphabetically	Pronounced "al fuh bed ick lee"
accidentally	Pronounced "axe uh dent lee"
actually	Pronounced "ak shuh lee"
basically	Pronounced "bay sick lee"
generally	Pronounced "Jen ruh lee"
practically	Pronounced "Prac tick lee"

Sentences:

I accidentally told my friend the secret.

She practically lost her mind when she saw the final episode of the season.

That's basically all I can remember from that meeting.

I'm actually impressed with your reports lately.

Syllabic Consonants

A syllabic consonant occurs when a consonant takes over and acts as the entire syllable itself; it takes over the vowel before it. A few consonants can do this, but let's focus on "L and N." The most common form of this is when an "L" or "N" becomes syllabic in unstressed syllables. The consonant does not sound any different than usual; it just allows you to delete the vowel before it altogether. For example, "chemical" is pronounced "kem uh kL," and the "a" is essentially dropped. The "L" takes on the syllable.

Syllabic "L":

cattle	"caa-dl"
bottle	"bah-dl"
chemical	"kem-uh-kl"
counseling	"cown-sling"
couple's	"cuh-plz"
double	"duh-bl"
isolated	"ice-layded"
journalism	"jern-lizm"
little	"lih-dl"
models	"mah-dlz"
penalty	"pen-lty"
personally	"pers-n-lee"
police	"plees"
poodle	"poo-dl"
saddle	"saa-dl"
successfully	"suck-sess-flee"

AL Words:

actual	bridal	cereal
aerial	brutal	choral
animal	burial	dental
annual	casual	dismal

facial	moral	rival
fatal	mortal	royal
final	mural	rural
fiscal	mutual	sandal
floral	nasal	serial
focal	naval	signal
formal	neural	social
frugal	normal	spinal
genial	plural	tidal
global	portal	total
herbal	postal	tribal
legal	primal	urinal
lethal	racial	usual
local	radial	verbal
loyal	rascal	viral
mammal	regal	visual
manual	renal	vital
medal	rental	vocal
mental	ritual	

Sentences:

A sloth is a mammal

Does it have facial recognition?

He's very social

I attended the annual global event

I had some dental work

I have a moral obligation

I try to be frugal

I'll log into the portal today

I'm a loyal friend

I'm watching lethal weapon

It was a verbal agreement

It' not normal to do that

It's a casual gathering

It's a mutual agreement

It's an actual original specimen

It's vital to the company

She had a spinal cord injury

She went to the formal gala

That's my favorite cereal
They are the rival corporation
What a brutal storm
What a cute animal
What a rascal!
What's the plural of goose?
What's the serial number?
What's your postal code?
Where is the local farmer's market?

ALLY words:	The "a" is dropped for all
Accidentally	Pronounced "axe uh dent lee"
Actually	Pronounced "ak shuh lee"
Basically	Pronounced "bay sick lee"
Generally	Pronounced "Jen ruh lee"
Practically	Pronounced "Prac tick lee"
Alphabetically	Pronounced "al fuh bed ick lee"

annually
brutally
casually
equally
facially
fatally
finally
fiscally
formally
globally
ideally

legally
lethally
locally
manually
mentally
morally
mortally
mutually
normally
racially
ritually

royally
serially
socially
totally
usually
verbally
visually
vitally
vocally

Sentences:
He casually entered the data
He was racially profiled
He's mentally drained
I accidentally told my friend the secret
I am equally surprised
I am finally finished
I totally understand

I'll be brut<u>ally</u> honest

I'll explain it verb<u>ally</u> to you

I'm actu<u>ally</u> impressed with your reports lately

Ide<u>ally</u> you would come along

It was actu<u>ally</u> agreed on mutu<u>ally</u>

It was done manu<u>ally</u>

It was fat<u>ally</u> executed

It was form<u>ally</u> presented today

It's a decision that was based on mor<u>ally</u> defined traits

It's not norm<u>ally</u> done that way

She practic<u>ally</u> lost her mind when she saw the final episode of the season

That's basic<u>ally</u> all I can remember from that meeting

The fruit was grown loc<u>ally</u>

Usu<u>ally</u> I'm more prepared

Syllabic "N"

<u>Syllabic "N" Words:</u>

appreci<u>ation</u>	"uh-pree-she-ehee-shn"
burd<u>en</u>	"bur-dn"
coul<u>dn</u>'t	"could-nt"
defi<u>ni</u>tely	"def-nit-lee"
di<u>dn</u>'t	"di-dnt"
ev<u>en</u>	"e-vn"
fast<u>en</u>	"fa-sn"
happ<u>en</u>	"ha-pn"
list<u>en</u>	"li-sn"
old<u>en</u>	"ohwl-dn"
oft<u>en</u>	"ah-fn"
reas<u>on</u>	"ree-zn"
recre<u>ation</u>	"reh-cree-ehee-shn"
relat<u>ion</u>ship	"ruh-lay-shn-ship"
ris<u>en</u>	"rih-zn"
sadd<u>en</u>	"saa-dn"
sec<u>ond</u>	"seh-knd"
shoul<u>dn</u>'t	"should-nt"

stud<u>ent</u>	"stew-dnt"
tigh<u>ten</u>	"tie-tn"
woul<u>dn</u>'t	"wood-nt"

Listening Exercise:

Now that you understand how these particular sounds change in words, you can start to listen to native English speakers in a whole new way. It's good to listen with focused attention to increase your ability to hear these syllabic sounds. Often it is just too difficult to parse apart rapid speakers' speech in real-time. You can listen to videos online and slow down the speaker's speed. Set the pace to a slow rate and listen for the syllabic sounds. You can even watch speakers with their script attached and read along, listening for the syllabic words as you go. The CBC and Ted Talk speakers online include scripts with each presentation so you can easily read along and do this exercise.

Reading and Conversation:

Now go and find your own reading passage to try out your new skills. Find your "L" and "N" syllabic words and try to drop the vowel before it. Read frequently to increase your speed and accuracy until you feel ready to use this new strategy when speaking. You might find it helpful to choose a few words to start with. Choose a few words you use frequently, and attempt your new pronunciation with those words until you feel comfortable adding more. Begin to use your new vocabulary, be it words with silent letters, homonyms, and syllabic "L" and "N" pronunciations, in your daily conversations. This process does take time, and only practice and familiarity will help with these "exception" rules in English. What you do have now is the information. The mysterious changes in English speech have been revealed to you. Knowing what the differences are is half the problem, and this is a problem you no longer have! Now, all you have to do is practice practice practice! Do a little every day, and you will see your pronunciation skills improve dramatically.

PART FIVE: Fluency in English

Chapter 32: Stress Patterns; Not The Kind of Stress You May be Thinking of!

What is Stress?

Stress in language is when we make a particular word or syllable louder, longer, and higher pitch than the others. Stress affects the rhythm of your speech. As listeners, native English speakers expect a predictable timing and rhythm in speech, and when the timing is off, it can affect your being understood. We know that speaking with correct stress patterns in English will have one of the most significant impacts on your ability to be understood by others, which is why it is so important.

Because many languages have very predictive stress patterns or equal stress patterns, the idea of having rules to adjust your speech seems quite daunting. Using the stress patterns in English is essential for ensuring that your meaning is clear. The rhythm or music of English is created by stressing some words and syllables and de-stressing others.

By practicing to improve your stress, you will be easier to understand, and you will be a more impactful speaker.

Let's learn some tricks to make English stress a lot easier!

Strong vs. Weak Sentence Stress:
In English, the content or meaningful words are **emphasized** (stressed) or made strong and long, and the function words (those little guys like a, the, to) are **de-emphasized** (unstressed). When you de-stress a word or syllable and make it weak,

364

you make the sounds quieter and very quick. It's almost as if the vowel is nearly gone. It's that fast.

Stress For Emphasis

A reason we might change the stress in a sentence is to emphasize a specific word. Below are examples of sentences that can be stressed in many different ways, each way changing the meaning of the statement:

I never told you she stole that money: The speaker never mentioned it.
I **never** told you she stole that money: The information was never told.
I never **told** you she stole that money: The speaker never explicitly said it.
I never told **you** she stole that money: The speaker may have told another person.
I never told you **she** stole that money: The speaker said someone did, not her specifically.
I never told you she **stole** that money: The speaker didn't say that the money was stolen.
I never told you she stole **that** money: She may have stolen different money.
I never told you she stole that **money**: She may have stolen a different item.

De-Stressed Words

Now we will go over some of the most common destressed words in English. These are the words to really rush through quickly, almost deleting the vowel in the word entirely. By de-stressing these function words, we can create contrast with the stressed words, giving our listener clearer information about what to pay attention to. Beside each word is how the term can be pronounced in its reduced form. Often, to destress a word, we neutralize the vowel to schwa "uh."

a "uh"
an "uhn"
and "uhn"
are "er"
as "uhz"
at "uht"
because "buhkuz"
can "cuhn"
for "fer"
in "n"

365

of "uhv and uh"
or "er"
our "ahr"
to "tuh" (if followed by a vowel, then it is "too")
you "yuh"
your "yer"
the "thuh"

Pronouns (he, she, me, they, we, I, them, etc.) become reduced or unstressed.

Destressed Sentence Practice: (Destressed words are underlined here)

Rush through the underlined words and stress the other words.
Where's the remote?
What's the time?
She can do it
I'm going to leave
She has a lot to say
I'm learning to speak Spanish
I'm going to go to the grocery store
You'll need to get there on time
He's one of a kind
Was that for you?
He's on his way to the store
I have to find a washroom right now
You are kind and sweet
It's as big as a mountain
You have to line up one at a time
Leave your umbrella at home today
I knew it because she told me yesterday
One by one, they came into the office
I can take your next order
It's for you
I can see you
Practice your pronunciation
I was going to pick you up later tonight
As far as I can tell, the show is canceled
There's one for you and one for me
It's one and the same

I found the document on my computer

You can come to **my** place, or I can come to **your** place

He can drive you there

How are you doing today?

He's been feeling pretty down and out lately

Was this piece of cake mine or yours?

You left your phone at **my** place

This is our favorite place to eat

A

The word "a" is a special function word. Because it is unstressed, English speakers tend to reduce the pronunciation to a simple "uh" rather than "aa" or "ey" when a consonant follows it. The result is a quicker, more natural reduction of the word. If the word "a" is followed by a vowel, however, the "a" will be pronounced as "an. " For example, "a door" is pronounced "uh," because there is a consonant after the word. "An author" would be pronounced "an" because there is a vowel after the word.

In the phrases below, practice reducing the word "a" to "uh," and "an" to "uhn."

Let's practice:

He had a plan

I grabbed a piece of paper

We had a deal

I learned a lesson

I held a cup in my hand

She sat in a chair

We're in a good place

That was a good decision

You had a great idea

We did a good job

What a beautiful place

Have a nice day

Have a great evening

What a day
What a great game
There's a letter for you
I had a report due today
A paper got jammed
I need a pen
Do you have a clock here?
I need a washroom break
I need to make a decision
We had a discussion
She won a prize
What an ordeal
He's an organized guy
I love an interesting story
That's a plan

To

The word "to" is a special function word. Because it is unstressed, English speakers tend to reduce the pronunciation to a simple "tuh" rather than "too" when a consonant follows it. If the "to" is followed by a vowel; however, the "to" will be pronounced as "too. " For example, "going to go" is pronounced "tuh," where "to our place" would be pronounced "too." Weirdly enough, the /t/ in "to" will also be pronounced as /d/ if it has a vowel before it as well since the /t/ then becomes the "flap /t/" when surrounded by vowels. E.g., "go to" becomes "go duh."

Let's practice:

according to legend
appeal to the masses
back to back
bound to happen
cater to you
come to terms with it
it comes down to you
cut to the chase

368

day to day
desire to love
down to earth
drink to that
end to end
eye to eye
face to face
fall to the ground
get to go
go to my place
go to our place
have to understand
he's dressed to the nines
head to toe
hold on to your hat
hot to trot
I'll see to it
in order to get there
it boils down to this
it's up to date
kept up to speed
lead to win
lean into it
learn to speak Mandarin
live up to your standard
look forward to it
look up to you
need to get around
next to me
not to mention
on to the next
people to see
places to explore
put down to paper
read to learn more
refer to the sign
resort to jokes
right to privacy
side to side

so to speak
speak to that point
stand up to him
stick to it
straight to the point
subject to reason
thanks to you
time to time
to and fro
to begin with
to no avail
turn to your partner
up to no good
used to do it
want to understand
way to go
what to do
where to go
will come to pass
willing to forgive
year to date
your right to vote

The

The word "the" is a special function word. Because it is typically unstressed, English speakers tend to reduce the pronunciation to a simple "thuh" rather than "thee" when it is followed by a consonant. This makes the pronunciation of this word even quicker. If the "the" is followed by a vowel, however, it will be pronounced as "thee." For example, "the cat" is pronounced "thuh", where "the end" would be pronounced "thee."

Let's Practice:

all the way out
at the end of the day

begs the question
but in the meantime
by the way
don't pass the buck
for the most part
get to the point
going off the grid
gotta face the music
have to bite the bullet
he kicked the bucket
he paved the way
he's all over the place
he's on the run
he's the cock of the walk
he's under the weather
I call the shots
I'm on the fence
I'm on the job
in the face of fear
it's all the time
it's in the air
it's in the making
it's off the hook
it's on the ground
it's the law of the land
just toe the line
let's clear the air
let's just cut to the chase
not on the spot
off the beaten track
on the contrary
on the go
on the other hand
one and the same
out of the way
over the counter meds
seize the day
she let the cat out of the bag
she made the cut

she's dressed to <u>the</u> nines
shooting <u>the</u> breeze
state of <u>the</u> art
that's beyond <u>the</u> pale
that's out of <u>the</u> question
that's over <u>the</u> top
that's so out of <u>the</u> blue
under <u>the</u> hood
we're on <u>the</u> same page
what a pain in <u>the</u> neck
you're on <u>the</u> ball

Our

The word "our" is a special function word. Because it is generally unstressed, English speakers tend to reduce the pronunciation to a simple "ahr" similar to "are" rather than "ow wer." This reduction in the pronunciation of "our" makes the word quicker and reduces it to one short syllable.

<u>Let's Practice:</u>

<u>our</u> family
<u>our</u> house
ran to <u>our</u> park
drove to <u>our</u> favourite place
go to <u>our</u> friend's house
dinner at <u>our</u> place
at <u>our</u> apartment
<u>our</u> last trip
<u>our</u> first dog
welcome to <u>our</u> home
eat in <u>our</u> lunchroom
one of <u>our</u> options
they're <u>our</u> friends
he's <u>our</u> boss
she's <u>our</u> sister
you're <u>our</u> last hope
we're having <u>our</u> lunch
you helped <u>our</u> cause

<u>our</u> printer is broken
<u>our</u> garden is looking great
<u>our</u> grass needs cutting
it's <u>our</u> turn
it's <u>our</u> right
<u>our</u> team did great today

In English, we stress or "linger" on the content words that hold meaning. We de-stress or speed through the function words or the words that carry less meaning.

Content words are the words that convey the actual meaning of a sentence. These words are what highlight what is important.

Content words are pretty much all the words that are not function words. For example,

- Nouns (e.g., paper, computer, Peter)
- (Most) main verbs (e.g., play, type)
- Adjectives (e.g., pretty, bright)
- Adverbs (e.g., often, quickly)
- Negatives including "nothing," "nowhere," etc.
- Words expressing quantities (e.g., a lot of, a couple, many, etc.)

Function words are typically little words that make the sentence grammatically make sense.

Example: the, a, an, it, she, he, of, in, on, about, around, this, there, have, had. These include:

- Prepositions (in, on, before, after)
- Pronouns (he, she, they, we, us, them, I)
- Determiners (the, a, some, an, a few)
- Verbs (have, be)
- Conjunctions (but, while, as, and)
- Auxiliary verbs (am, can, were)

Here are a few sentence examples: Notice the content stressed words are bold and held longer, while the de-stressed function words are small and sped through:

State *of the* **art**

On *the* **go**

By *the* **way**

One *and the* **same**

Out *of the* **bag**

All *the* **way**

On *the* **fence**

Shoot *the* **breeze**

Over *the* **coun**ter

Clear *the* **air**

Out *of the* **blue**

Survi**val** *of the* **fit**test

Under *the* **wea**ther

I **look for**ward *to it*

Get *to the* **point**

I **go there** *from* **time** *to* **time**

I've **come** *to* **terms** *with it*

We **see eye** *to* **eye**

Get *me* **up** *to* **speed**

He's a **pain** *in the* **neck**

I'm **on** *the* **fence**

I'll **keep** *an* **eye** *on it*

He's **on** *a* **roll**

As a **mat**ter *of* **fact**

I'll **give** *it a* **whirl**

Once *in a* **blue moon**

Take *a* **look** *at it*

John met Sarah

Go *to* **work!**

How *are* **you?**

How *did you* **get there?**

The **boss** *is in the* **office**

She **beat** *me*

I'm **eat**ing *my* **break**fast

I **walked** *to the* **beach**

Don't forget *your* **water bottle**

I'm **almost done** *with my* **work** *for the* **day**

I **wish** *I* **had**n't for**got**ten *my* **bag**

I **love go**ing *for a* **walk** *on a* **bright sun**ny **day** *in the* **ci**ty.

I've been **lear**ning **Eng**lish *for a* **year**.

I have **so much** *to* **do** *this* **week**end.

Peter *and* **Sa**rah *will* **spend** *the* **week**end *at the* **co**ttage *with their* **friends**.

I would **not** *have* **ea**ten *if I had* **known Dinner** *was* **al**most **rea**dy.

Test Your Stress: (answer key below)

Pick the meaningful words and add your stress:

Speak of the devil

That's the last straw

The best of both worlds

Nice to meet you

Where are you from?

What do you do?

Are you on Facebook?

Thanks so much

I really appreciate it

Excuse me

What do you think?

That sounds great

Never mind

I don't understand

Thank you

How do you spell it?

What do you mean?

Where is the washroom?

Can I have this delivered?

375

How can I help you?

When is our meeting?

When is the deadline?

Don't beat around the bush

Better late than never

You've got to bite the bullet

Break a leg

Let's call it a day

Cut him some slack

Don't let it get out of hand

Get out of my office

You missed the boat

She's on the ball

You're pulling my leg

That's the last straw

Your guess is as good as mine

Answer Key: (Bold are stressed and lingered on, the other items are de-stressed and sped through)

Speak of the **de**vil

That's the **last straw**

The **best** of **both worlds**

Nice to **meet** you

Where are you **from**?

What do you **do**?

Are you on **Face**book?

Thanks so **much**

I **rea**lly a**ppre**ciate it

Ex**cuse** me!

What do you **think**?

That sounds great

Never **mind**

I **don't** under**stand**

Thank you

How do you **spell** it?

What do you **mean**?

Where is the **wash**room?

Can I **have** this de**liv**ered?

How can I **help** you**?**

When is our **mee**ting?

When is the **dead**line?

Don't beat around the **bush**

Better **late** than **nev**er

You've **got** to **bite** the **bull**et

Break a **leg**

Let's **call** it a **day**

Cut him some **slack**

Don't let it **get out** of **hand**

Get out of my **office**

You **missed** the **boat**

She's **on** the **ball**

You're **pull**ing my **leg**

That's the **last straw**

Your guess is as **good** as **mine**

New Information Stress

Generally, new information is going to have the greatest stress. When someone asks a Wh-question, the content word that carries the meaning in the answer will hold the stressed syllable.

Examples:

What's your **name**?   My name is **Sa**rah.

Where are you **from**?   I'm from **Ger**many.

Where do you go to **school**?   I go to **Har**vard.

What do you **do**?   I'm a **tea**cher.

12 Syllable Stress Rules

What is a Syllable?:

A syllable is a chunk of a word that has a vowel sound in it. You can think of a syllable as a clap in the word. For each vowel set, there is a syllable. If you are having an issue identifying syllables, look for the vowels.

In English, we don't give equal stress to each syllable in a word. We STRESS one syllable in each word and speed through the other syllables, and de-stress them.

A one-syllable word could only be "clapped" with one clap. With one-syllable words, there needs to be a clear wavy pitch change from high to low. Think of it as singing up on the vowel then down at the end.

Eg.

pen
bear
hair
just
that

A 2-syllable word would have 2 vowels, so 2 claps: For each 2-syllable word, you must still STRESS one syllable.
E.g.

pa-per
pen-cil
car-pet
o-pen
af-ter

A 3-syllable word would have 3 vowels, so 3 claps: You must still STRESS one syllable.
E.g.

e-le-phant
oc-to-pus
le-mon-**aid**
af-ter-math
won-der-ful
bo-ttle-neck

A 4-syllable word would have 4 vowels, so 4 claps: You must still STRESS one syllable.

E.g.

he-li-cop-ter

el-e-va-tor

wa-ter-me-lon

a-lli-ga-tor

te-le-vi-sion

pre-**dic-**ta-ble

We also have 5 and 6 syllable words. You must still STRESS one syllable.

E.g.

re-**frid**-ger-a-tor

hi-ppo-**pa**-ta-mus

su-per-in-**ten**-dent

in-ter-**na**-tio-nal

The point here is that we can only choose ONE syllable in each word to be stressed or "lingered" on. A one-syllable word is simple since there is no choice. But, when we have multi-syllabic words, we must choose the correct syllable to stress (make louder, longer, and higher-pitched).

<u>Practice stressing and de-stressing a syllable:</u>
You can practice this by using the nonsense word "da."
Stress the first syllable and de-stress the second syllable by making the first louder, longer and higher pitched. You can think of stressing a syllable as really lingering on the vowel longer. Destressing would involve speeding through the vowel as quickly as possible.

When a word has only one syllable, there is no guessing where to put the stress. That one syllable will be stressed (e.g., book, pen, light, man). The difficulty arises when you must decide where to put stress in words with more than one syllable. There are a few helpful rules that can help you navigate the complex nature of English stress. Here are some helpful tips:

<u>1. Nouns and adjectives</u>

When a noun (a word referring to a person, place, or thing) or an adjective (a term that <u>describes</u> a noun, e.g., "pretty, happy") has two syllables, the stress or "lingering" is usually on the **first** syllable.

Examples:

DA-da

Nouns:
TA ble
SCI ssors
WIN dow
PRIN ter
PEN cil
PA per

Adjectives:
PRE tty
CLE ver
BO ring
PUR ple
JEA lous
CRA zy

Exceptions: Unfortunately, there are exceptions to this rule. Exceptions occur because English often borrows vocabulary from other languages. You have to memorize these outsiders.

Here are a few words you can start with:
hotel   "hoe-**TELL**"
extreme   "x-**TREEM**"
concise   "cun-**SISE**"
police   "puh **LEES**"

2. Verbs and prepositions with two syllables

When a verb (an action or state of being) or a preposition (a relational word, e.g., "behind, around") has two syllables, the stress is usually (around 65% of the time) on the second syllable.

Examples:

Verbs:
pre **SENT**
ex **PORT**
pre **TEND**
a **PPROACH**

Prepositions:
a **SIDE**
be **TWEEN**
a **ROUND**
su **RROUND**

3. Words that are both a noun **and** a verb

Some English words can be used as a noun and a verb depending on the context of your sentence. In those cases, if the word is used as a noun, its word stress will be on the first syllable. If the word is used as a verb, the stress falls on the second syllable.

Examples:

PRE sent (noun)	vs. present pre **SENT** (verb) give something formally
EX port (noun)	vs. export ex **PORT** (verb) to sell goods to another country
SU spect (noun)	vs. suspect su**s** **PECT** (verb) to believe that something is true
PER mit (noun)	vs. per **MIT** (verb) to allow
IN vite (noun)	vs. in **VITE** (verb) asking a guest to come to a party
OB ject (noun)	vs. ob **JECT** (verb) lawyer says after a witness has spoken
RE cord (noun)	vs. re **CORD** (verb) to document something
RE bel (noun)	vs. re **BEL** (verb) to go against the rules
IN sult (noun)	vs. in **SULT** (verb) to put someone down
CON tract (noun)	vs. con **TRACT** (verb) to get or be infected with
PRO gress (noun)	vs. pro **GRESS** (verb) to improve or move further along
CON flict (noun)	vs. con **FLICT** (verb) to disagree with or go against

Use each of the words above in a sentence. Change your stress depending on how the term is used (noun vs. verb form). Focus on pronouncing one syllable louder, longer, and higher pitched than the other.

E.g., "I want to pre**SENT** you with this **PRE**sent."

There are exceptions to this rule. For example, the word "reSPECT" has stress on the second syllable both when it's a verb **and** a noun.

4. The suffix rule:

A suffix is the "tail" of a word. Each word has a nucleus or root, and a tail or suffix can be added to the end of a word to elaborate on the meaning. "tion" is an example of a suffix as "tion" can be added to many words: "deTENtion, aFFECtion, reLAtion." Suffixes are usually unstressed, and the stress is generally placed on the syllable just before the suffix. Here are some other examples of stressing before the suffix or "tail" of a word:

AGE	dis-**cour-**age	per-**cent-**age	ad-**vant-**age
ANCE/ENCE	ac-**quaint-**ance	o-ver-a-**bund-**ance	in-de-**pend-**ence
TED	un-ex-**pec-**ted	pre-**sen-**ted	sub-**mit-**ted
ENCY	in-con-**sist-**en-cy	com-**plac-**en-cy	in-ef-**fici-**en-cy
ENT	in-de-**pend-**ent	cor-re-**spond-**ent	in-can-**desc-**ent
EOUS	cour-**ag-**eous	si-mul-**tan-**eous	ad-van-**tag-**eous
IAL	con-se-**quent-**ial	fi-**nanc-**ial	ar-ti-**fic-**ial
IAN	ve-ge-**tar-**ian	ma-the-ma-**tic-**ian	am-**phib-**ian
IC	pho-to-**graph-**ic	i-**con-**ic	**trag-**ic
ICAL	**Log-**ic-al	e-co-**nom-**ic-al	ster-e-o-**typ-**ic-al
IFY	**just-**i-fy	e-**lectr-**i-fy	ob-**ject-**i-fy
IOUS	har-**mon-**i-ous	**glor-**i-ous	con-sci-**ent-**i-ous
ITY	com-**mod-**i-ty	**DIG-**ni-ty	re-spec-ti-**bil-**i-ty
GRAPHY/PHER	pho-**to-**gra-phy	ge-**o-**gra-phy	bi-**o-**gra-phy
SION	com-**mi-**ssion	per-**mi-**ssion	**pa-**ssion
TION	ad-min-i -**stra-**tion	re-cre-**a-**tion	re-ex-a-mi-**na-**tion
UAL	un-**us-**u-al	in-te-**llect-**u-al	mul-ti-**ling-**u-al
LOGY	psy-**cho-**lo-gy	the-**o-**lo-gy	mi-cr-bi-**o-**lo-gy
METRY/METER	ge-**o-**me-try	tri-go-**no-**me-try	**sy-**mme-try
LOGIST	i-de-**o-**lo-gist	psy-**cho-**lo-gist	an-thro-**po-**lo-gist
ISH	es-**TA-**blish	re-**FIN-**nish	dis-**TING-**uish
IBLE	in-**cred-**i-ble	in-com-pre-**hens-**i-ble	**terr-**i-ble

382

| MENT | co-**mmit**-ment | en-ter-**tain**-ment | en-**gage**-ment |

There are a few Suffixes that do **not** affect stress:

ABLE	de-**MON**-stra-ble	un-**break**-a-ble	**PLEA**-su-re-able
HOOD	**PA**-rent-hood	**NEIGH**-bour-hood	**WO**-man-hood
NESS	a-**TTRAC**-tive-ness	**HA**-ppi-ness	**FRIEND**-li-ness
ISM	i-**DEAL**-ism	**FE**-men-ism	**TERR**-or-ism

Three syllable words ending in "er" and "ly."

Words that have <u>three</u> syllables and end in "-er" or "-ly" usually have stress on the first syllable.

Examples:

OR-der-ly

QUI-et-ly

Ha-ppi-ly

MA-na-ger

O-pe-ner

Car-pen-ter

5. Compound Nouns vs. Compound Verbs:

A compound noun is a noun made up of two or more existing words. In most compound nouns, the stress occurs on the first word.

Example:

BUS stop	**SUN**set	**AIR**line
CHALKboard	**WASHING** machine	**NOTE**book
FLASHlight	**WATER** bottle	**BASE**ball
FOOTball	**ASH**tray	**HOT** dog
HAIRcut	**DOWN**time	**KEY** chain
KEYboard	**OUT**come	**POLICE** car
LIGHTbulb	**CUT**back	**SAVINGS** account
OVERboard	**NEWS**paper	**BANK** teller
PAPERweight	**GREEN**house	**MOUTH**-watering
SCIENCE test	**WHITE**board	**THOUGHT**-provoking
SMALLtalk	**BATH**room	

Compound Verbs and Adjectives:

Compound verbs and adjectives are made up of more than one verb or adjective. The stress in these types of compounds occurs in the second word.

Example:

absent-**MINDED**	kind-**HEARTED**	second-**HAND**
brand-**NEW**	left-**HANDED**	self-**CONSCIOUSLY**
brightly-**LIT**	long-**LASTING**	short-**HAIRED**
deeply-**ROOTED**	narrow-**MINDED**	slow-**MOVING**
densely-**POPULATED**	never-**ENDING**	strong-**WILLED**
early **ON**	old-**FASHIONED**	under–**STAND**
far-**REACHING**	open-**MINDED**	well-**BEHAVED**
forward-**THINKING**	out-**DATED**	well-**EDUCATED**
good-**LOOKING**	over**BOOK**	well-**KNOWN**
highly-**RESPECTED**	over**REACT**	well-**PAID**
high-**SPIRITED**	quick-**WITTED**	

6. Abbreviations and Acronyms:

An acronym is when letters represent a phrase. Abbreviations are short forms of longer words.

For example, a CEO is an acronym for **C**hief **E**xecutive **O**fficer. If the acronym has two letters, both will be equal stress:

Example:

BA

MA

ID

PR

MD

OD

If the acronym has three letters, the stress will be placed on the final letter.

MB**A**

AK**A**

FA**Q**

RI**P**

TB**A**

FY**I**

DN**R**

DNA**A**

PD**A**

ES**L**

GS**T**

Acronyms and abbreviations that are pronounced as a single word would follow the stress rules for nouns. E.g., **NA**-TO "nay dow," **TE**-SL "tess uhl."

<u>7. Stress Shifts:</u>

According to the previous rules, when we add a suffix to a word, the word's stress will move to another syllable.

O-per-ate	o-per-**a**-<u>tion</u>
Re-**me**-di-ate	re-me-di-**a**-<u>tion</u>
Po-li-tics	po-**lit**-<u>i-cal</u>
Hi-sto-ry	his-**tor**-<u>i-cal</u>
Tech-**no**-lo-gy	tech-no-**log**-<u>i-cal</u>
Pro-duct	pro-**duc**-<u>tive</u>
A-ddict	A-**ddic**-<u>tive</u>
A-**vail**-a-ble	a-vai-la-**bil**-<u>i-ty</u>

<u>8. French origin words</u>

Words that originate from French have stress in the suffixes.

ETTE	Ma-ri-o-n**ette**
AIRE	Ques-tio-nn**aire**
IQUE	An-t**ique**
EER	Pio-n**eer**
ESQUE	Gro-t**esque**
EUR	En-tre-pre-n**eur**

<u>9. Number Stress</u>

Tens and numbers that are multiples will often have stress on the first syllable.

Twenty

Thirty

Forty

Fifty

Sixty

Se-ven-ty

Eighty

Ninety

Multiple digit numbers often have stress on the last syllable

Twenty-**Six**

Thirty-**Four**

Eighty-**Nine**

Fife hundred ninety-**Eight**

Two thousand three hundred forty-**Two**

10: "Self" Pronouns

When a word includes the "self/selves," such as "myself," the stress will be on the "self" portion of the word.

Him**self**

Her**self**

Your**self**

My**self**

Them**selves**

Your**self**

Our**selves**

11. Stress on names of streets, roads, avenues, drives, circles, courts, and crescents

Streets and Roads:
The stress will occur on the actual name of the street or road.
Fourth Road
Elm Street

Avenues and Drives, Circles and Courts:
The stress will occur on the type of roadway.

Fourth **Avenue**

Elm **Drive**

Plumb **Crescent**

Birch **Court**

Greenway **Circle**

12. Proper names and titles with multiple words.
Names with two words will receive the primary stress on the last part.

Niagara **Falls**

New **York**

Prince **George**

West **Nile**

Elvis **Presley**

Stress Practice

Let's do a little practice to find the correct stressed syllable. Remember, nouns and adjectives have stress on the first syllable, whereas verbs and adverbs stress the second syllable. If the word can be either a noun or a verb depending on its use, then you can change the stress accordingly. If the word has a suffix (see the suffix list above), move the stress to the syllable before it. Practice the words below.

Word	Stress on Syllable	N=Noun V=Verb A=Adjective AV=Adverb
a-gain	2	AV
be-lieve	2	V
Christ-mas	1	N
coun-try	1	N
de-vote	2	V
di-rect	2	V
em-brace	2	V
Fri-day	1	N
fu-ture	1	A/N
ha-ppy	1	A
Hea-ven	1	N

Mon-day	1	N
ne-glect	2	V
peo-ple	1	N
per-fect	1 OR 2	A/V
pi-zza	1	N
prin-cess	1	N
pump-kin	1	N
pur-ple	1	A
qui-et	1	A
sca-ry	1	A
sel-dom	1	A
se-ven	1	A
sil-ver	1	A/N
spe-cial	1	A
sus-pend	2	V
twen-ty	1	A
wa-ter	1	N
a-tten-tion	2	Suffix "tion"
a-chieve-ment	2	Suffix "ment"
a-gree-ment	2	Suffix "ment"
ack-nowl-edge	2	Suffix "edge"
ad-mi-ssion	2	Suffix "sion"
ad-vant-age	2	Suffix "age"

Common Differences:

Many speakers commonly place equal stress on all words and syllables, especially those whose first language does not have these stress differentiations. It can take time to hear these stress changes and grasp the complexity of the rules that exist in English. If a speaker places stress on the wrong syllables in words, it can confuse the listener and impact meaning. If you struggle with placing stress on the correct syllables in English, it is important to focus on understanding the rules and improve your ability to hear the stress in others' speech. When you improve your English stress patterns, your message will significantly improve in clarity and naturalness.

Hear it!

Go through the word lists above and try some "negative practice." Listen to how words sound when you stress the wrong syllable, and compare what they sound like when you stress the correct syllable. Listen to native speakers and pay careful attention to the stress in their speech. Some speakers exaggerate the high pitch and loudness far more than others, and there is an element of personality that goes with this variation. Often, those who want to sound energetic and enthusiastic about a topic will increase their stress in words and add to the high and low patterns in their speech intonation (the music of their voice). Choose a stress level that you feel comfortable with, but be sure to make at least some stress variations.

Do it!

As you get comfortable with listening and attending to the stress patterns of native North American English speakers, begin to work up the ladder of complexity. Focus on word level practice until you feel you understand the rules and have mastered this level. Move on to the phrase and sentence level and read aloud. Read scripts of speakers as they speak. Pause videos and read aloud as you predict how you think they would add stress, and then listen to the speaker use their stress in the sentence. Stress practice will help you test your abilities and knowledge and improve your listening skills. Finally, begin to implement your new skills into daily conversation. As with any new skill or habit, you must push yourself out of your comfort zone. It will feel like you are exaggerating slightly, and this is normal. With time, and practice, your naturalness will increase, and your confidence will improve with it.

Chapter 33: Intonation: A Music Lesson of Sorts

What is Intonation?

Intonation refers to the variation in pitch or "highness and lowness" of our voices when we speak. There is a sort of music to English speaking patterns that conveys meaning. It is important to understand and be able to replicate this music of intonation to speak with confidence and clarity. Intonation helps English speakers convey their intentions (questions versus statements), their type and level of emotion, as well as the meaning of the speaker. Intonation is extremely important!

Types of Intonation

There are various types of intonation in English to be aware of. Many non-native English speakers will use their first language intonation patterns when speaking, marking a distinct change in the sound of their speech from typical Native English speakers. Let's talk about the intonation patterns of English and why they are so important. Many speakers will use a great deal of variation (up/down/up intonation) within the music of their speech to increase the energy or interest when speaking. However, the amount of variation you use in your speech is related to personality and excitement related to the topic. You might go higher and lower with your pitch and intonation if you're trying to convey emotion and energy. A flat intonation, where there is no upward or downward intonation change, often indicates disinterest or boredom. Bueller? Bueller? (This is a well-known quote from a pop culture movie, *Ferris Bueller's Day Off*.) This is just an example of a teacher who had very little interest and his intonation indicated how very disinterested he was. It was quite flat. Being aware of what your intonation conveys to other English speakers is important in ensuring your message is clear and accurate.

Falling Intonation

Falling intonation is when the pitch of your voice rolls down to a low pitch at the end of an utterance. The falling pitch occurs on the last stressed syllable of the sentence. Falling intonation is the most common type of intonation used in English since it is used for nearly everything except specific questions and incomplete information. We use falling intonation for statements, commands, as well as WH questions. Falling intonation indicates certainty; it suggests that a message is complete. If your goal is to show others that you are speaking with confidence, then your intonation is extremely important. If you want others to know when you're still talking and not done with what you're saying, then your intonation is also very important. We also use falling intonation at the ends of lists to suggest to the listener that the list is complete.

Here are some examples of Falling intonation:

Hello!
Good morning.
How nice of you.
I'm working at my
computer right now.
She was late today.
You won the race!
It's already 9:00!
I'm allergic to dairy.

It was nice to see you
yesterday.
Please sit down.
Go home.
Shut the door.
Who is that?
Where did he go?
Why did she go there?

When will you be
home?
Why were you at the
office?
Who is in the corner?
Where were you last
night?
How old are you?

Rising Intonation

Rising intonation is when the pitch of your voice rolls up to a higher note at the end of an utterance. The rising intonation is an invitation for the speaking partner to complete the interaction. Remember, it is the pitch or music of our voice we are talking about. We usually use this upward pitch to indicate that we do not have the information, like yes/no questions. Yes/no questions are like a half interaction; the answer is the completion of the exchange. Since the question means there is incompletion, it will end in a high rise:

Did you finish your homework? -Yes.

Examples of rising intonation:

Did you do your homework yesterday?
Doesn't he like ketchup?
Didn't you get my texts?
Did she give him his money back?
Jen has a fever?
He has a snake as a pet?
Can you believe he did that?
Can you pass me that book?
Do you need a printed copy?
Could you bring it with you tomorrow?
Do you want to go to the movies tonight?
You want to grab a coffee?

A sentence can be said with either a falling or rising intonation. You will choose the intonation based on whether the sentence is a statement or a question that's not a WH-question. Say the following sentences with a rising or falling intonation.

Statement: He wasn't embarrassed when he tripped in the gym.
Question: He wasn't embarrassed when he tripped in the gym?

Statement: You got a haircut.
Question: You got a haircut?

Statement: Your mom is going shopping.
Question: Your mom is going shopping?

Statement: We have to fly to Florida.
Question: We have to fly to Florida?

Statement: I'm early.
Question: I'm early?

392

Statement: No one knows the answer.

Question: No one knows the answer?

Statement: Alex couldn't get his door open.

Question: Alex couldn't get his door open?

Statement: The boss said we couldn't leave early today.

Question: The boss said we couldn't leave early today?

Statement: She plays the flute.

Question: She plays the flute?

Statement: I was late to work today.

Question: I was late to work today?

Intonation In Lists

Intonation drops when a speaker has finished their list. This drop in intonation signals that the speaking turn is complete. If the pitch of the intonation has not fallen, it tells the listener you have not yet finished, and there is more for you to say. When you make a list or give more information, the pitch should not drop until the end. This drop signals completion.

Example of a list:

Leanne bought a shirt, some jeans, and a pair of shoes.

I need some pens, paper, and a comfortable computer chair.

She ate the cake, cookies, cupcakes, and even the doughnuts!

When I retire, I want to visit Greece, Paris, and Rome.

Intonation With Choices

When you provide choices, the upward intonation or rising intonation happens on the choices offered, and the downward intonation or falling intonation occurs on the last choice. The downward intonation helps the listener know you have finished offering options.

Would you like tea or coffee?

Are you coming Wednesday or Thursday?

Do you want to go to my place or your place?

Unsure Intonation

The more uncertain a speaker is about their statement, the more the pitch intonation will rise. You will notice the high pitch will show just how unsure a speaker is in their statement.

Did you go to that party last night?!! (extreme uncertainty)

Intonation With Tag Questions

A tag question is when a statement is presented in the form of a question. Since the speaker tags on an extra little "tail" answering the question like "isn't it?" they are not actually asking for an answer at all. You, as the listener, will have to decide if they really want an answer or if they are answering their own question or just agreement. You will have to listen to the intonation. If the speaker raises the intonation at the end, you will know they are hoping for an answer.

My new jeans are great, aren't they?   (no answer required, they want an agreement)

My baby is adorable, isn't she!   (no answer required, they want an agreement)

Sarah didn't come back yet, did she?   (Speaker is not sure, they want an answer)

Practice

Work through this dialogue below. Practice rising and falling intonation for each part. You will notice that as you get the hang of what kind of utterance it is (statement, yes/no question, list, etc.), your intonation will be markedly different. Try it out!

A. Help! I'm lost!
B. Where are you?
A. I don't know. I can see a store and a lake here.
B. Oh, I think I know where you are! Can you see a train track?
A. Yes.
B. Okay, go across the train track and make a left.
A. Go left?
B. Yes. Now, can you see some houses on the right?
A. Yes.
B. Okay, make a right turn after the houses.
A. What, in front of the gas station?
B. Yes. In front of the gas station. You'll see my house right behind it.
A. Oh, It's across the street.
B. That's it. Great, I see you now!

Stress and Intonation

When trying to convey a message by stressing a word in your sentence, you will make the vowel in the syllable or word longer, louder and higher pitch. The higher pitch element is the intonation. When we stress a vowel in a syllable, it will sound like a change in pitch going up to down like a wave. Of course, you can choose which word to stress depending on your meaning, but be sure to add an upward and downward wave of music to help create clear stress.

Hi (up and down)!

How are YOU?

Oh, I'm doing WELL

Where did the DOG go?

I had to go the LONG way

PLEASE sit down!

Reading:
To get a good grasp of the intonation patterns of Native English speakers, I highly recommend reading the scripts of presenters as they speak. An excellent resource for this is to listen and read Ted Talk scripts. You can read the script of the speaker as they talk and listen to the intonation patterns. Some speakers use a greater variation in their pitches, using higher and lower pitches than others. As you recall, there is an element of personality in the use of intonation in speech. Listen for a speaker that you admire and like the sound of, then listen to their intonation carefully as you read the script along with them. Pause the audio or video before each phrase and decide for yourself how you would use your falling intonation or rising intonation for each part and listen for what the speaker does. You can even slow down the playback rate to 0.75 or slower to hear the intonation at a more manageable speed. Try to mimic the speaker's intonation as best you can to get a good grasp of how much of a difference this new way of speaking feels for you. For many, using even just slightly more pitch variation can feel crazy! Often clients will report that they think they sound significantly different as a result of this one change. Work with what feels comfortable for you, just reaching slightly outside your comfort zone, and you will notice the impact of greater intonation.

Conversation:
Once you feel that you have a good grasp of the types of intonation patterns to use, whether it be falling, rising, or list types of intonation, you should begin to use them in speech. Your meaning will be significantly enhanced when your falling intonation shows your listener that you are speaking with confidence and certainty. If your rising intonation yes/no questions are understood as requests for information, you

will be less likely to be cut off mid-utterance. Similarly, your intonation will let your listener know when you are finished talking. Of course, with any new habit, this will take time and practice. Being intentional in your listening and knowing what to listen for is an essential first step.

Now that you have this skill, it is time to go out and use your new English intonation patterns with confidence!

A Note About News Broadcasters and Politicians

Many of my clients ask me about the way most news broadcasters and hosts on TV speak. Even politicians have very distinct patterns of speech. Many speakers wish to sound more confident and want to mimic some elements of this authoritative speaking style. Many aspects of this speaking style differ from everyday conversational speech, but I will discuss a few important differences, one being the intonation and pitch used.

Like politicians and news broadcasters, many public speakers use a distinctly different intonation pattern. The overall mean or average pitch of their voice, be it male or female, is slightly lower than the average pitch of a typical speaker. What this means is that these public speakers are purposefully lowering their voices! Reasons for this lower pitch may vary; to convey credibility, confidence, authority, attention, charisma. Many believe, however, that this "broadcaster" style developed over time as speakers mimicked successful iconic predecessors from the past.

Another element of this speaking style includes brief "extra-low" voice use. Think of those curvy lines in the sentence examples above that show you when to raise and lower your intonation pitch. For broadcasters, the curvy lines that go down in falling pitch utterances would reach even lower than normal pitches. The research indicates that these very low bursts in pitch seem to convey authority to their listeners.

So a typical person would say:

Good evening!   Where a news broadcaster would say: Good evening!

397

One other distinction between regular speech and professional speakers is their use of pausing. Pausing is the use of a break between phrases in a sentence. Public speakers such as politicians and news broadcasters use more frequent and more prolonged pauses in their speeches. Research indicates that it is not fast speech that engages a listener or gains people's attention, but <u>more pauses</u> between phrases are the key!

In the next chapter, we will talk about "Phrasing" or "Pausing" in speech in greater detail. We will learn why it is important, what to do, and how to achieve phenomenal pausing when talking to enhance our clarity and confidence.

Chapter 34: Linking & Phrasing: The Key to Sounding "Au-Naturel!"

Learning to produce speech sounds accurately and using accurate stress and intonation patterns are all important in improving clarity and confidence when speaking any language. Let's discuss a few more elements that have a significant impact on how natural-sounding your speaking will be; these are "Pausing" and "Linking."

To sound natural, you must be able to have flow or fluency in your speech. Fluency is accomplished by creating appropriate pauses and linking or blending your words to increase the flow of everything you say.

The Pausing/Phrasing Technique

When you listen to native English speakers, it can seem like all the words jumble together as one, so you can't really discern where one word ends, and another begins. But, native English speakers do not speak continuously without breaks. Rather, they take tiny pauses between groups of words. These groups of words are called phrases or thought groups. Being aware of the pauses between phrases is an important first step toward more natural-sounding speech. Pausing is a tool to help you speak clearly and be better understood.

An excellent way to look at pausing is to think of speech in terms of reading. When you see a period or comma, you stop reading for a split second. You take a pause. This pause is short but highly effective. Using pausing requires that we place short pauses between our phrases, just like when we see commas and periods when we read. So you can think of pausing as putting commas and periods between your thoughts. A short sentence has no pauses. It is a single thought group. We segment longer sentences into phrases or thought groups, divided by a pause. Each thought group has at least one stressed word (louder, longer, higher pitched).

Let's look at an example:
Why would you commute to work when you could stay home and work virtually?
[Why would you commute to **WORK**]*PAUSE*[when you could stay **HOME**]*PAUSE*[and work **VIRTUALLY**]?

The second sentence is much simpler to understand, conveys greater meaning, and has more impact on listeners. The reason it is easier is that there is a slight pause between the groups of thought. By pausing, the speaker also unconsciously emphasizes or stresses the last content word in the thought group, which adds to the listener's ability to understand your meaning.

Why should I learn about Pausing?

Aside from sounding more natural and fluent when talking, there are other very important benefits to using the pausing technique. One reason is that pausing between your thought groups helps your listener better understand what you are saying. Because you separate your words into meaningful chunks, your listener can understand your organized speech much easier. You might have noticed many politicians and public speakers using these pauses consistently in their speeches. Politicians and news broadcasters statistically use a greater number of pauses and longer pauses in their speech for this very reason. Now, it may seem counterintuitive to place pauses in your speech as you may think it will slow you down. In one way, yes, pauses add time to your utterances. However, the following strategy called "linking" will help you speed right back up. So, in the end, the total length of your speech will ultimately be the same. The difference is, you will be significantly better understood, and you will sound much more confident.

Most people believe that if they just speak quicker, they will sound more confident and natural. Unfortunately, speaking faster does not achieve this goal. Research indicates that the chunking of thought groups (linked together) and separating thought groups by pauses helps one be better understood and rated as having greater confidence when speaking. So, instead of speaking quickly, use your phrasing/pausing technique to achieve your speaking goals!

When we pause, we give our listeners time to understand what we have said, and since we separate our ideas into thought groups, it helps our listeners better organize what we say. Another reason that pausing helps us is that we tend to stress the last word in the thought group, adding to the ability to highlight with stress.

Example: [I didn't get there on **TIME**] *PAUSE* [because there was so much **TRAFFIC**].

Notice how I linked the words together and paused in the middle. The final words in each thought group were stressed.

Pausing rules:

Now I will go into a few "rules" about pausing, but truly, this is something our brain is ready to do for us automatically. We can "feel" exactly where a good place to pause would be when we hear a sentence.

The best places to pause in speech are the same as in reading.

- When you see a punctuation mark (comma, period, etc.)
- When you see a conjunction (words like 'and,' 'but,' 'or,' etc.)
- When you see a preposition (words like 'on,' 'in,' 'around,' 'at,' etc.)

For example, in the sentences below, I want you to think about where you might pause to take a break.

I went to work on my computer but then realized it was not working.
[I went to work on my **computer**] *PAUSE* [but then realized it was not **working**].

She went outside, grabbed a huge rake, and started to clean up the yard.
[She went **outside**], *PAUSE* [grabbed a huge **rake**], *PAUSE* [and started to clean up the **yard**].

You can try for yourself to put a pause in a different place. You will notice somehow, it just does not "sound" or "feel" right. The reason is that our brain likes to organize things into thought groups or meaningful chunks. It makes our brain feel good or comfortable when we can organize something with meaning. Here's an example below with pauses in "unnatural" locations. Notice how it doesn't "feel right."

[She went outside grabbed] *PAUSE* [a huge rake, and started to clean up] *PAUSE* [the yard].

Practice:
Let's do some practice placing pauses in a natural location. The brackets have been placed in each sentence to see a good spot to pause. You might find a better place to pause that feels better for you, and that is fine! Decide for yourself what feels like the right place to pause.

[Excuse me,] [where's the bathroom?]
[Now that I think about it,]   [I think I changed my mind.]   [I like the second one.]
[He didn't say so specifically,]   [but I think he's going to be looking for a new job.]
[They bought a new place]   [and will probably move in next month.]
[I ordered the chicken,]   [but now that I see your pasta,]   [I wish I picked that instead.]
[You'll have to pick up the kids after school,]   [I have a meeting scheduled.]
[Our dining room has a table,]   [a few simple chairs,]   [and a lamp in the corner.]
[I bought a burger,]   [fries,]   [and a milkshake for lunch.]
[The weather is way too cold]   [so I'm not going outside.]
[I went to the store to get groceries,]   [but then I realized]   [I forgot my wallet.]

Reading aloud is great to help you practice pausing. First, you will need to visually scan the sentence before you start to read it aloud. Punctuation marks are always pausing or phrasing breaks. When you see conjunctions (e.g., and/but/or) and prepositions (e.g., in/on/about), those are great spots to pause as well. Read the words aloud. Take a pause or easy breath between each "thought group."

Below is an excerpt of Dr. Martin Luther King, Jr.'s "I Have A Dream" speech. This passage purposefully has no punctuation marks. Read it out loud and practice placing your pauses to separate the thought groups in the passage.

"And so even though we face the difficulties of today and tomorrow I still have a dream it is a dream deeply rooted in the American dream I have a dream that one day this nation will rise up and live out the true meaning of its creed we hold these truths to be self-evident, that all men are created equal I have a dream that one day on the red hills of Georgia the sons of former slaves and the sons of former slave owners will be able to sit down together at the table of brotherhood I have a dream that one day even the state of Mississippi a state sweltering with the heat of injustice sweltering with the heat of oppression will be transformed into an oasis of freedom and justice I have a dream that my four little children will one day live in a nation where they will not be judged by the color of their skin but by the content of their character I have a dream today"

Linking

Linking refers to sliding words in a phrase or thought group together. Some people like to call it "blending" because you blend the words together into one. It means that we say all of the words together in one breath, so they blend into one another. Linking involves avoiding any pauses or stops between words within the thought group. The only pause that would exist is the pause BETWEEN phrases or thought groups.

Example: [Iwentoutforlunch] *PAUSE* [withmyfriends.]

We link our words in English to speak more efficiently. However, there is slightly more to linking than just squishing all the words together within the phrase or thought group. There are a few things to consider when we link our words together.

<u>Linking consonants to vowels:</u>

You can look at linking in a few ways. It's like squishing the words together. Ultimately what you are doing is keeping your voice going without turning it off as you move from one word to another. If you think of your voice like a motor, just keep it going and never turn it off within the phrase. Put your hand on your throat and say, "ahhhhh." You should feel your voice vibrate on your throat. Linking means that this vibration should stay on for the whole phrase.

Try to "keep your voice motor running" for these phrases without any pause or gap between the words:

How are you doing?
What's up?
Great weather today!
Nice to meet you!
How do you do?
It's a pleasure to meet you.
It was great to meet you.
Have a good day!
What's the time?
What a lovely day today!
Good evening.
Talk to you soon.
I hope you're doing well.
Great talking to you.
Good afternoon.
Thank you.
Thank you very much.
I'm doing well.
I'm good.
I'm doing great!
What a day!
I hope you had a nice weekend.
Have a great week.
Have a great weekend.
Have a great afternoon.
Have a great evening.
Talk to you later.
See you later.
Talk to you soon!

Consonants to Vowels:

You can look at linking as pushing the consonants at the ends of words forward to the next vowel in a word:

Examples:

Add and subtract	A dand subtract
All alone	A lalone
Bad apple	Ba dapple
Bid a large amount	Bi da lar jamount
Calm and peaceful	Cah mand peaceful
Cob of corn	Cah bof corn
Come on	co mon
Crawl away	Craw laway
Curl a string	Cur la string
Do we have it?	do we ha vit?
Farm animal	Far manimal
First in line	firs tin line
From a friend	Fro ma friend
Germs are everywhere	Germ za reverywhere
Give it away	Gi vi daway
Good afternoon	Goo dafternoon
Good evening	Goo devening
Grab a bag	Gra ba bag
Grab it	Gra bit
Hard answers	Har danswers
Have a great day	Ha va great day
Have a try	Ha va try
Hazel eyes	Haze leyes
Hid away	Hi daway
How are you?	Ho ware you?
Hug a friend	Hu ga friend
I'm alright	I' malright
I'm over it	I' moverit
It's over there	It' sover there
Just a minute	Jus ta minute
Kept it up	kep ti dup
Last one standing	las twun standing
Love is beautiful	Lo vis beautiful
Mad about you	Ma dabout you

Movies are amazing	Movie za ramazing
My job is awesome	My jo bi zawesome
Pay a fee	Pa ya fee
Red apple	Re dapple
Sad emotion	Sa demotion
Skipped a beat	skip ta beat
Take it away	Ta ki daway
Team approach	Tea mapproach
That's amazing	That' samazing
Where are you?	Whe rare you?

Either way you look at it, the point is to avoid any real pauses or breaks between the words.

Linking identical consonants together:
When two words start and end with the same sound, you don't say it twice, only once!

Examples:

a sad driver	asadriver
add doughnuts	adoughnuts
all lonely	alonely
bad direction	badirection
bad dog	badog
basal leaf	basaleaf
bed duvet	beduvet
black car	blacar
cab broke	cabroke
calm moment	calmoment
cob bite	cobite
crawl low	crawlow
curl long hair	curlonghair
drum master	drumaster
farm mammal	farmammal
film my life	filmylife
frail limbs	fralimbs
from me	frome
germ mite	germite
grab bag	grabag

grim moment	gri_moment
had dark hair	ha_darkhair
harm me	har_me
hazel likes him	haze_likeshim
hid down below	hi_downbelow
hug Gus	hu_Gus
ice skating	i_skating
job bank	jo_bank
just too tricky	jus_tootricky
libel lawsuit	libe_lawsuit
mad dad	ma_dad
mid-decision	mi_decision
mod design	mo_design
motel light	mote_light
mud dive	mu_dive
my friend's zipper	myfriend_zipper
odd decision	o_decision
off field	o_field
oil leak	oi_leak
pay yourself first	pa_yourse_first
rag gone	ra_gone
red devil	re_devil
seem melancholy	see_melancholy
slam my door	sla_mydoor
sod dried	so_dried
swell large	swe_large
team member	tea_member
that tornado	tha_tornado
the kid did it	theki_didit
their raincoats	thei_raincoats
top professional	to_professional
trim my hair	tri_myhair
vocal leader	voca_leader
warm mist	war_mist
will let you know	wi_letyouknow
with three of them	wi_threeofthem
worm movement	wor_movement
yell loudly	ye_loudly
zoom meeting	zoo_meeting

Even sounds that are really similar to each other will follow this rule above. In English, there are "sister sounds," or nearly identical sounds; only one sound has the voice on, and the other does not. Below are examples of sister sound pairs:

If a word ends and another starts with these pairs, you would pronounce the sound once. Generally, the voiceless sound prevails. In some cases you transition from voiced to voiceless, but essentially you make the sound once, not placing a pause between the sounds.

Examples:

p/b: Step brother > ste**p**rother
s/z: six zippers > si**x**ippers
t/d: had to > ha**t**o
k/g: big canoe > bi**c**anoe
sh/ch: catch shrimp > cat**ch**ripm
f/v: have four > ha**f**our
θ/ð: with them > wi**th**em

Y and W Shadows

Linking Two Vowel Sounds:
Words that end in an "eee/aheee" (like /i/ "eee", /ai/ "AH EE", /ei/ "EH EE, /oi/ "OH EE") vowel: add a "y" sound
e.g.

see it   see **y**it
pie over there   pie **y**over there
say a word   say **y**a word
boy at home   boy **y**at home

Words that end in an "ow/oo" (like /o/ "oh", /au/"ow" /u/"oo") vowel: add a "w" sound
e.g.

no one   no **w**one
how is it   how **w**is it

go over   go **w**over

Remember, you must link the words together to successfully add the "y" and "w" shadows.

Ho**w w**often
Wh**o w**are you?
Yo**u w**are awesome
G**o w**away
D**o w**over
D**o w**unt**o w**others
Compare apples t**o w**oranges
If it comes t**o w**it
Add insult t**o w**injury
D**o w**I have your number?
S**o w**I decided to do **w**it!
It takes one to kno**w w**one
T**o w**everyone I know
Ho**w w**about another drink?
N**o w**one really knows
Kno**w w**all about it
Yo**u w**are the best
Just d**o w**it
Gro**w w**up
Tw**o w**apples
Argu**e w**over it
Caribo**u w**antlers
He **y**is
My **y**apartment
We'll se**e y**about that
Fre**e y**at last
My **y**other half
Th**e y**end of the road
Judge a book b**y y**its cover
Be **y**open to possibilities
I **y**only have eyes for you
He **y**isn't that bad
By**e y**everyone!
The**y y**are here

408

We **y**aren't going
Sa<u>y</u> **y**it aint so!
M<u>y</u> **y**only choice
Me **y**and my friends are going
See **y**everyone tonight!
Onl<u>y</u> **y**you would know!
Wa<u>y</u> **y**over there
Da<u>y</u> **y**after day

Linking consonants to consonants:
When you are linking words that end and start with consonants, we generally don't release the stop sounds (like /t/ /p/ and /k/). For example, if you place a tissue in front of your mouth when pronouncing the sound, the tissue would not move because no air was blown or released.

Examples:
le<u>t</u> go > le(-t)go -the /t/ doesn't release with any aspirated airflow
ste<u>p</u> down > ste(-p)down -the /p/ doesn't release with any air
bla<u>ck</u> paint > bla(-ck)paint –the /k/ doesn't release with any air

Simplifying Complex Clusters of Consonants

When speakers talk quickly in connected speech, some clusters are sometimes too tricky and time-consuming to produce completely. The result is that English speakers drop a consonant to get through the word easier and quicker.

We tend to drop the last consonant in clusters with "xt," "st," and "nd" when followed by yet another consonant.

Examples:
Ne**xt** year   "nexyear"
Bo**xed** wine   "boxwine"
Te**xt**book   "texbook"
Ha**nd**shake   "hanshake"

Hi**nd** legs	"hinlegs"
Ki**nd** man	"kinman"
Go fu**nd** me	"gofunme"
Se**nd** you	"senyou"
Sa**nd**paper	"sanpaper"
Po**nd** water	"ponwader"
Be**nd** the rules	"bentherules"
Ki**nd**ness	"kiness"
Sa**nd**wich	"sanwich"
Pou**nd** cake	"pouncake"
Pe**st** control	"pescontrol"
Ea**st** coast	"eascoast"
La**st** call	"lascall"
Ju**st** do it	"jusdoit"
Mu**st** have it	"mushaveit"
Pa**st** lives	"paslives"
Lo**st** puppy	"lospuppy"
Re**st**room	"resroom"
Be**st**seller	"Beseller"

Practice Sentences:

See you ne**xt** year

You mu**st** have had a lot of fun

I forgot my te**xt**book

I'll se**nd** you the email tonight

You ju**st** need to do it

I'm not a fan of bo**xed** wine

He will se**nd** you a pou**nd** cake

I don't want to swim in the po**nd** water

She's known to be**nd** the rules in politics

I fou**nd** my lo**st** puppy in the re**st**room

Let's get started on ne**xt** year's agenda

We have no choice but to call pe**st** control

That ki**nd** man is mo**st** known for his ki**nd**ness

La**st** call mu**st** have pa**ssed** because it's 4 am!

Ne**xt** year I'm going to write a be**st**-selling book!

I love the sa**nd**wiches they make on the Ea**st** coast

The box did not la**st** long once it fell in the po**nd** water

Reading:

You very rarely see the changes that occur in spoken language due to linking reflected in written speech. When reading, there are many reductions that you will learn (which we will discuss in detail in a future chapter). You will rarely see any reflection of linking while reading texts. It would be too difficult to identify what the words would be if they were! Spend some time reading dialogue books, emails of dialogue, even scripts of favorite shows, movies, and speakers. Look at how natural spoken English is adjusted to include your new linking knowledge. Practice reading using your phrasing technique, linking all the words together within the phrases, and considering some of the linking rules discussed above to practice more fluent natural speech.

Conversation:

Now that you have had practice reading many different kinds of dialogue, you can listen to these linking rules with native English speakers. Listen as you talk to friends, colleagues, and characters on television and in movies. Try to imitate the linking that you hear. Begin to be intentional about your speaking with others. Include your new linking skills as much as possible. It can be helpful to start with a few phrases that you regularly use as a foundation to work from. Slowly incorporate more and more phrases that include your linking rules and naturally insert them into your daily conversations. Working with an accent modification instructor and speech-language pathologist will help you identify your skills and provide feedback on your pronunciation and linking strategies. It is important to practice with the people around you regularly. If you are not quite ready to use your new skills with people close to you, you can try to record yourself speaking freely to yourself. Tell yourself about your day or about that crazy dream you had last night. Listen to yourself and review your speech sounds, your intonation, your linking, your phrasing. Make notes and practice some more. With every new interaction and every chance to practice speaking, you are much closer to speaking English clearly and confidently.

Chapter 35: Contractions & Reductions; Don't Worry, We All Do It!

Consider the sentence:

He'll arrive at the time we've agreed upon.

Notice the apostrophes? Notice how two words have been put together as one?
He'll > He will
We've > we have

Those are contractions.

Contractions

In English, it is common for speakers to reduce words to speak more efficiently. We call these processes reductions and contractions. It is important to know that reducing or contracting words in English is not considered informal or impolite. Reductions and contractions in typical speech are appropriate in all speaking situations; in formal, professional, academic, and social situations. The degree and frequency of reductions used, however, may differ depending on the level of formality of your speech. You may notice slightly fewer reductions as you increase formality.

Reductions and contractions are just fancy terms to explain in even more specificity what is changing in words when we speak naturally. Knowing these terms is unnecessary; what is key is to identify and mimic these changes in your everyday speech to enhance your naturalness and fluency when speaking English.

Contractions:
Let's take a look at the contractions that we frequently use in English. Contractions are when two words are put together as one word. Compare these in the full form versus the contracted form. Begin to get familiar with their use.

FULL FORM	CONTRACTION	EXAMPLES
Would		
I would	I'd	I'd love to go
You would	you'd	You'd love it there
He would	he'd	He'd love to go to the movies tonight
She would	she'd	She'd have to ask her dad
We would	we'd	We'd love to come if we knew where it was
They would	they'd	They'd have loved this movie
Who would	who'd	Who'd like to come?
It would	it'd	It'd be wise to bring a coat
Have		
I have	I've	I've got an idea
You have	you've	You've never been there?
We have	we've	We've never been there before
They have	they've	They've never been there before
Why have	why've	Why've you not answered?
Who have	who've	Who've you asked?
Who has	who's	Who's been there before?
How have	how've	How've you been?
Will		
I will	I'll	I'll be there
You will	you'll	You'll have to bring your ticket
He will	he'll	He'll be late
She will	she'll	She'll be late
We will	we'll	We'll be late
They will	they'll	They'll be late
Who will	who'll	Who'll be going with me?
What will	what'll	What'll you say to him?
It will	it'll	It'll be cold tonight
Did		
Why did	why'd	Why'd you go without me?
Who did	who'd	Who'd you bring?
Are/am/is		
I am	I'm	I'm definitely going
You are	you're	You're coming with me
He is	he's	He's a friend
She is	she's	She's a friend
We are	we're	We're bringing the tickets

They are	they're	They're bringing the tickets
Why are	why're	Why're you taking the car?
Why is	why's	Why's he coming?
Who is	who's	Who's driving?
It is	it's	It's for her

Not

Cannot	can't	He can't go
Will not	won't	He won't go
Did not	didn't	He didn't go
Do not	don't	Don't you dare go!
Has not	hasn't	He hasn't given it to me yet
Should not	shouldn't	She shouldn't go
Would not	wouldn't	She wouldn't go
Could not	couldn't	She couldn't go

Others

Have to	Spelling-there is no change,	"Haftuh"
Going to	Spelling-there is no change,	"Gonna"
Has to	Spelling-there is no change,	"Hastuh"
Give me	Spelling-there is no change	"Gimme"

Reductions

Typically Reductions result in more neutral pronunciations, with the vowels turning to "uh."

FULL FORM	REDUCTION	EXAMPLES
a	/ə/ "uh"	What "uh" shot!
an	/ən/ "uhn"	That's "uhn" understatement!
and	/ən/ "un"	shirts "un" shorts
as	/əz/ "uz"	"uz" white "uz" snow
for	/fər/ "fer"	It's "fer" her
have	/əv/ "uhv" or /ə/ "uh"	Could "uh" said so! Or Could've
of	/əv/ "uhv" or /ə/ "uh"	Film "uh" the year
or	/ər/ "er"	red "er" blue?
to	/tə/ "tuh"	going "tuh" the store
he	/i/ or "ee"	Did "ee" go?
her	"er"	Give "er" the prize!
him	"um" or "em"	Give "em" the keys
his	"Iz"	Use "iz" computer instead
you	/jə/ "yuh"	I wanted "yuh" "duh" know

the	/ðə/ "thuh" or /ði/ "thee (vowel after)	That's "thuh" part I wanted "thee" **o**ther day (when there is a

Hear it!
Now that you have a greater understanding of the changes that occur in rapid English speech, listen to native English speakers talking. As you watch a favorite TV show or movie, spend some time doing some "intentional listening." Focus on one contraction at a time, listen for the change. Often this can be too quick to hear when you're starting out. I recommend watching YouTube videos. If you look at the settings "gear" symbol in the bottom right hand of the screen, you can adjust the speaker's speed. Change the speed to slow, and listen. You can go back and listen to words over and over, then speed up the rate to hear in real-time. Reviewing recordings is a great exercise to increase your ability to discriminate between these contractions and reductions. Work towards listening for these changes faster and faster until you can notice them in conversations with others.

Do it!
Once you feel you can hear these contractions and reductions in other English speakers, you will need to work on your own productions. Repeat and record yourself using these reductions and contractions at the word and phrase-level first. Practice until they feel natural. Move up the complexity ladder until you are ready for conversation.

Words:
Go through each of the contractions and reductions above. Compare the full form versus the reduced form for each and listen to the difference.

Phrases:
Once you have worked through all the words, go to the right-hand column with the simple phrases and short sentences. Say each phrase/sentence in the full form, then in the reduced/contracted form. Try testing yourself by covering up the written answers.

Sentences:
Let's do a little more practice at the sentence level to get yourself used to the contractions and reductions in speech. The sentences below are in full form. Try to insert as many reductions and contractions as you can in each sentence. Give it a try!

Example:
Would <u>you</u> like <u>to</u> ride with <u>her</u>? I <u>can</u> <u>not</u> drive. > Would "yuh" like "tuh" ride with "er"? I "can't" drive.

I am definitely going

Send her paperwork to him

I do not know where you have gone!

She has not RSVP'd yet because he will not go with her

There is an exam this Thursday. I have got to study!

Who will bring the tickets and who will be driving?

You could have told me you would be going to the store

Who did you bring to the party and where did you go?

He is going to give me his files when they are complete

She did not go to the party, so he should not ask about it

Carlos would have gone, but he has never been there before

She would have gone to the movies with him if he had asked her

It will be cold tonight, so it would be wise if you would bring your jacket

It is for her so she could go to the store and buy whatever she would want

We would have finished the report if they had given us the figures we needed

I wanted you to know that the part I wanted in the play was not the part I got

I have to make lunch for my daughter, but she has not brought her lunch box home

Sentence Answer key:

I'm definitely going

Send er paperwork to um

I don't know where you've gone!

She's not RSVP'd yet because e won't go with er

There's uhn exam this Thursday. I've got tuh study!

Who'll bring thuh tickets n who'll be driving?

Yuh could've told me you'd be going tuh thuh store

Who'd yuh bring tuh thuh party and where'd yuh go?

He's gonna give me iz files when they're complete

She didn't go duh thuh party, so he shouldn't ask about it

Carlos would've gone, but ee's never been there before

She would've gone tuh thuh movies with em if he'd asked er

It'll be cold tonight, so it'd be wise if you'd bring yer jacket

It's fer her so she could go tuh thuh store n buy whatever she'd want

We'd have finished thuh report if they'd given us thuh figures we needed

I wanted yuh duh know that thuh part I wanted in thuh play was not thuh part I got

I have tuh make lunch fer my daughter, but she's not brought er lunch box home

Reading:

Most fictional reading includes lots of dialogue, and this is where you are more likely to see the reductions and contractions discussed above. If you look at more academic-type reading samples, you will be far less likely to find these contractions and reductions. As with learning stress patterns, linking, and phrasing, it is best to find transcripts of real speakers to use as your reading practice. Transcripts of dialogue from movies can be found easily online. Transcripts of speakers' speeches and talks are readily available if you search. Go through dialogues and read the contractions. Remember, many reductions will not be written as such, so you will have to identify them yourself and insert the reduced form in your speaking practice. Read aloud and record yourself. Listen to your speech and look for your reduced and contracted forms as you speak. With time and practice, these will come with ease, and you will feel increased confidence when you use them in conversation.

Remember, reduced forms and contracted forms are not used 100% of the time. You can choose to use or not use them as much as you like. Generally a typical conversation will include at least some form of reductions and contractions. So, decide for yourself what level you would like to use them and use them accordingly.

Conversation:
Finally, it's time to put your practice to use! You'll want to try to insert these reductions in your speech, especially in natural, informal conversations. Not to say that you must speak formally to your colleagues or bosses. Listen to how your conversation partners talk. Often we mirror what we hear and mimic the formality of our speech to match the tone of our speaking partner. Try to identify if your speaking partner is using many reductions and contractions or not. If in your workplace, for example, it is the culture to speak informally in your industry, then match that level of informality. On the other hand, if you notice only formal speech being used even in conversations, then you are best to save these reduced forms for your informal conversations with friends and family. Of course, this is not a rule. Do what feels comfortable to you. Reduced forms are just elements of speech to consider when determining the tone of your environment. Remember, using contractions and reductions is deemed appropriate for nearly all settings, so you will likely not break any rules by using them. However, each setting has its own rules, so you will need to change accordingly; it's called code-switching. Using reductions and contractions with someone implies familiarity and connection with your listener, so consider this when talking to others. Happy practice!

Chapter 36: Going Forward!

Phew!

I'm guessing that right now you probably feel a bit overwhelmed. This book is definitely not what I would call "light reading." You have just completed a full-on immersion course in General North American English pronunciation, and you should feel so proud of yourself! Not just for finishing this guide, but for taking the time to really investigate and assess your own speech patterns. I am betting it has been a real eye-opening experience!

It might sound strange, but being a bit overwhelmed by this information is actually a good and normal process. Even though this information may feel like a big jumbled mess, your brain has and will continue to make connections. When you speak to others, your brain will now make more connections regarding the sounds you hear. Your ability to listen to what you have learned will improve. Little lightbulbs will go off in your mind when you're speaking to someone or when you hear someone speak. You will be better able to discriminate between sounds and understand rapid native English speakers so much better. You now know the rules! Those mysteries of the General North American English accent are revealed, and it doesn't seem so impossible and daunting anymore, does it? Most importantly, you now understand your problem areas and how to adjust your pronunciation to speak with clarity when you need to the most.

You now know what is standing in your way of clear, confident speech. As you work through the exercises one by one, you will better understand where your pronunciation is breaking down. You will work up the ladder of complexity from sounds, syllables, words, phrases, sentences, reading, and conversation practice. You now know that each step along the way is paving a solid foundation for more precise articulation. No activity you do will be a waste of time, as it will help you reach your goals little by little. If you feel overwhelmed by the information, that's okay! I genuinely believe that you will surprise yourself at just how much you have retained. I urge you to review this book again in a few weeks. If you forget a concept, that's okay too. Just go back and refresh yourself on the information.

So What in The World Should I Work on First?

This is something you might be asking yourself.

Here's what I suggest:

1. Pick out two of the sounds you are painfully aware of as being your most challenging sounds. Go through the directions, practice up the ladder from isolation, syllable, word, phrase, sentence, reading, to conversation level.
2. Dedicate 20 minutes each day to reviewing the words and sentences in the worksheets
3. Dedicate 20 minutes each day to reading out loud. Choose whatever interests you, or choose what is most convenient in your day. Record yourself as you practice and listen to yourself as you focus on clear pronunciation.
4. Pick out a few commonly used words with those sounds and make up a sentence to repeat throughout the day. I recommend ten times quickly, ten times a day to promote rapid pronunciation.
5. Dedicate 20-60 minutes each day to using your new sound in conversation. Clients who start working with me nearly always say that this feels slow at first. They feel self-conscious and realize that it is a tedious process. Do your best to let yourself fail! It's okay!! You're not a robot, and you can't be great at your first few attempts. Keep working at it, and catch yourself as much as you can.
6. After you feel like you have got the hang of those first two sounds, add another two to the mix! Just keep going and work on accuracy and improving more and more of your goal sounds and strategies.

This book is your English pronunciation playbook. The point is not to read it like a novel and move on with your life. This is the kind of book you refer to regularly; it's your personal version of a folded, creased, highlighted, filled with post-it notes and circled passages kind of book. Keep this book handy and refer to it as often as you can! Once you have gone through all of the chapters and worked through them, do it again! Pay special attention to your trouble sounds and goals. There will always be new little pieces of information that you didn't notice the first time around.

Super-Charge Your Goals!

The clients who contact me directly want to work with a knowledgeable professional through one on one instruction. These people understand the extreme value that their communication skills have in their career and personal lives. I work with many individuals who recognize the need for a fully tailored program with an instructor who can provide the feedback and knowledgeable instruction required to achieve their pronunciation goals. I am able to provide the most in-depth speech analysis through an IPA transcription. This transcription allows me to identify with succinct accuracy precisely what is holding clients back from speaking English clearly and confidently. I provide the direct and tailored instruction needed to implement the information you just learned in this book. My clients see significant improvements in their English pronunciation clarity and confidence through individualized plans and feedback. The clients I work with receive unlimited support and feedback during the coaching program, which is why my clients achieve such incredible results.

What I love so much about what you've just learned in this book is that all of the information is now in your hands! You have discovered the concepts that you can apply with time and practice. The results can be extraordinary and have incredible effects on your career and social connections; it's immeasurable!

I've created a way for people who have important goals, just like you, to chat with me for 30 minutes and talk about individual coaching. It's a chance to see firsthand what a session with me/my team looks and feels like. If you are interested in being a part of my Individualized program, I want to invite you to apply with me. You can review the specifics of the program (including price) and book a free consultation to discuss how to start here:

https://proactivepronunciation.com/

The consultation is a virtual video session that takes place online. We will talk about the individualized PROactive 13-session Accent Modification Program to see if it's a good fit for you. If it is, then we could be chatting together really soon! And with that, I will end this book. Thank you so much for reading. I truly wish you all the success in the world!

Rebecca Bower MHSc.
Speech-Language Pathologist (C) Reg. CASLPO